Anthropology Handbook

A Basic Introduction

Frank Robert Vivelo

Department of Social Sciences
University of Missouri at Rolla

McGraw-Hill Book Company

New York   St. Louis   San Francisco   Auckland   Bogotá
Düsseldorf   Johannesburg   London   Madrid   Mexico
Montreal   New Delhi   Panama   Paris
São Paulo   Singapore   Sydney   Tokyo   Toronto

CULTURAL ANTHROPOLOGY HANDBOOK
A Basic Introduction

567890   DODO   8987654

This book was set in Times Roman by National ShareGraphics, Inc.
The editors were Lyle Linder and Susan Gamer;
the cover was designed by Nicholas Krenitsky;
the cover photograph was taken by Al Green;
the production supervisor was Charles Hess.
The drawings were done by Fine Line Illustrations, Inc.
R. R. Donnelley & Sons Company was printer and binder.

Library of Congress Cataloging in Publication Data

Vivelo, Frank Robert.
    Cultural anthropology handbook.

    Includes index.
    1. Ethnology. I. Title.
GN316.V58   301.2   77-9324
ISBN 0-07-067530-9

ACKNOWLEDGMENTS

In addition to the citations given in the text and the bibliographies, these credits have been requested for quotations on the following pages:

Pages 16 and 19: From "A Scientific Concept of Culture" by Gerald Weiss. Reproduced by permission of the American Anthropological Association from the *American Anthropologist*, 75(5):1381, 1396 and 1397, 1973.

Page 13: From *Anthropology Today: An Encyclopedic Inventory,* prepared under the chairmanship of A. L. Kroeber, © 1953 by The University of Chicago, University of Chicago Press.

Page 13: From "We and They," *Rudyard Kipling's Verse: Definitive Edition.* Copyright 1926 by Rudyard Kipling. Reprinted by permission of Doubleday & Company, Inc.

Pages 38, 92, and 199: From *Theory of Culture Change: The Methodology of Multilinear Evolution* by Julian H. Steward, © 1955 by The Board of Trustees of The University of Illinois, University of Illinois Press.

Page 72: Copyright © 1963 by Wesleyan University. Reprinted from *Puritan Village: The Formation of a New England Town,* by Sumner C. Powell, by permission of Wesleyan University Press.

Pages 121 and 179: From *Cultural Anthropology* by William A. Haviland. Copyright © 1975 by Holt, Rinehart and Winston, Inc. Reprinted by permission of Holt, Rinehart and Winston.

Page 118: From *Age, Prayer and Politics in Tiriki, Kenya* by Walter H. Sangree, published by Oxford University Press for the East African Institute of Social Research (1966). Reprinted by permission of the publisher. (Excerpted as "The Bantu Tiriki of Western Kenya" in *Peoples of Africa,* edited by James L. Gibbs, Jr., Holt, Rinehart and Winston, 1965).

Extracts quoted in Chapters 9, 11, 12, 13, and 14. From *New Perspectives in Cultural Anthropology* by Roger M. Keesing and Felix M. Keesing. Copyright © 1971 by Holt, Rinehart and Winston, Inc. Reprinted by permission of Holt, Rinehart and Winston.

Pages 129, 178, and 189: From *Comparative Cultural Analysis: An Introduction to Anthropology* by Keith F. Otterbein. Copyright © 1972 by Holt, Rinehart and Winston, Inc. Reprinted by permission of Holt, Rinehart and Winston.

Pages 191 and 200: From *Social Anthropology* by Paul Bohannan. Copyright © 1963 by Holt, Rinehart and Winston, Inc. Reprinted by permission of Holt, Rinehart and Winston.

Page 220: By permission. From "Inhibition of Son-Mother Mating among Free-ranging Rhesus Monkeys" by Donald S. Sade, in *Science and Psychoanalysis,* vol. 12, pp. 18–38. Bound as *Animal and Human,* edited by J. H. Masserman. Copyright © 1968 by Grune & Stratton, Inc., New York.

Page 220: From "The Biological Basis of Human Sociality" by Earl W. Count. Reproduced by permission of the American Anthropological Association from the *American Anthropologist* 60:1075, 1958.

Page 225: From "The Origin of Incest Rules" by Wilson Wallis. Reproduced by permission of the American Anthropological Association from the *American Anthropologist* **52**:277–279, 1950.

Several of the photographs in this book are my own. Of the others, some are from published sources and some are from the private collections of friends and colleagues who have generously granted me permission to reprint:

Four photographs (pages 34, 149, 185, and 189) belong to Ingrid Deich, a sociologist.

Five photographs (pages 12, 15, 48, 61 and 63) belong to Erwin H. Epstein, a sociologist.

One photograph (page 126) belongs to Nelson A. Ossorio, an anthropologist and professional photographer.

One photograph (page 128) belongs to Jacques Zakin, a chemical engineer.

The photograph on page 41 is from *The Gentle Tasaday,* by John Nance (Harcourt Brace Jovanovich, 1975). Reprinted by permission of Magnum Photos, New York.

The photograph on page 59 is from *The Dugum Dani,* by Karl G. Heider (Aldine: Viking Fund Publications in Anthropology, No. 49, 1970). Reprinted by permission of Robert G. Gardner, Director, Carpenter Center for the Visual Arts, Harvard University.

The photograph on page 84 is from *The Social Organization of the Marri Baluch,* by Robert N. Pehrson (Aldine: Viking Fund Publications in Anthropology, No. 43, 1966). Reprinted by permission of the Wenner-Gren Foundation for Anthropological Research.

The photograph on page 168 is used with the permission of Tony Howarth, Woodfin Company and Associates.

The photograph on page 181 is used with the permission of the American Museum of Natural History, New York.

Contents

Chapter 10
Economic Organization

· Chapter 11
Political Organization

Preface

To The Instructor

RATIONALE: INTRODUCING ANTHROPOLOGY

In recent years there has been a growing trend among teachers of anthropology to use ethnographic case studies, supplemented by journal articles, in lieu of large texts. Others, who would like to abandon the textbook altogether but do not, argue that a series of readings, no matter how extensive ethnographically, cannot provide an adequate framework for neophytes and may leave the student with the impression that anthropology is indeed a hodgepodge of pots and sherds. Moreover, a series of readings may not supply students with the basics they need to know if they are to continue in anthropology, a foundation on which advanced courses and training can be built. On the other hand, the size and cost of textbooks often preclude the simultaneous use of extensive supplementary readings. This handbook represents my attempt to resolve these difficulties. It is neither a full-scale text nor a series of ethnographic accounts. It is designed, instead, to be used primarily with a series of ethnographic case studies or other modular readings.

I have made this handbook as short as possible; simple in style, tone, and organization (but not oversimplified to the point of distortion); comprehensive (but certainly not exhaustive; see below); and unified (through the explicit concept of sociocultural evolution in Part Two and an implicit, modified functionalism in Part Three). To increase further the unity and coherence of the book, a unique feature has been added: a summary table is provided as Appendix 1. This table lists the salient material from the handbook in one overall design so that the reader can, at a glance, relate the various pieces of information to each other within a single framework. No other introductory book in anthropology, regardless of size, does this. There is also a brief appendix that lists an eight-step self-study program for attaining an initial familiarity with the field: this is Appendix 3, Learning about Anthropology.

OBJECTIVES

This volume is a *handbook;* that is, its objectives are simplicity and breadth. The presentation is in simple language without, I hope, being condescending. It is short yet broad in scope; it attempts to introduce the student to an entire field. It aims to convey a number of complex issues and ideas within cultural anthropology in a brief, clear manner, without becoming bogged down in an excessive number of ethnographic examples and theoretical debates. It presumes no more than to be a coherent elementary presentation, concentrating mainly on fundamentals.

It can serve on its own as a summary of any of the major introductory texts currently in use in cultural anthropology (about two dozen of which were consulted in writing this handbook), and thus of the discipline itself; and it can serve as a succinct compendium of concepts and terms that facilitates understanding of professional monographs and journal articles. But it is emphatically not a glossary—not a simple listing of terms and their definitions—though students who use this handbook will find that, by and large, they can go on to explore the scholarly works of anthropologists without being hindered by terminology.

PRESENTATION

The primary value of this handbook is the straightforward summary it provides of major topics, terms, and concepts in cultural anthropology. (For some subjects, such as marriage and family, this is not an easy task, since anthropologists do not even agree on terminology. I have tried, however, not to take sides and to present each subject in such a way that it will be acceptable to most anthropologists.) To this end, I have been at pains not to indulge in lengthy theoretical discourses and to resist the temptation to cite an ethnographic example for every assertion (though brief ethnographic sketches are included in Chapters 4 through 8). Either of these can be handled more elaborately by the instructor in class or through collateral readings.

If I were to get involved in these pages in extended theoretical discussions, I would defeat my own purposes. This would no longer be a handbook; it would be a textbook. Theory simply cannot be adequately and *fairly* handled within the limits set for this book. Theory deserves its own volume. The only way to treat theory briefly in a handbook such as this would be to take sides, to choose one interpretive framework and relegate all others to ancillary status; but this would result in a perspective much too narrow to serve as an adequate introductory guide to a field as diversified as cultural anthropology. Hence, I restrict my mention of theory to that which is necessary to order my exposition. For instance, I mention in the text such issues as postpartum sex taboos, couvade, fear of menstrual blood, and initiation rites; but I refrain from discussing the various interpretations of these phenomena. I do, however, provide the appropriate references. Also, I do not discuss the history of anthropology (a topic also suited for a handbook of its own), for history means chiefly theories, their advocates and opponents. Thus unilinear versus multilinear evolution, functionalism, historicism, and so on, are avoided. Similarly, even though I use an evolutionary framework for ordering my presentation in Part Two (as I use an institutional overview in Part Three), I do not discuss the history of the concept, its broad theoretical implications, or highly moot related issues such as causal influences in transitions between evolutionary levels. Again, these are topics for the instructor to handle in class or through the assignment of appropriate readings.

But, on the other hand, the handbook is not only a summary, for it is also unified in presentation. One may read about rites of passage, for instance, on page 80 of a standard text but not encounter a discussion of rites of intensification (if they are mentioned at all) until page 250. I have attempted throughout the handbook to avoid this fragmentation. I use two devices. One is contrasting pairs: rites of passage–rites of intensification; shaman–priest; animism–animatism, etc. Such pairs are treated together instead of being scattered haphazardly throughout the book. The other device is classificatory schemes. For example, focusing on a subject like political organization, I try to discuss variations in such a way that the many types relate to, and build on, each other. (Unhappily, it is not an uncommon practice for authors to scatter such information through several chapters, without making explicit connections. For instance, one of the most popular recent texts—popular at least with instructors—fragments political organization into two different chapters separated by three intervening chapters on other subjects.)

USES: SUPPLEMENT AND STIMULANT
TO CLASSROOM ACTIVITY

This handbook is intended to be both short enough and broad enough to allow the instructor latitude to cover, either in class or through additional readings, those particular topics he or she is fond of or thinks especially important. The handbook does not—cannot—cover them all. It is a barebones, core presentation of the basic essentials of cultural anthropology. By design, it must cover a great deal of information in a few pages to provide students with what they need in order to understand the monographs and journal articles assigned by the instructor. Its aim is thus to facilitate a course of learning, to serve as a teaching aid, to supplement and inform in-class activity.

My inclusion of ethnographic sketches may serve as a case in point. At the end of each of the chapters describing adaptive strategies (hunting-gathering, horticulture, herding, etc.), a very brief description of an appropriate social group is provided. These "sketches" are purposely not well integrated with the preceding general "model." They are merely examples, and there is value in that alone. The comparison of the example group with the model is an appropriate exercise for the instructor and students to perform *in the classroom*. Such an exercise has a twofold pedagogical function: it forces the students to examine critically not only the sketch but also my model to judge how useful they are. Building on this exercise, the instructor may then wish to choose one of the ethnographies listed in Table II (at the end of the front matter), assign it to students, and have them write a paper comparing that ethnographic description of a particular society with my corresponding general model of that "type" of society. (It is for this reason that I chose to do sketches of obscure societies or those described in ethnographic monographs not likely to be assigned in an introductory course.) This ought to help students to develop a healthy skepticism toward generalization (and generality), since no particular society will be found to correspond closely, point for point, with the "model." The exercise can also encourage students to use their analytic faculties by asking them to account for or "explain" divergences between the particular case and the model.

For example, the Tasaday, who are the subject of the first ethnographic sketch (Chapter 4), are primarily gatherers in a tropical environment and may be fruitfully compared with an Arctic group, such as the Netsilik Eskimo, who rely largely on hunting for their livelihood (Balikci 1970), or with other forest-dwellers, such as the Mbuti Pygmies, for whom hunting is a major activity (Turnbull 1961). Contrasts and similarities among the various societies that are lumped together as "hunter-gatherers" are then more readily apprehended. Or one might assign an ethnography, such as Newman's book on the Gururumba of New Guinea (1965), to provide a comparison with the Dugum Dani, also a horticultural group in New Guinea, described in Chapter 5. Peasant societies (such as those described in Beals 1962 and 1974) might be contrasted with the ethnographic sketch of New England Puritans supplied in Chapter 6; or one might choose to focus on similarities by assigning an ethnography on, for instance, the Amish (Hostetler and Huntington 1971). In another short ethnography, *Tonalá* (1966), Diaz describes the social system of a Mexican town located on the outskirts of the city of Guadalajara. Though Tonaltecans are most likely to be classified as agricultural peasants and artisans, nevertheless many of the features Diaz notes for this society (sex-role differentiation, economic activities, the structure of domestic authority, attitudes toward politics) correspond to those found among the West Enders, Italian-Americans living in Boston who are described in Chapter 8. Hence, *Tonalá* provides informative parallel reading. Unfortunately, anthropologically useful general treatments of industrial society are hard to come by. It has been left primarily to sociologists and historians to generalize about such societies. One of the most comprehensive treatments of modern societies—though in many respects unsatisfactory from an anthropological perspective—is by Harvey (1975). Another is by Schneider (1969). And, in *Human Societies,* an anthropologically oriented sociology text, Lenski and Lenski (1974) provide extensive coverage of industrialism. Theirs is perhaps the most comprehensive and yet balanced textbook treatment available. A selection of the works mentioned above should be used as a counterpoint to my ethnographic sketches.

My unorthodox use of footnotes also exemplifies the practical intentions of this handbook. Footnotes are addressed to *both* instructors *and* students. In addition to the normal function of supplying supplementary information and references without interrupting the flow of in-text narrative, footnotes offer comments on useful in-class techniques appropriate to the subject under discussion in the text, suggest related topics which the instructor might pursue in class or which students might wish to read about on their own, and point out issues of theoretical concern. (That footnotes are not addressed solely to one part of the audience but to both sets of readers should produce consternation in neither the serious student nor the competent instructor. The nice thing about footnotes—and the strongest argument for their inclusion, since they occupy little space—is that they can be ignored by those who choose to do so.) Moreover, I attempt to keep the tone of the footnotes informal, almost conversational, because I think this facilitates their use and thus adds to the utility of the book as a whole. I judge it preferable to offer such footnotes in combination with this preface in place of a separate instructor's manual. I can see no real value in a device that excludes the student. I give away no "trade secrets" in my footnoted remarks.

There is also a deliberate pattern in the use of italics and boldface print. Italics are used for a term when it is being defined or when enumerating secondary or descriptive attributes of a subject under discussion. Defining characteristics and special or primary features, when first mentioned, are printed in boldface type. The aim is to emphasize key bits of information by having them stand out visually on the printed page.

To add further to the utility of this handbook, a glossary is included, (it begins on page 234). My objective was not to invent definitions that satisfied *me,* but rather to reflect current usages in anthropology. And some terms, for which it was not considered necessary to provide definitions within the body of the book, are nevertheless defined in the glossary. The resulting glossary is more detailed than any I have seen in an anthropology text.

In sum, I have tried to write the kind of concise book that I as a student would have liked for reference when reading monographs, articles, or writing papers—the kind of book my own students have repeatedly asked for. I have tested the book by using its contents as the substance of lectures in several (about a dozen) introductory courses, and it has so far proved successful. I hope that, because of its simplicity, brevity, and breadth, this handbook will be useful to students at all levels as a sort of quick-reference, hip-pocket guide to the field of cultural anthropology.

OMISSIONS AND JUSTIFICATIONS

Not included in this handbook are three areas that have become almost traditional topics in introductory treatments of cultural anthropology: social change; culture and personality; and art, music, and folklore. Their absence, and the departure from tradition it represents, therefore requires some explanation.

I have omitted social change because any single-chapter treatment in a handbook such as this would surpass acceptable limits of superficiality, even for an introductory volume (besides, the entire handbook may be said to be concerned, if only implicitly, with the subject). Moreover, there is such a lack of agreement concerning theory, methods, appropriate data, and even an accurate definition of social change, that I felt the student would be better served if this area was omitted as a separate topic in the handbook and instead left in the hands of the instructor. Anthropology has done far better in documenting social change than in explaining it. (This is a major shortcoming it shares with the other social and behavioral sciences.)*

Similar reasons led me to omit a treatment of the field of culture and personality (or psychological anthropology). There is really no accepted body of "fundamentals" to summarize (either in anthropology or in the psychology of personality). Terminology is often contradictory (how many researchers will agree on what a "value" is or what a "personality trait" is?). The field is in a state of flux, to say the least, with both methodology and theory under attack (cf. LeVine 1973). A summary would consist of a catalog of ethnographic research and methods in this area (such as Barnouw 1973), thus defeating the purpose of this handbook.

Moreover, there is an even more cogent basis for omitting these two areas as separate topics. Neither culture and personality nor social change represents a sphere of belief and behavior or a societal type, as the chapter

---

*In a review of Bee's (1974) book on sociocultural change, Heath (1975:212) says, "Few social scientists would be willing to say that the subject of cultural change is no longer important, but I, for one, am convinced that little new has been said in this connection in the past decade or so, and it is far from the focal position it held in anthropological thinking at mid-century. At that time, Felix Keesing wrote, 'Studies of culture in its time-dimension aspects are as old as cultural anthropology itself. Yet, paradoxically, this field of theory and method is currently weak and not well integrated. . . .' It may seem strange to readers who have not systematically followed the relevant literature, as Bee apparently has done, to find that Keesing's statement applies equally today."

divisions within Parts Two and Three of this handbook do. They are not ways of organizing social relations or sociocultural institutions themselves but are cross-cutting, wide-ranging subjects with their own orientations toward the study of human social process. In fact, they may be conceived as theoretical and methodological approaches to the study of society. In other words, one uses the basic concepts of cultural anthropology as tools to aid in the study of culture and personality and social change. The major objective of the handbook is to provide these basics; how they are combined in application to particular problems is left to the classroom. Coverage of these topics requires the introduction of theory or a series of ethnographic cases—both of which, it should by now be clear, controvert the aims of this handbook.

A treatment of art (which *does* represent a fairly well-defined sphere of belief and behavior comparable to others discussed in this handbook) was rejected because this field, too, is in general descriptive—reports of who did what, when, and how. I do not mean to denigrate the importance of documentation. We of course need such data on which to build an anthropology of art. But until the field has something conceptually more substantial to offer about the relation of art and sociocultural systems, its inclusion in a handbook such as this seems hardly warranted.

CORRESPONDING MATERIALS: TEXTS, ETHNOGRAPHIES, READERS

As was stated above, this handbook is meant to function principally in conjunction with other materials. To facilitate this use, Tables I and II on pages xviii and xix are provided. Table I correlates the chapters of this handbook with corresponding sections in large textbooks. Table II suggests several pertinent ethnographies available in paperback, as well as some widely used anthologies of introductory readings.

Frank Robert Vivelo

Table I   Chapters in Other Introductory Texts Corresponding to Chapters in This Handbook

Other texts:	Chapters in this handbook: 1	2	3	4	5	6	7	8	9	10	11	12	13	14
Barnouw 1975	1	2-5	6	7	7	7	7	7	13, 14	8	15, 16	11, 12	9, 10, 12	17, 18
Beals & Hoijer 1971	1,4	4		7	8	8	8	9	11	10	13	11	11, 12	14
Bock 1969	1	2	7,9	9	9	9	9	9	3,4, 7	4,7	4,5, 11	4,5, 10	4,5, 10	11
Bohannan 1963	1	2,3	13	13	13	13	13	13	10, 11	14, 15	16, 17	4,9	5-7	18-20
Collins 1975	Intro	13, 14	15	15	15	15	15	15	19	16	20-22	17, 18	17	23
Hammond 1971	1	1, 17	2	2	2	2	2	2	8,9	4,5	10, 11	7	6	12, 13
Harris 1975b	1	8	12	12	12	12	12	12	19, 26	14	13, 17, 18	16	15	23, 24
Haviland 1975	1	1,4	1,6	6	6	6	6	6	9	10	11, 12	8	7	13
Hoebel 1972	1	2	12	12	12	12	12	12	18, 19, 24, 25	17	26, 27	22, 23	20, 21	29, 30
Keesing & Keesing 1971	1	2,4	5,7	5,7	5,7	5,7	5,7	5,7, 11	10	12	13, 14	8	9	15
Kottak 1974	1	2	2,8	8	8,9	8,9	8	10, 21	10	18	10, 11, 17	14, 16	14, 15	19
Otterbein 1972	1	1	2	2	2	2	2	2	3,5	2	4	3	3	5
Pearson 1974	Intro	13	2, 22	23, 25	24, 29, 30	29, 31	26, 27	32	18	17	14, 16	15	15	19, 20
Richards 1972	8	8	1	1	2	2	2	2,3	5	3	4	6	6	7
Schusky 1975	1,2	1	7	8	8	8	8	8	6, 11	7	5,6	4	4	10
Spradley & McCurdy 1975	2,3	1	9	9	9	9	9	9	4,6, 7,8	10	11, 12	5	5	13
Stewart 1973	1,2	1,2	3, 17	5	6	8	7		9	(5-9)	12, 13	11	10	14, 15
Swartz & Jordan 1976	1	2		9, 10	10	10	10		3	12	13	14	14	16
Taylor 1973	1,5	2	3,7	8	8	8	8		12, 18	9	13	11	10	15

Table II   Collateral Readings

SUGGESTED ETHNOGRAPHIES

Hunter-Gatherers
Balikci (1970), *The Netsilik Eskimo*
Chance (1966), *The Eskimo of North Alaska*
Downs (1966), *The Two Worlds of the Washo*
Hart & Pilling (1960), *The Tiwi of North Australia*
Ohnuki-Tierney (1974), *The Ainu of the Northwest Coast of Sakhalin*
Turnbull (1961), *The Forest People*
Vanstone (1974), *Athapascan Adaptations*

Horticulturists
Chagnon (1968), *Yanomamo*
Dentan (1968), *The Semai*
Dozier (1965), *Hano*
Harner (1972), *The Jivaro*
Holmes (1974), *Samoan Village*
Meggers (1971), *Amazonia*
Middleton (1965), *The Lugbara of Uganda*
Newman (1965), *Knowing the Gururumba*
Verrill & Verrill (1967), *America's Ancient Civilizations*
von Hagen (1960), *World of the Maya*
von Hagen (1961a), *The Aztec*
von Hagen (1961b), *Realm of the Incas*

Agriculturists
Beals (1962), *Gopalpur*
Beals (1974), *Village Life in Southern India*
Geertz (1971), *Agricultural Involution*
Hsu (1965), *Ancient China in Transition*
Lewis (1960), *Tepoztlan*
Smith (1959), *The Agrarian Origins of Modern Japan*

Pastoralists
Barth (1961), *Nomads of South Persia*
Cole (1975), *Nomads of the Nomads*

Ekvall (1968), *Fields on the Hoof*
Klima (1970), *The Barabaig*

Industrialists
Bennett (1971), *Northern Plainsmen*
Gans (1965), *The Urban Villagers*
Garretson (1976), *American Culture*
Keiser (1969), *The Vice Lords*
Nakane (1970), *Japanese Society*
Norbeck (1965), *Changing Japan*
Spradley & Mann (1975), *The Cocktail Waitress*

NOTE: In addition, two useful volumes of ethnographic sketches are:
Service (1971), *Profiles in Ethnology*.
Oswalt (1972), *Other Peoples, Other Customs.*

SUGGESTED ANTHOLOGIES OF INTRODUCTORY READINGS

Bernard (1975), *The Human Way*
Cohen (1971), *Man in Adaptation: The Institutional Framework*
Cohen (1974), *Man in Adaptation: The Cultural Present*
Gould (1973), *Man's Many Ways*
Hammond (1975), *Cultural and Social Anthropology*
Hughes (1976), *Custom-Made*
Hunter & Whitten (1975), *Anthropology*
Poggie, Pelto, & Pelto (1976), *The Evolution of Human Adaptations*
Spain (1975), *The Human Experience*
Spradley & McCurdy (1974), *Conformity and Conflict*

Part One

Introduction

Chapter 1

What Anthropology Is

(Photograph by the author.)

Anthropology (literally, "man-study") is the study of humanity. One of the best single-sentence definitions to appear in recent years is that offered by Gerald Weiss, who describes anthropology as "the study of the sum total of all human phenomena, everywhere across the face of this planet and beyond, and through all time . . ." (1973:1381).

Anthropology has been referred to as (1) a *natural* or *biological science*, in that it studies the physical evolution and biological nature of human beings; (2) a *social science*, in that it studies the behavior of human beings as members of social groups; (3) a *historical discipline*, in that it seeks to reconstruct sequences in cultural development; and (4) *one of the humanities*, in that it studies art, folklore, oral tradition, and so on (Mead 1966:3).

Hence, anthroplogy is probably the most presumptuous of scholarly pursuits, for it is the only discipline that attempts to embrace *all* of humanity, biologically and culturally. Other disciplines focus on one or more of the biological or cultural dimensions of human beings; but none claims, as anthropology does, to study all of what is human or related to being human, throughout all of time and over space, wherever human beings are found.[1]

CHARACTERISTICS OF ANTHROPOLOGY

The two major characteristics of anthropology are that it is *comparative* and *holistic*.

Comparative approach

First of all, anthropology emphasizes a **comparative approach** to the study of humanity. It attempts to see human beings in the broad view, not just in isolated societies or even in one societal tradition. It compares society with society, tradition with tradition, over time and space. It tries to identify *likenesses* and *differences* in order to arrive at generalities. It seeks scientifically valid explanations for variations in social forms and to document the origins and development of human beings and their customs. Descriptions of a hunting society in southern Africa, tribal horticulturists in New Guinea, politically complex horticulturists in Mesoamerica, herdsmen in Asia, agriculturists in Europe, and industrial nation-states are all *necessary* to the anthropological endeavor. A serious anthropologist would not think of formulating generalizations about human beings and society based only on a study of Western societies, regardless of how intensive and complete that study was. Anthropologists insist that any proffered generalizations about humankind (whether they refer to biology, psychology, patterns of social behavior, or systems of belief) must hold up under cross-cultural examination. If such generalizations are asserted to be true of *human beings* or *human society*, they must be true of human beings or society *everywhere*. To an anthropologist, Western society is only one set of cases, a subset of a larger phenomenon. Of course, anthropologists would also react against generalizations about, say, the nature of human familial organization based only on a study of the Eskimo family. What, they want to know, has been the evolution of the family since the origin of the species? How did "the family" come into being? How and why did it change over time? How does it differ and how is it alike from place to place? And how does it relate to economy, political organization, child rearing, socialization, religion, recreation, and so on? Thus when anthropologists attack a particular problem concerning family organization in a given society—for example, how will greater participation by women in the national economy affect the American family?—they bring to the problem a broad understanding gained from investigation of "the family" in its larger context.

Integral to this approach, of course, is an acceptance of the proposition that human societies are comparable across space and time. No society, at least in its gross characteristics, is unique. The history of any given society *is* particular to that society, just as is the life history of a particular individual. But both human societies and individual human beings share some general attributes as members of a species, i.e., as members of a taxonomic category. Or, to alter the analogy, human societies, like lion societies or ant societies or baboon societies, evince similarities—"things they have in common." It is necessary to attempt to enunciate and understand the general characteristics of the larger class before one may hope to "understand" any of its representatives. Differences among human societies are *subclass* differences, and before we can adequately appreciate such differences and attempt to account for them, we must have some grasp of overall *similarities.*

What I am here opposing is the notion held by some historians (and other scholars) that each society must be treated as something special, unique, not truly comparable to what other human societies have done or believed in other times and places. As an anthropologist and as a social *scientist,* I must reject such a position. To deny comparability and emphasize uniqueness is to deny the possibility of valid generalizations and, hence, of scientific understanding of human beings and their behavior.

The comparative perspective also entails a time dimension. That is, it asserts that in order to understand present-day, industrial, state societies, we must be familiar with what has gone before, with the nonstate, nonindustrial societies from which modern societies have evolved. We have at our disposal a fairly complete record of the human species stretching back in time nearly 5 million years. The first food-producing societies did not appear until about 10,000 years ago; the first state societies appeared only about 6,000 years ago; and the large-scale implementation of industrialism appeared only about 200 years ago. Surely we cannot ignore the earlier record and still hope to understand ourselves. Once again, modern societies constitute only one subset of cases of the larger phenomenon we are attempting to examine, describe, and understand. For example, one cannot fully understand the exercise of power in modern political institutions without some familiarity with societies in which political power is *not* exercised and in which formal, legal institutions are nonexistent. To take another example, one cannot understand the social ramifications of a *complex* technology without some acquaintance with the social consequences of a *simple* technology. One "works up" to this understanding by stages, progressing from the simplest to the most complex. How are we to understand the current changes in "the family" if we do not know something about the evolution of, and sociocultural variation in, human familial organization as a general phenomenon?

Holism

The other major characteristic of the anthropological approach to analyzing and understanding human belief and behavior is the insistence that societies be treated as wholes, as functional units, or—in the terms of cybernetics—as systems. There are many variations of this **holism,** which have gone under a number of names. The most common of these names is "functionalism," although that label is now considered an epithet in some circles. Most simply stated, holism means that anthropology tries to cover the *whole* scope of what humankind is, in order to arrive at generalizations; it attempts to provide a total or composite view. More specifically, the holism of anthropology has two primary aspects.

First, anthropologists try to see human culture as a single, interconnected web, an ordered entity, a functional whole, in which all the parts relate to each other as components of one system. What happens in any component of the system invariably has some effect on the structure and operation of the whole. Though we can isolate or separate elements of the total system for purposes of analysis, exposition, or discussion, we will achieve at best only a surficial understanding of these parts unless we relate them to each other in an effort to see how they are tied together. Religion, economic organization, the political system, spatial organization, kinship, education, marriage, etc.,—all these are related, interwoven parts of a sociocultural system. An anthropologist studies all these—although he or she may specialize in or concentrate on one or two—and is trained to be observant for their interconnections. For instance, an anthropologist who is political specialist will nevertheless be conversant as well in kinship and marriage, though perhaps choosing not to emphasize these aspects of a sociocultural system. In other words, we have in the discipline ecological anthropologists, psychological anthropologists, political anthropologists, and economic anthropologists, as well as specialists in the study of law, religion, cognitive systems, art, and music; but all these specialists are first of all *anthropologists* in the broad sense.[2]

Anthropology is also holistic in the sense of attempting to comprehend humans as animals in addition to humans as cultural beings. It studies both the physical or biological characteristics of the species, as well as the social and cultural. The physical evolution of *Homo* and human cultural evolution are not viewed by anthropologists as unrelated or discontinuous. Both are necessary for an adequate understanding of the kind of creature we are.

Focus of Study

Another attribute of anthropology that has frequently been identified as a major characteristic is the traditional concern of cultural anthropologists with studying, primarily, nonliterate (or preliterate, or "primitive") peoples.[3] Contemporary anthropologists, however, no longer confine themselves to such societies. Increasingly, anthropologists are turning to their own societies to conduct field research. Several factors are responsible for this trend. The major ones seem to be the absence of financial support currently available for field expeditions to remote corners of the globe; the existence of fewer isolated, primitive societies in the world (the traditional ways of tribal peoples are fast disappearing as both cultural and geographical distances are shortened in the supersonic age, and many of these peoples resent being "studied" by anthropologists); and the pressure of immediate problems in our own society demanding the attention of social scientists.

To the task of alleviating pressing problems on the home front, anthropologists bring a special expertise. Their familiarity with various lifeways and with the evolution of human society helps them to approach particular problems we face here and now with a broad range of testable alternatives for meeting modern contingencies. That anthropologists are in some ways being compelled to conduct investigations within their own societies, then, is not an entirely infelicitous situation.

DIVISIONS OF ANTHROPOLOGY

Any discipline that claims to study *all* of anything (and in this case, moreover, all of *humanity*) is claiming a great deal. Such an ambitious endeavor is obviously beyond the capabilities of any single individual, for no one person could possibly master the knowledge needed to study human beings in their entirety. Therefore, as was stated above, within anthropology there are "specialties," or divisions, and each anthropologist elects to concentrate on only some of these. Still, most anthropologists receive a general education in the entire discipline, and most graduate programs require that candidates for the doctoral degree in anthropology demonstrate at least a minimal level of competence in three broad areas: physical anthropology, archaeology, and cultural anthropology.

In Figure 1.1, I have tried to indicate something of the major divisions of the discipline. The chief division is between physical and cultural anthropology. Some anthropologists prefer a threefold division, with archaeology as one-third of the whole. The reason for doing so is that archaeology is a kind of bridge between physical and cultural anthropology. An archaeolo-

8

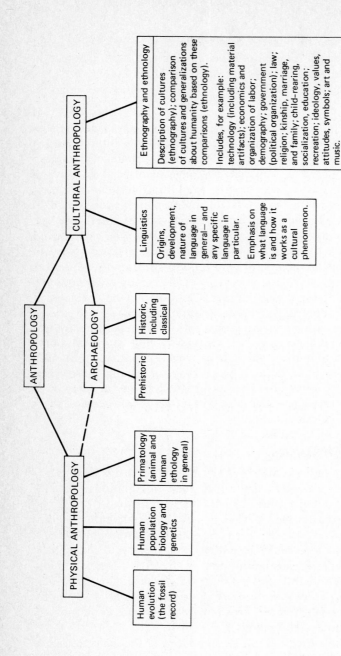

Figure 1.1 Major divisions of anthropology.

gist, on the one hand, needs a good working knowledge of paleontology, both human and nonhuman, and of geology, in order to be able to recognize fossils and evaluate their significance. On the other hand, archaeologists often form theories about the social organization of a past people based on the remains they unearth; and for this archaeologists must be knowledgeable in cultural anthropology generally. Though I prefer a simple dual division of anthropology, I have tried to indicate the central importance of archaeology by its placement in the diagram and by the connecting lines from physical and cultural anthropology. (That the line from physical anthropology is broken and the one from cultural anthropology solid merely reflects my bias that archaeology is more closely related to cultural than to physical anthropology.)

I will not deal in this handbook with physical anthropology or archaeology. Instead, I will concentrate on cultural anthropology—though not all of it, since I will not be concerned with linguistics as a separate specialty. (Linguistics is in fact so specialized an enterprise that some anthropologists place it on a par with physical and cultural anthropology instead of listing it as a subdivision of the latter.)

Cultural anthropology is used in three senses. It may designate a major division of anthropology, as it does in Figure 1.1. It may be used in a narrower sense to mean only what is contained in the large box at the extreme right in Figure 1.1, the box labeled *Ethnography and ethnology*. And, finally, it may refer to a particular theoretical approach, in contradistinction to "social anthropology" (the distinction is based on a particular view of "cultural" and "social" which is discussed in the next chapter).

GATHERING ANTHROPOLOGICAL DATA: FIELDWORK

Fieldwork in cultural anthropology may be defined as the firsthand study of a community. This is the basic experience of nearly all cultural anthropologists. Characteristically, cultural anthropologists do their research in natural settings, among a group of people carrying out their daily activities in their usual way and under usual conditions (except for the presence of the anthropologist). In general terms, this anthropological field method has come to be called **participant observation.** It consists of living among a group of people, doing what they do to the extent that they will allow, and recording faithfully as much of what occurs as is possible; i.e., it consists of *participation* and *observation*. In addition, of course, anthropologists conduct both formal and informal interviews with members of the society they are trying to understand. These individuals from the native group are referred to as *informants*.

The resultant description provided by an anthropologist is called an **ethnography.** Ethnography is usually contrasted with **ethnology,** which may be described as theorizing or generalizing based on comparative ethnography, descriptions of a number of societies.

One of the main tasks of the ethnographer, either before actually enter-ing a field situation or while doing fieldwork, is to learn the native lan-guage. Learning a people's language entails learning to think to some extent the way the people being studied do (or at least it is a major step in that direction). This is of inestimable help in understanding and interpreting their behavior. Without a firm knowledge of the native language, there is great danger that the anthropologist's understanding of an exotic way of life may be distorted by trying to "translate" it into more familiar terms. (This problem will be dealt with further in Chapter 2.)

USES OF ANTHROPOLOGICAL DATA: CULTURAL RELATIVISM VERSUS ETHNOCENTRISM

What is the utility of the information anthropologists gather? First, there is the hope that by learning the way of life of others, we can better understand ourselves. All societies are faced with certain problems (how to feed their members, how to keep order, etc.). By examining alternative solutions and the conditions under which they have been tried—by learning about the responses of others—we may benefit by building upon them.

We can also become less self-centered as a group. *Ethnocentrism* is the term used for group-centeredness; it is the tendency to see one's own cul-ture as the center of everything, the measure or standard against which all other lifeways are evaluated. It is the tendency to consider one's own cul-ture superior to, or "better" than, all others. This attitude (the attitude which exhorts us to "civilize" the "savages," to bring Christianity to the "pagans") is not confined to Western societies but appears to be present in all societies. For instance, many nonliterate societies do not have a name for themselves other than "The People," the implication of course being that no one outside their group is quite human.

The opposite of ethnocentrism is *cultural relativity:* the practice of *not* judging other cultures on the bases or standards of one's own culture. It involves an effort to remain unbiased in one's observations. In other words, cultural relativism acknowledges that cultures are *different* but not ranked, with one better than another, for there is no absolute scale. Cultural relativ-ism is perhaps seen most clearly with regard to morality. Cultural (or, in this case specifically, ethical) relativism—as opposed to ethnocentrism—does not hold that one culture is "right" while another is "wrong"; cultures are simply different. For example, killing your baby (infanticide) is "wrong" in the United States. Among many Eskimo groups, it is not wrong under certain conditions. Killing your grandfather because he is too old to care for himself is "wrong" in the United States. Among some aboriginal Ameri-can Indians, it often was not. Having more than one spouse is "wrong" in the United States. But for the majority of the world's societies polygamy is the *preferred* form of marriage. Among Americans, overtly demonstrating affection for one's mother-in-law is met with approval. Among Australian

Aborigines it is thought disgraceful. Among Americans, a close brother-sister relationship is prized. Among the Trobrianders, it is considered the height of iniquity. Cultural relativism sees these customs not as moral issues but as answers to problems people face (what to do with economically unproductive members of the group in a harsh environment, how to minimize competition for spouses, etc.) and as adjustments to certain kinds of conditions; and it advances the view that if they are to be evaluated at all, then it is to be by their efficacy in meeting these problems.

It does not follow, as Spradley and McCurdy (1974:7) suggest it does, that cultural relativism "absolves the believer from the responsibility of finding some way to resolve conflicts among the world's different value systems." Neither does cultural relativism mean, as they also assert (p. 6), that "it is possible to remain aloof and free from making value judgments." It simply means that anthropologists are aware of the human predilection for evaluative judgments and attempt to minimize these in their own work. ("Conscious involvements," as Hortense Powdermaker observed in her book *Stranger and Friend,* "are not a handicap for the social scientist. Unconscious ones are always dangerous.") It means that for purposes of inquiry judgments regarding rightness or wrongness are suspended in order to understand lifeways dissimilar to our own. As professionals, anthropologists are committed to discovering how customs that seem bizarre to the uninitiated or untrained actually "make sense" when treated as part of the complex of human life under, say, a different set of ecological conditions from our own. Hence, anthropologists as a rule do not (any longer) speak of "the repugnant practices of senseless savages"; for such evaluative declarations depend on applying a standard of values in one culture to pass judgment on practices based on values in another culture. Such a practice obviously impedes understanding exotic lifeways (as well as our own). But understanding foreign practices in no way implies approval of them. In fact, "approval" is as alien as disapproval to a position of cultural relativity. Cultural relativity means only that the anthropologist is aware of the tendency to pass judgment and tries actively to refrain from doing so for the purpose of study. It does *not* mean that, as members of a society and as concerned citizens of the world, individuals (whether or not they happen to be anthropologists) do not make value judgments at all, that they do not have preferences, that they do not have notions of good and bad, that they do not apply their own standards in reacting to foreign practices which threaten them personally or threaten their culture—or practices which do not. It would be absurd to maintain such a posture.

One of the first serious practitioners of anthropological fieldwork, Bronislaw Malinowski, exemplifies this. Malinowski worked among the Trobriand Islanders in the Pacific and left us a wealth of first-rate ethnographic description of the Trobrianders. One cannot guess from Malinowski's monographs that he personally was far from liking or admiring the Trobrianders, their customs, and their values. We did not learn this until the publication of his diary fifty years after his fieldwork. Malinowski did not let his own dislike and repulsion interfere with his work, which was to "make sense" out of Trobriand life, to understand it in its own terms and to present a reasonably fair and unbiased picture of it. *That* is cultural relativism.

On a personal level, anthropology may help to broaden one's outlook by showing one how other people live and judge the world. An acquaintance with the human species through time—going beyond a knowledge of Western civilization—is likely to affect a person's values and philosophy. A narrow-minded anthropologist should be—but of course is not always—a contradiction in terms. By broadening one's perspective to include societies throughout the world and throughout time, anthropology helps one to detect fallacies in generalizations about human behavior when such generalizations are based only on a familiarity with Western society.

In short, living in an exotic society, and making a sincere effort to understand another culture without judging it, compels one to suspend culturally influenced tenets temporarily. It has the effect of bringing into consciousness many of the assumptions one holds as a member of a particular

Quechua Indians in the Uros Islands, Lake Titicaca, Peru. *(Photograph by Erwin H. Epstein.)*

group with particular norms, beliefs, and attitudes. Learning about other, and perhaps drastically different, assumptions made by people in other societies serves to highlight many of one's own assumptions and thus helps to make explicit what was previously implicit. Once this occurs, the way is open to a fuller understanding of one's own sociocultural system.[4]

It is with the hope of facilitating your familiarity with anthropology, to help you take the first steps to acquire the anthropological perspective, that this handbook is written. It is designed to ease your introduction to a discipline that has as its goal the understanding of the most fascinating of all creatures—the most fascinating, at least, to human beings themselves.[5]

FOOTNOTES

1 Here, the instructor might wish to contrast cultural anthropology with other social or behavioral sciences. There have been several attempts to do this (nearly every introductory text provides some information on this score); see, for example, the comments offered by Kottak (1974:10–14) in his recent text. Beattie (1964:16–33) provides a British perspective; a sociologist's view is supplied by McGee (1975:4–8); and a social psychologist's view is given by Lindesmith, Strauss, and Denzin (1975:15–18). See also the pertinent references in Mandelbaum, Lasker, and Albert (1967).

2 A. L. Kroeber (1953:xiv) made the following pertinent comments: "It is evident that anthropology—however specific it may often be in dealing with data—aims at being ultimately a co-ordinating science, somewhat as a legitimate holding corporation co-ordinates constituent companies. We anthropologists will never know China as intensively as a Sinologist does, or prices, credit and banking as well as an economist, or heredity with the fullness of the genetic biologist. But we face what these more intensive scholars only glance at intermittently and tangentially, if at all: to try to understand in some measure how Chinese civilization and economics and human heredity, and some dozens of other highly developed special bodies of knowledge, do indeed interrelate in being all parts of 'man'— flowing out of man, centered in him, products of him."

3 Anthropologists, in an effort to avoid bias, have agonized over a term to indicate the non-Western, nonstate, nonindustrial societies in which they have conducted the majority of their research. No completely satisfactory term has found currency. I will use "primitive" and "nonliterate" in this handbook. The reader is reminded that nothing pejorative or derogatory is intended by these terms.

4 In the poetic phrases of Rudyard Kipling (*The Collected Works of Rudyard Kipling,* vol. 27, pp. 375–376, Doubleday, Doran, & Company, 1941):

> All good people agree,
>   And all good people say,
> That all nice people like Us are We,
>   And everyone else is They;
> But if you cross over the sea,
>   Instead of over the way,
> You may end by (think of it!) looking on We
>   As only a sort of They!

5 It should be made clear to the student that anthropology is learned by relating
   basic concepts to personal observations and that it is not simply a set of abstract
   ideas. Committing to memory the contents of this handbook will not be productive unless the student learns to relate the material to his or her own experiences.
   This goal, however, is not itself a major objective of this handbook and is better
   pursued by the instructor in the classroom and through collateral reading.
        Accordingly, I have found it useful at this point to introduce students to
   "One Hundred Per Cent American" (Linton 1937) and to "Body Ritual among
   the Nacirema" (Miner 1956), either by assigning these articles to be read or by
   reading them aloud to a class. The latter is more effective and usually engenders
   intense discussion, the tone of which can then be sustained throughout the
   course.

Chapter 2

Culture and Society

(Photograph by Erwin H. Epstein.)

Culture, perhaps the most central concept in anthropology, has resisted rigorous definition. Anthropologists have had the same difficulty defining culture in precise terms as biologists have had with "life" and physicists have had with "electricity."

Before discussing what anthropologists mean by *culture*, we ought to get straight what is *not* meant. Anthropologists do not use the term in the sense of "cultivation," "refinement," "sophistication," or the like, as in, "He is a cultured man." In the anthropological sense, all people are "cultured" in that they are born, are raised, and live in social groups.

TWO MAJOR VIEWS OF CULTURE

I will not go into all the definitions of culture that have been propounded; they are too numerous. (A book called *Culture,* by Alfred Kroeber and Clyde Kluckhohn, was published in 1952; in it they listed about 175 separate definitions.) But I do want to discuss the major ways culture is viewed in anthropology today.

Most definitions of culture, despite minor differences, fall into one or the other of two general categories which I shall call the *totalist view* and the *mentalist view.*

The Totalist View

In this view, *culture* is used to refer to the totality of a people's "way of life." According to the classic definition of this type, culture is "that complex whole which includes knowledge, belief, art, morals, law, custom, and any other capabilities and habits acquired by man as a member of society" (Tylor 1871:1). A recent formulation along these lines defines culture as "the generic term for all human nongenetic, or metabiological, phenomena" (Weiss 1973:1396).

Cohen (1974:46) defines culture as "the artifacts, institutions, ideologies, and the total range of customary behaviors with which a society is equipped for the exploitation of the energy potentials of its particular habitat." In Levine's (1975:213) words, "Culture is composed of the energy systems of a population and its methods of exploiting them, of the organization of social, political, and economic relations, of language, customs, beliefs, rules, and arts—of everything that is *learned* from other people or their works." This view emphasizes the functional importance of culture as an adaptive mechanism, as a generic term for the sum total of the ways a society organizes its relations to its environment and the way it is internally organized.

Cohen defines a population's adaptation as "its relationship to its habitat" (1974:3) and states that "the adaptation of man is accomplished by cultural means, through the harnessing of new sources of energy for productive ends and through the organization of social relations that make it possible to use these energy systems effectively" (p. 4). And elsewhere (1968:41) he says that "adaptation in man is the process by which he makes effective use for productive ends of the energy potential in his habitat."

Looking at culture as an adaptive mechanism—as that totality of tools, acts, thoughts, and institutions through which a population secures and maintains itself—is, in my opinion, the most useful view of culture; for it focuses our attention on the *organization* and *function* of a people's way of life rather than on the "peculiar" or "curious" nature of its "customs," but does not obscure significant cultural differences between populations.

The Mentalist View

A second major, and less comprehensive, way to view culture is as an ideational or conceptual system, i.e., as a shared system of knowledge and beliefs by which people order their perceptions and experiences and make decisions, and in terms of which they act. It is a shared system of ideas, a kind of conceptual code that people use to interpret themselves and the world and to formulate behavior. That is, people act in reference to the code (Goodenough 1961:521–522; see also Goodenough 1951 and 1968). It is a system of rules or a pattern *for* behavior, rather than an observed pattern *of* behavior (Keesing and Keesing 1971:20).

Young Herero woman; southern Africa. *(Photograph by the author.)*

In this view, "culture" does not include tools, acts, or institutions—only thoughts. It is not the actual behavior of people but their standards of, or guides for, behavior. It is their conceptualization of *appropriate* behavior (Frake 1964).

Those who view culture in this second way have chosen to focus on only a part of the totalist view of culture. And they have done so because they are interested in investigating particular types of problems: those related to the nature and operation of the human mind, the conceptual apparatus. No one would deny the importance of such an enterprise; but it is unfortunate that the term *culture* was chosen to identify the subject matter because this use conflicts with the traditional usage. We need another term, but none has been suggested and widely accepted. (It is probably too cumbersome to speak of "culture 1, the ideational view," and "culture 2, the totalist view"; see Goodenough 1961:522.)

It might also be pointed out that "culture" in the mentalist sense may be employed as an adaptational concept. But in this sense we would be speaking of a people's shared ideas, the conceptual or mental code *for* behavior, as a tool for maintaining their relationship with their environment. It is a way of thinking about things. It is an ordering device for making sense out of perceptions and experience and an organizational frame of reference in terms of which persons behave (just as magical-religious and scientific ways of thinking about things are).

Another recent definition combines the core ideas of both views of culture. LeVine (1973:3–4) says that

> culture can also be seen as constituting an environment for members of a population. . . . The individuals in a human population do not adapt directly and simply to their physical and biological environment but to the cultural (or sociocultural) environment that includes means for their individual survival and guides their adaptation along established channels. I use the term *culture* to mean an organized body of rules concerning the ways in which individuals in a population should communicate with one another, think about themselves and their environment, and behave toward one another and toward objects in their environment.

Though my personal preference is toward the totalist use of the term *culture,* I find the distinction between ideas about behavior and actual behavior an extremely useful one for presenting an introduction to the field of cultural anthropology. By employing this distinction, I will be able to structure most of the material in this handbook. Once the distinction between "the cultural" and "the social" (to be discussed shortly) is understood, all subsequent information (by being divided into the cultural realm or the social realm) is that much more easily grasped.

To avoid confusion, I will use the term *sociocultural* when I mean the totalist view. Strictly speaking (from the totalist perspective) this term is nonsense because "the cultural includes all that is humanly social plus all other human nongenetic phenomena" (Weiss 1973:1386); thus the term *sociocultural* is redundant.

SOCIETY

In order to grasp the distinction between the cultural and the social realm, we must first discuss the term *society*.

A society is usually defined as a group or population of people separated physically or by its culture (especially by its language) from other, similar units. The important thing to note is that it is a *group* or *population* of people. A difficulty arises, however, when we try to identify any particular group as "a society." Where do we draw the lines between societies? It has been suggested that the modern world is no longer divisible into distinct societies, for the groups of the world have become so interdependent and engage in so much interaction that it is almost impossible to designate the boundaries of any particular society. But Gerald Weiss (1973:1397) has offered a definition that will serve us well here.

> A human society: a group of human organisms constituting a breeding population or a maximum political entity, whichever is greater in the given instance. In those cases where these two criteria coincide, where a single breeding population is controlled by a single political authority, the population is a human society. In those cases where, as is typical among foragers, a breeding population consists of several politically autonomous but intermarrying bands, it is the breeding population that constitutes the human society by this definition. In those cases where several breeding populations are under a single political authority, as in a caste situation or at least initially after conquest or confederation of several previously separate societies, it is the group of populations thus forming a maximum political entity that comprises the human society. [For Weiss' rationale, see pp. 1397–1398.]

THE CULTURAL AND THE SOCIAL: INFLUENCE OF LINGUISTICS

Having provided the above mentalist definition of "culture" and a definition of "society," I am now able to indicate what is meant by "the cultural" as opposed to "the social."

When I speak of something as being "cultural," I am referring to ideational things, conceptual codes, something in people's minds. When I speak of something as "social," I am referring to behavior, behavior patterns, regularities in interaction between persons as members of a society.[1] Thus, the phrases *social organization* or *social system* refer to descriptions of people in interaction, whereas *culture* refers to the set of ideas with reference to which people carry out their interactions. A culture comprises the *standards* for behavior, but it is not the behavior itself. Just as the grammar of a language is a set of rules or principles for appropriate speech, a culture is a system of rules or principles for appropriate behavior.

Let me elaborate briefly on this analogy with linguistics. A **language** may be seen as a system of rules or a code governing the production of intelligible oral communication. It is composed of those rules or principles that govern the proper or appropriate way of producing sounds and arranging them so that a hearer understands the message being communicated. In short, language is the conceptual code for proper speech.[2] But **speech** is the actual behavior, the sounds produced when employing the rules. Speech is *what* is said; language is *how* something is to be said—what one needs to know to produce intelligible speech.

This distinction is important. If we denied the existence of a conceptual code governing speech and concentrated only on actual speech behavior, then we could analyze only *what* is said. We could talk only about actual, observable speech behavior. We could examine what is said, how often, to whom, under what conditions, and so on. But we could not learn how people manage to put these sounds together to express a meaning so that hearers can understand it. For this we have to look beneath the speech sounds themselves to find the code which allows people to create and string together meaningful sounds to create intelligible speech. Otherwise we could not predict speech that, though completely acceptable, we had not already heard in the past.

This reasoning has important implications, beyond language, for all forms of sociocultural interaction. If we limit our interest to observable behavior—i.e., simply to what people actually do—we will know who does what, when, how often, with whom, in what situations, etc. That is, we can construct statistical charts of behavior showing that this person or class of persons performs this behavior this often. But we cannot predict what should be done, what is appropriate or acceptable behavior in the particular culture, under certain conditions. We will never know how one is *supposed* to act in a given situation. We can only observe how persons actually *do* act, as opposed to how they *may* act.

An example should make this clear. The following passage is taken from a paper written by Roger Keesing in 1967 (p. 2):

> If we are planning a wedding, and the bride's parents are divorced or she is an orphan, we want to know who appropriately would give away the bride (or who can give legal consent if she is under age). A statistical table telling us the frequency with which fathers, uncles, mothers, etc. give brides away simply will not tell us what we need to know.

Those who advocate this view say that what we have to do if we want to "understand" behavior from the actors' perspective (what is called the *emic* approach) and not just record it for analysis by an outsider (the *etic* approach) is to try to construct a system of rules or a conceptual code which if applied in a particular social context will result in culturally appropriate behavior. Now, according to cognitive anthropologists or ethnoscientists—those, like Keesing, who support this approach—we all carry such an ideational code or "theory of culture" around in our heads. When you come into a classroom, you *expect* the instructor to act in a certain way. You do not expect to find the instuctor naked, or asleep, or tap dancing; any of these situations would constitute inappropriate behavior.

The point of view which ethnoscientists advocate holds that the job of anthropologists is to learn that code also, to learn what behavior is *appropriate* in what contexts—just as a linguist tries to learn a grammar in order to produce appropriate speech. Ward Goodenough was the first to point out that learning a culture is like learning a grammar. He has said that the purpose of ethnographic description is to "give the reader a basis for learning to operate in terms of the culture described in somewhat the same manner that grammar would provide him with a basis for learning to speak a language" (1951:10).

The object is to learn to act in a culturally acceptable way, to learn the culture just as the native actors learn it. This will not allow you to predict exactly what behavior will occur, but it will allow you to predict what range of behavior is appropriate (Frake 1964). Thus in a certain situation you will expect to find a certain kind of behavior which is appropriate, but you do not know specifically which appropriate behavior will occur. To use language as a model again, one can say: "He is writing a poem," or "he writes a poem," or "a poem is being written by him." All are acceptable; but we cannot predict just which form will be used, though here a statistical table can tell us what the probability is that one form will be chosen over another.

How do investigators learn the cultural grammar?

First of all, they note actual behavior. They observe people doing things, make up charts of who does what when. Then they analyze the charts and look for patterns and underlying logic. They try to formulate rules that would account for or generate the observed behavior, rules of the nature: "In such-and-such situation, such-and-such behavior is proper." They test such a rule by asking their informants if it is correct. They try it out by actually performing the behavior. They will know soon enough if it is "ungrammatical," or not culturally acceptable. The native actors will express disapproval, laugh, perhaps even become overtly hostile.[3]

Again, this is similar to what linguists do. They observe and record what people say and how they say it. They try to formulate rules to account for or generate such speech. Then they ask informants, "Can you say this?" They try out the rules by creating sentences. Again, their informants will indicate when the grammar is, or is not, correct.

I have devoted considerable space to the mentalist view of culture because it is essential in order to grasp the dichotomy between rules about behavior and actual behavior, to which I will refer throughout this handbook. I do not advocate either a cognitive or a behaviorist approach to the study humanity. It is probably a distortion of reality to place too much emphasis on either. Yet the two approaches are useful expository and mnemonic devices—i.e., they make it easier for me to talk about the topics that follow (especially in Part Three), and they make it easier for you to understand and remember this material.

FOOTNOTES

1 There is a similarity between these terms and *norm*, though I have avoided using the latter because it has no uniform meaning. To Bohannan (1963:284) a norm is "what people ought to do, . . . a guide to social action"; whereas for Hoebel (1972:30) it refers to "the average or modal behavior of a given type that is manifested by a social group. Statistically, it means either the average or the greatest frequency of a variable." Thus, one may legitimately speak of "ideal norms" and "descriptive norms." The former term refers to ideas about appropriate behavior; the latter, to statistical expressions of actual behavior.

2 Language is usually more broadly described as the totality of rules *and behaviors* involved in human communication. By equating language with grammar, I am here following the limited definition of many cognitive anthropologists in order to emphasize the distinction between rules and behavior.

3 The best account for students of the ethnoscientific (or "emic") approach may be found in the first five chapters of Spradley and McCurdy (1972). The material is presented in nontechnical, easy-to-read prose which not only outlines theory but offers a number of suggestions regarding research methodology. Following this presentation are twelve short papers by students who used Spradley and McCurdy's suggestions to conduct small-scale field projects.

Good examples for students of a more "etic" approach are Netting (1971) and Cohen (1968, revised 1974, and 1971). The latter has strongly influenced my presentation in Part Two of this handbook.

Part Two

Evolutionary Overview

Chapter 3

Preliminaries: Evolutionary and Institutional Overviews

(Photograph by the author.)

There are two major ways to present an introductory overview of human sociocultural diversity, and of cultural anthropology as well. One is the *institutional approach* (Chapters 10 through 14) favored by the authors of most introductory texts; the other is the *evolutionary approach* (Chapters 4 through 8).

THE EVOLUTIONARY APPROACH

An evolutionary or *adaptational* approach examines the types of organization characteristic of each major developmental stage in human history, from the "simplest" to the most "complex." In such a scheme, the characteristics often used to categorize these stages or types are based on how people organize themselves to extract a living from their habitat. The complex of factors which I use to identify these levels of adaptation includes the energy resources a society relies on, the tools used to extract these resources from the habitat and to convert them into usable products (technology), and the ways people organize themselves to use these tools (organization of labor). In simple terms, I identify the different evolutionary stages on the basis of how people make a living.

Each of these levels or stages in sociocultural evolution is variously described as a level of social (or cultural) evolution, a level of sociocultural integration, a technological or technoeconomic level, a subsistence level or type, a level of adaptation, or simply an economic level. The phrase *ecological types* (suggested by Kottak 1974:147) is most appropriate in this presentation, since my focus is really not on evolution per se, or the process of transformation in human sociocultural organization, but on describing the overall characteristics of each adaptive strategy and its consequences for the organization of social relations within a given level. (In other words, I am "freezing" time for a specific pedagogical purpose.)

Anthropologists usually identify five major levels or ecological types, subsumed under two broad categories: *food collectors* and *food producers*. These are listed in Table 3.1.

Table 3.1   Major Adaptive Strategies

Food collecting:
Hunting-gathering (including fishing)

Food producing:
Horticulture
Pastoral nomadism*
Agriculture
Industrialism

*There is some disagreement over whether or not pastoralism stands alone. See Chapter 7.

Six-month-old Herero girl; southern Africa. *(Photograph by the author.)*

Since we cannot go back in history and study the first hunter-gatherers, horticulturists, etc., we study modern peoples who today make their living in these ways, so that we can make inferences about the earlier stages. This is not to say that contemporary societies are exactly like those that existed originally in these earlier stages. Obviously, they are not; the people in these societies are as "modern" as you or I in that they are living now.

But if we are going to learn about our forebears—and, hence, about ourselves—we must start somewhere. We try, therefore, to combine ethnographic descriptions of contemporary peoples with archaeological evidence concerning past societies to arrive at generalizations about humankind's sociocultural evolution. Without a time-travel machine, this is the best we can do.

This approach—i.e., looking at the overall evolutionary picture of human development and using examples of contemporary societies *as if* they were antecedent to other stages—has been termed *general evolution*; whereas *specific evolution* deals with the actual evolutionary progression (or, loosely, history) of a society or set of societies.[1] I will deal in this handbook not with specific evolution but only with general evolution, in that I will concentrate on depicting major similarities found among societies within a given ecological type.

A related evolutionary approach is based on characteristic social structure as the defining attribute for each type or level. Thus, we might speak of societies with band organization (primarily hunter-gatherers), or those having tribal organization, chiefdoms, or state systems (food producers). I will be dealing with characteristics of social organization, but I will not base my initial overview on it. (I will use this type of progression in Part Three, when, for instance, I discuss types of political organization.)[2]

In Chapters 5 through 8 of this handbook, I will discuss each of the major levels of sociocultural evolution. But before doing so, since my discussions will pivot on food-getting (or subsistence) techniques, a few terms must be defined.

Ecology is the study of the interrelations of populations of living organisms (such as human beings) with their environment. The environment for any particular human population includes other groups of people (as well as nonhuman organisms and physical features). When I speak of this aspect of ecology—i.e., intergroup relations—I will call it *social ecology*. All the populations or species in a particular habitat form a network of interconnections and interdependencies, and this network is usually referred to as an *ecosystem*.

Adaptation refers to a particular aspect of ecological relationships. "Adaptation in man is the process by which he makes effective use for productive ends of the energy potential in his habitat" (Cohen 1968:41). That is, how people in a particular environment characteristically extract and use the resources of that environment—especially, which sources of energy they use—in order to provide for their survival and maintenance (food getting, shelter, protection and nurturance of their young, and so on) constitutes their *adaptive strategy*.

Theorists who advocate an ecological point of view usually see environmental circumstances in combination with a group's technology and organization of labor as primary—i.e., as being of first importance in, and perhaps even determining, forms of social organization, which they see as superimposed on (or epiphenomena of) technological-economic necessity and as reinforcing patterns of technological-economic organization. (One plausible way to diagram a basically ecological view of a sociocultural system, one which attributes priority to "economic organization," is shown in Figure 3.1, pages 30–31.) Those who advocate a cognitive or ethnoscientific approach in anthropology (see Chapter 2) usually see integration in a sociocultural system as being provided by conceptual codes or a system of ideational rules. They view conceptual systems as something distinct in themselves, as interactive with ecological factors but not determined by them. This is an issue for you, the reader, to resolve to your own satisfaction as you become more sophisticated in anthropology and better acquainted with the arguments from both camps and their effectiveness in application.[3]

THE INSTITUTIONAL APPROACH

The other comparative approach an author might employ is an institutional overview. This method of presentation (used in Part Three of this handbook) deals with more or less arbitrary divisions of a sociocultural organization—such as economic organization, political organization, religion, and kinship—and compares how these are structured and how they operate in different societies.[4]

For example, one focuses on "political organization" and compares how the need for order and conformity is handled in different societies. Other such "institutions," or sectioned-off complexes of belief and behavior in an overall sociocultural system, are then similarly treated. Hence, in an institutional approach, we are primarily interested in elaborating *differences* in comparable spheres of activity in various populations.

In an evolutionary or adaptational overview, however, we are chiefly interested in characterizing the overall *likenesses* among societies which we identify as being in the same stage or level—i.e., we are concerned with describing an ecological type—though we are also secondarily interested in the major differences among societies at different levels.

For instance, when I talk about hunter-gatherers, I will describe some general characteristics of sociocultural organization shared by most hunter-gatherers. I will not dwell on exceptions to this general model (i.e., how various hunter-gatherer societies differ from each other). Thus, I am sacrificing ethnographic detail for a general introduction.[5]

It should be understood that I use sociocultural evolution as an organizing framework for presenting certain information—information that concerns the organization of social relations characteristic of societies at each adaptive level—just as I use an institutional framework in Part Three. Since I am reluctant to become bogged down in theory, I do not discuss transitions between the levels. Instead, I focus on describing given adaptive strategies or ecological types.

That humanity as a species moved through various sociocultural stages—or, to phrase it differently, that human beings have used various adaptive strategies throughout their existence—is incontrovertible. It is no more moot than physical evolution. *How* and *why* humanity moved from one stage to another—how and why these transitions between adaptive strategies were accomplished—are highly disputable matters. As yet, anthropologists simply *do not know*. Several plausible ideas have been advanced; Carneiro's suggestions (1968, 1970), for example, come immediately to mind. But in order to discuss the hows and whys of these transitions, too much interpretive and speculative material would have to be included, altering the nature of this handbook, and I would finally reach a point at which I would have to take sides, to choose a theoretical platform.[6]

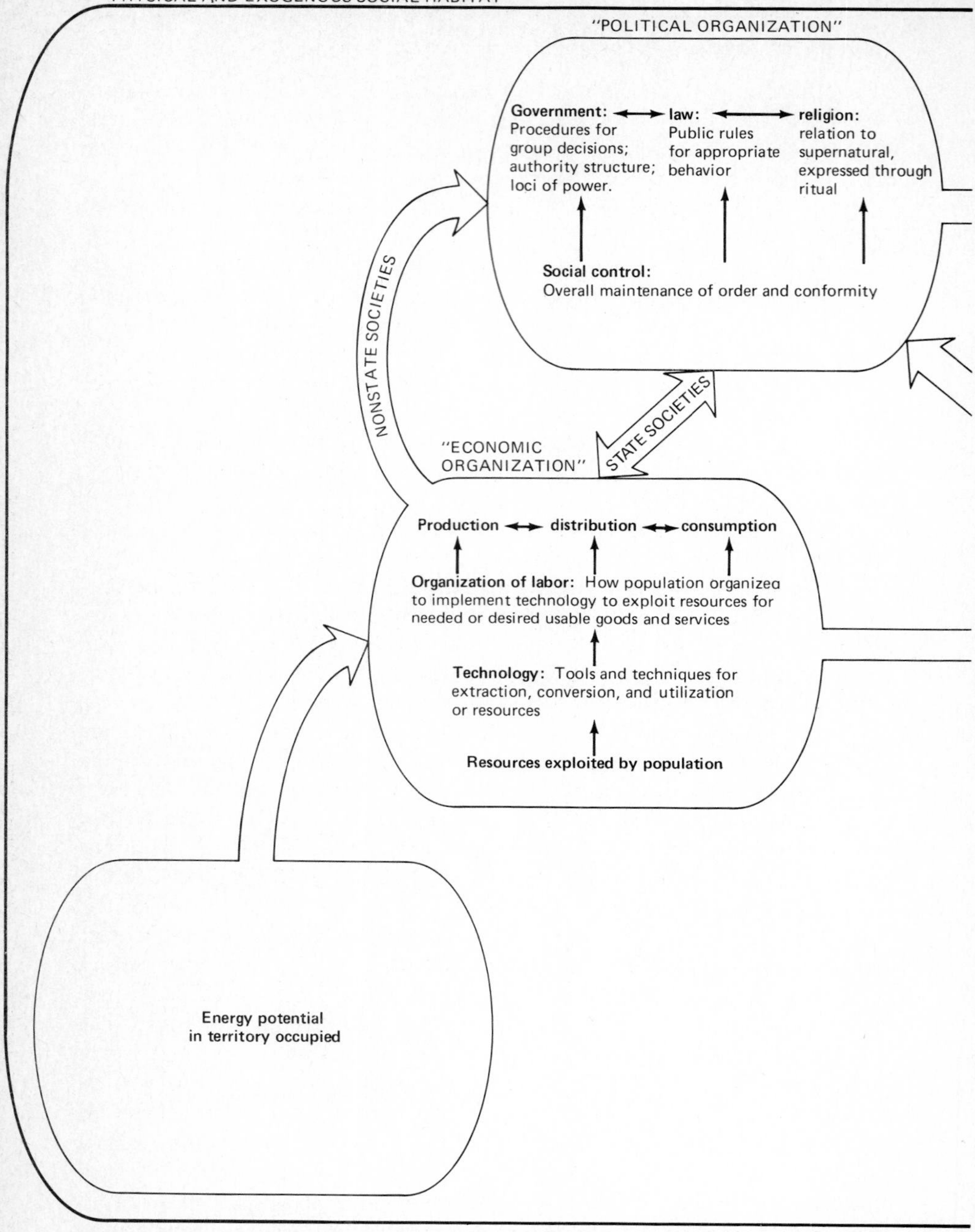

"POLITICAL ORGANIZATION"

NONSTATE SOCIETIES

Government: Procedures for group decisions; authority structure; loci of power.

law: Public rules for appropriate behavior

religion: relation to supernatural, expressed through ritual

Social control: Overall maintenance of order and conformity

STATE SOCIETIES

"ECONOMIC ORGANIZATION"

Production ←→ distribution ←→ consumption

Organization of labor: How population organized to implement technology to exploit resources for needed or desired usable goods and services

Technology: Tools and techniques for extraction, conversion, and utilization or resources

Resources exploited by population

Energy potential in territory occupied

Figure 3.1 Possible conceptualization of a sociocultural system from an ecological point of view. Arrows indicate the assumed directions of major causation. In such a system, feedbacks and even reversals occur; but these have been omitted in order to simplify.

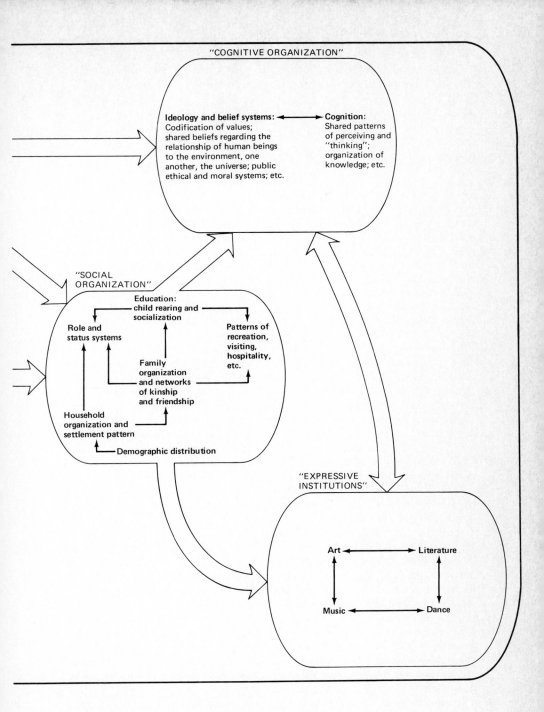

"COGNITIVE ORGANIZATION"

Ideology and belief systems: ←————→ Cognition:
Codification of values; Shared patterns
shared beliefs regarding the of perceiving and
relationship of human beings "thinking";
to the environment, one organization of
another, the universe; public knowledge; etc.
ethical and moral systems; etc.

"SOCIAL
ORGANIZATION"

Education:
child rearing and
socialization

Role and
status systems

Patterns of
recreation,
visiting,
hospitality,
etc.

Family
organization
and networks
of kinship
and friendship

Household
organization and
settlement pattern

Demographic distribution

"EXPRESSIVE
INSTITUTIONS"

Art ←————→ Literature

Music ←————→ Dance

31

Therefore, in Chapters 5 through 8, I describe, in general terms, each of the adaptive strategies, sticking closely to the "facts" that almost all anthropologists acknowledge. I leave most of the theoretical issues to instructors, to handle as they deem appropriate.

FOOTNOTES

1 For a fuller and more exact account of specific and general evolution, see Sahlins (1960), the originator of these terms.

2 Perhaps the instructor should make clear that this choice represents a bias on the author's part. It reflects my view that sociocultural systems cohere around, and must be compatible with, a central core that consists of "economic organization"—or, in Cohen's more apt phrase, a group's "adaptive strategy." As was pointed out in the previous chapter, Cohen's series of readers is probably the best available presentation of this approach.

3 The book that may very well become the *opus classicus* for the ecological (or "etic") argument is Harris's *Rise of Anthropological Theory* (1968). The "emic" argument has not as yet been so fully expounded, but Goodenough's statements are probably the most comprehensive to date (especially 1968, but see also 1961, 1969, and 1971).

4 No rigorous definition of the term *institution* has achieved currency among social scientists, but Spiro's description (1966:98) comes closest to the way I use the term: "All institutions consist of *belief systems*, i.e., an enduring organization of cognitions about one or more aspects of the universe; *action systems*, an enduring organization of behavior patterns designed to attain ends for the satisfaction of needs; and *value systems*, an enduring organization of principles by which behavior can be judged on some scale of merit." (See Glossary.)

5 Each of Chapters 5 through 8 is a thumbnail sketch of a major ecological type and is intended to present a very general picture of societies at that level. Strictly speaking, none of these characterizations can properly be considered a "model," since major variables are not given much more attention than minor ones and the complex relationships of the variables to each other are not examined in great detail. (This reflects both omissions in the literature and the difficulty of accurately encapsulating in a few pages a wide range of phenomena and their diverse manifestations.) These chapters are, instead, suggestive descriptions of adaptive strategies, abstracted from a composite of several ethnographic cases but strictly applicable to none. This is a reasonably acceptable way to introduce someone to sociocultural levels in the broadest of terms, but it will be found wanting when compared with any actual ethnographic examples. To encourage such comparisons, at the end of each chapter a brief description is provided of at least one actual society exhibiting the adaptive strategy under consideration. *These descriptions are only sketches.* They are not intended to be complete ethnographic accounts but are only meant to convey some flavor of the society under discussion.

6 Carneiro (1968; in Cohen 1974:162) has noted that "looked at from a distance, an evolutionary advance appears to be the logical unfolding of an inherent tendency. But examined more closely, it always proves to have been mediated by

particular ecological conditions." Unfortunately for our understanding of evolutionary process and the mechanisms and influences involved in transitions between adaptive strategies, anthropologists—with only a few exceptions, such as Carneiro and Robert McC. Adams (1966)—have concentrated mostly on the long view at the expense of close inspections. This is really not surprising, for the transitions (except to industrialism) occurred in prehistoric times, and our understanding of them must be based on reconstructions and inferences made from historical and contemporary data. This sort of retrodiction is risky as well as difficult, for, as was pointed out above, contemporary societies, no matter how "simple" they may seem to some of us, are not themselves actually antecedents of more complex adaptive strategies.

Chapter 4

Hunter-Gatherers

(Photograph by Ingrid Deich.)

By means of fossil evidence, physical anthropologists have been able to trace human biological evolution back nearly five million years without any great time gaps. For most of this five-million-year period—for nearly all of it, in fact—humankind has made its living by hunting-gathering. Only comparatively recently (9,000 to 11,000 years ago) have humans begun *producing* food.[1]

Hence, considering this time depth and the obvious adaptive significance food collecting has had for humanity, I will begin this overview of ecological types with a discussion of hunter-gatherers.

CHARACTERISTICS OF HUNTER-GATHERER GROUPS

Hunter-gatherers are food collectors. They hunt wild game (or fish) and forage for wild plants. They do not rely on domesticated plants or animals for subsistence. They live off the land as they find it.[2]

Small Groups

Hunter-gatherers characteristically live in *small groups* (usually only a few families and rarely exceeding a total of fifty individuals) called *bands* or *camps*.

Flexibility

Hunter-gatherer groups are very loosely structured and unstable; their membership is continually changing; persons frequently drop out of one group and join another. Though these groups are generally small, hunter-gatherers sometimes form larger groups during certain seasons. For example, during the dry season, when water is scarce, the Bushmen of the Kalahari Desert in southern Africa congregate around the few remaining waterholes; and the Eskimo of North America come together in large groups to hunt caribou during the migrating season. (The practice of small groups' coming together into larger aggregations is referred to as *fusion*, and their splitting up is called *fission*.) Thus, group *flexibility* is characteristic of hunter-gatherers. This flexibility is necessary in order to adapt to the vicissitudes of the habitat, to take advantage of game and vegetation.

Mobility

Hunter-gatherers are also *highly mobile*; they are generally nomadic. This, too, is in order to go where the resources are—to follow game, to seek out edible plants and water deposits. Hunter-gatherers may be seen as very much a "part of nature"—more so, probably, than those who practice any other way of making a living, from primitive farmers to modern industrialists. Hunter-gatherers must adapt to changes in seasons; they move where the animals they hunt move; they go where water and plant life occur naturally. They do not raise animals for subsistence or cultivate plants but merely use what is already available. They take what they need from the environment. They do not replace what they take or reinvest in their environment—though they are conservationists; they have to be to survive. And they make simple tools (spears, bows and arrows, etc.) from the same sources from which they get their food. Given these characteristics, it is easy to understand why hunter-gatherer bands have a loosely structured, highly flexible social organization and a high rate of mobility: because they, so to speak, "follow nature around," taking what is needed. In this they are much like the animals they hunt, which move about in search of grass and water. Social organization must be flexible to allow the group to take advantage of the growth of vegetation, of the movement of game.

Leadership: *Primus Inter Pares*

Another characteristic of hunter-gatherer societies is their *lack of formally defined positions of leadership*. No one in a hunting-and-gathering society has any power or authority (as opposed to influence) over the group. Nobody can tell anyone else what to do, because no one would listen; and no one has the power to make others listen.[3]

There is, however, a kind of informal leadership known as *primus inter pares* ("first among equals"). A leader of this type does not exercise coercive authority. "Neither he nor any other leader has the power or the right to compel compliance. He can only advise or persuade" (Murdock 1959:33). A person accorded the status of *primus inter pares* is one who demonstrates proficiency in hunting or some other valued endeavor, who provides well for his or her family, behaves judiciously, and so on. He or she is, in short, an individual who does well what a person is expected to do and who exhibits those qualities and personality characteristics admired by the group.

For emphasis, it should be repeated (since we in modern state societies find it difficult to conceive of societies without an authority system) that such a person has no formal authority, cannot tell anyone what to do, and cannot issue orders and force others to obey them. He or she is merely a respected individual whose advice and opinions are often sought.

Division of Labor

Accordingly, in hunting and gathering societies every person's labor is, for the most part, under that person's own control. No one can tell another what work to do or not to do. And no one can demand a percentage of the products of labor—i.e., there is no taxation.

But there is sharing of food among hunter-gatherers. If a man or a small group of men kills a large animal, the meat will be divided among all the members of the band. In this way, everyone gets some protein. Since the group is never sure when, where, or how much game will be available in the future, the sharing of meat serves as a distribution mechanism for an unpredictable food source. If I am fortunate enough to kill a deer today, I will share it with you because the next time I may not be so lucky. But *you* may be; and I will expect you to share your luck with me.

This band-wide sharing, however, usually does not extend to gathered plants. Women normally gather in groups (for protection against predators, care of the young, companionship, etc.), but each woman brings the food she has collected back to her own household. This is probably related to the fact that, where gathering is important, the supply of wild plants is somewhat more dependable than the supply of game. Consequently, there is less need to share.

There is no *specialization of labor* in hunting-and-gathering societies. That is, there are no full-time specialists who do predominantly one thing, such as artisans (carpenters, metallurgists, etc.). Instead, there is a *division of labor based on sex*, with men generally doing the hunting and women the gathering. Within each sex there is usually also a breakdown of tasks based on *age* (certain tasks, however, such as those assigned to young children, may not be sex-related). The elderly, persons in their prime, and children of various ages perform different but complementary chores.

In essence, each household, the basic social unit within the band, supplies most of its own needs—makes and repairs most of its own tools (though a limited amount of trading may occur with persons who have special skills, such as arrow making), gets most of its own food (though, as noted, sharing is practiced), and performs most of its own religious functions (but see the comments on shamans below).

Much of the earlier literature on hunter-gatherers focused on man-as-hunter. Lately, however, more attention has been paid to women's role in food procurement. Though hunting is primarily men's work, gathering is not. Gathering is done by the women. The importance of gathering wild plant foods is only now being explored. It seems that wild plant foods may contribute as much as 60 to 80 percent of some, perhaps most, hunter-gatherers' diets. This makes women's role in subsistence seem indispensable. Though hunting may appear more dramatic and exciting, it is becoming increasingly evident that collecting plants is more central to daily survival, at least among many hunter-gatherers (Lee and DeVore 1968).

Equality

In such societies, there is no social stratification, and there are no social classes (defined by access to resources). Hence, hunter-gatherer society is usually characterized as *egalitarian*—i.e., everyone, at least theoretically, has equal access to resources, limited mainly by a person's own ability.[4] Anyone in the society may go out and hunt game and gather plants. No one in the group controls these resources. (It is this characteristic, lack of control over resources, which in large part accounts for the absence of positions of power.)

Kinship

The basic ideological construct (or notion or idea) upon which groups are built is *kinship*. That is, although almost anyone can drop out of one band and join another, people usually support their move into a group by invoking a kinship relationship with some person already a member of that group. It often is not important if a person is "really" related to a member (what is called *real* or *actual* kinship); one simply claims to be related (this is called *putative* or *fictive* kinship) to legitimize a move. Kinship, it must be stressed, is a device that people manipulate for social ends. It normally does not represent an overly rigid constraint on behavior.

Kinship provides an obvious means for ordering social relations. All societies recognize "relatedness" between parents and children, between siblings, and so on, though precisely how they conceive of this "relatedness" and which relationships they tend to emphasize and for what purposes are matters subject to a great degree of variation (see Chapter 12). Hence, all societies use notions of kinship to some extent to regulate behavior. In small-scale, nonliterate societies, however, kinship—along with sex and age—is a primary structuring principle. Watson and Watson (1969:64) comment on the significance of kinship among hunter-gatherers:

> The advantages of social organization along kinship lines is that it formalizes and extends patterns of sharing and cooperation. It makes possible a more versatile and complex, and thus more efficient, attack on the problems stemming from basic human needs than is possible in other primate groups. The institution of kinship is, then, a major way of interacting with the physical environment and, hence, a *cultural* concept that makes the society of men distinctly different from that of protohuman and nonhuman primates.

Territoriality and Property Rights

Hunting-and-gathering bands usually do not "own" land or resources (as we would understand "ownership"). In essence, they travel about, using any available resources as long as someone else is not already using them. Characteristically, then, there is *little, if any, formal territoriality* among hunter-gatherers (though there is a general sense that the group is entitled to access to the overall area in which they forage, and they will resist efforts by other groups to restrict their activities).

As regards property, Steward's comments (1955:107) concerning the Shoshoni Indians of the Great Basin area are generally applicable to most other hunter-gatherers and so are worth reproducing:

> The concept of property rights among the Shoshoneans was directly related to their mode of life. These Indians assumed that rights to exclusive use of anything resulted from work expended by particular individuals or groups and from habitual use. This is a rather obvious, simple, and practical concept, and it seems to have entailed a minimum of conflict.
>
> In most parts of the area, natural resources were available to anyone. The seeds gathered by a woman, however, belonged to her because she had done the work of converting a natural resource into something that could be directly consumed. If a man made a bow or built a house, these were his, although prior to making objects of them, the trees he utilized belonged to no one. Any family might fish in a certain river or stream, but if a group of families built a fish weir, it alone had the right to use that weir.

Fighting

Because of the lack of territoriality, hunter-gatherers usually do not engage in large-scale conflict or *war* among themselves (but they will make war against an invading power that threatens their autonomy or their access to resources). However, *feuding*, a smaller-scale and more individualistic form of conflict, does exist. (Feuding between individuals or small groups of related individuals may arise from accusations of adultery, laziness, aggressiveness, sorcery, and so on. See the section on feuding and conflict resolution in Chapter 11).

Religion

As for religion, hunter-gatherers are typically *polytheistic*—that is, they have many gods.[5] Not only do many deities exist, but people maintain a relationship with all of them (this is not always true, as will be pointed out, in societies at other evolutionary levels).

Each sphere of nature or activity is governed by its own deity (thus, for instance, there may be a god of rain, of sunshine, of sickness, of rabbits, etc.). Each deity is autonomous and has no right to tell any other deity what to do—just as in human social relationships there is no formal political authority. And there is usually no high god, no supreme deity.

Also in accord with the rest of social organization, the relationship to the supernatural is maintained primarily on an *individual* basis. That is, there are no priests (or full-time religious practitioners); each person, for the most part, is his or her own religious functionary. Though group rituals do occur, mainly in reference to "life cycle" ceremonies (Chapter 9), much religious activity is perfomed by individuals in a more or less spontaneous manner.

Though a formal priesthood is absent among hunter-gatherers, part-time religious and magical practitioners, called *shamans* (see Chapter 14), are often found. These are persons who have a special talent or predilection for dealing with the supernatural or with crises. Perhaps they are prone to having visions or going into a trance, or they may claim the ability to converse readily with spirits or to cure sickness. Other members of the community, therefore, may seek their help from time to time. It is important to remember, however, that shamans do not "make a living" from their special talents. They hunt, collect, and perform the same basic tasks for their livelihood that other members of the community perform. In other words, shamanism may be described as an avocation or a sideline rather than as a vocation.[6]

SUMMARY OF CHARACTERISTICS

Small groups: bands or camps
Fluid or unstable group organization (fission and fusion)
High mobility; nomadism
Taking from the environment rather than replenishment of it

No authoritarian leadership (primus inter pares instead)
No specialization
Division of labor by sex and by age
Egalitarian society (no social stratification)
Ideology of kinship, but not rigid
No "ownership" of resources
Lack of strict territoriality
Feuding, but not large-scale war
Polytheistic religion

ETHNOGRAPHIC SKETCH: The Tasaday—Cave-Dwellers in the Philippine Rain Forest

Some time during the early or middle 1960s an adventurous Filipino hunter named Dafal wandered deep into the rain forest. He happened upon three near-naked men digging roots. After considerable difficulty, Dafal succeeded in making friends with the frightened men. They exchanged some food, conversed as well as they were able, and parted. For the next few years Dafal met several times with these people of the forest.

In 1971 Manuel Elizalde, the head of the Private Association for National Minorities in the Philippines, met Dafal while visiting in a tribal community at the edge of the rain forest. Dafal told Elizalde about the reclusive forest people. Fearing what might befall these people when happened on by loggers, miners, settlers, and assorted entrepreneurs, Elizalde asked Dafal to contact the forest people and to try to persuade them to meet with him. This was accomplished in June of 1971, and thus began an association that introduced the outside world to an isolated group of simple, cave-dwelling foragers called the Tasaday. (It also, of course, exposed the Tasaday to the ways of the outside world and so altered forever their simple lives.)

The following brief sketch of the Tasaday is based on John Nance's (1975) report of the information gathered during the first three years of intermittent contact between the forest people and outsiders. Throughout this description the ethnographic present refers to the time, as well as it can be reconstructed, before contact. This sketch should be viewed as highly tentative, since the data on which it is based are meager and are extracted from a nontechnical publication.

WHO ARE THE TASADAY?

The term *Tasaday* properly refers to only one of at least three (and probably more) separate but intermarrying bands. The other two bands specifically named in Nance's account are the Tasafeng and the Sanduka. All three groups of people take their names from the geographic designations they apply to the locations of their base camps. Thus the Tasaday band are the people who live in the caves in Mount Tasaday. (Apparently no generic name exists for all the bands taken together.)

The Tasaday band totals about two dozen persons, including those women acquired in marriage from other bands. The Tasaday speak a Malayo-Polynesian language (their historical origin is still unknown). The group consists of related males, their wives, and their unmarried daughters. Figure 4.1 diagrams the claimed kinship composition of the Tasaday. Fangul, the apical ancestor, is the legendary founder of the band and is referred to as the original "owner" of the caves in which the group lives. (The Tasaday say that today the caves and the surrounding forest are communally "owned" by the band as a whole.)

The researchers who have worked among the Tasaday (anthropological field research, conducted by about a half-dozen investigators, totals less than four months spread over a three-year period), and others who have learned of these forest people, have puzzled over their small population. At this stage of our knowledge no satisfactory answer has been established, but there are indications in Nance's report that fission and a high mortality rate are important factors in limiting group size.

With the possible exception of snakebite (which one person in the group, a man named Udelen, is said to be able to treat), the Tasaday appear not to treat their sick. They have no curing ceremonies, medicinal herbs, or the like. Sick persons are simply allowed to die or recover on their own. (This is not so unusual. For an example of another forest people who have few or no curing rites, see Holmberg 1969.) During the contact period, 1971–1974, visitors to

A group of Tasaday at the back of a cave; Philippines. *(Photograph: John Nance/Panamin/Magnum.)*

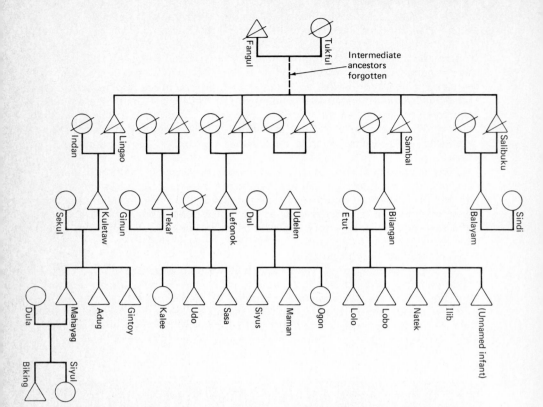

Figure 4.1 The Tasaday. Total population in 1974: twenty-eight, including women obtained in marriage from other groups. Age range: infancy to mid-sixties (estimated). An oblique line through a symbol indicates that the individual is deceased; for an explanation of the symbols, see Chapter 12. (*Note:* All adult women are originally from other bands and are Tasaday by marriage. Sekul, Ginun, Dul, and Dula are from the Tasafeng; Etut is from the Sanduka. Sindi is from a tribal group located outside the forest; she accompanied one of Elizalde's early expeditions to the Tasaday and later returned to take up residence with the Tasaday as Balayam's wife.)

the Tasaday, including a medical doctor, reckoned that at least three individuals (Sasa, Siyus, and Lobo in Figure 4.1) would have died without outside intervention. One boy (a son of Lefonok named Ukan, not shown in Figure 4.1) did die during this period. Another male, an adult, currently suffers from a hernia that may soon strangulate. If this situation is characteristic for the Tasaday, it helps to explain their low population.[7]

Another factor is fission. During the latter part of the initial three-year contact period, there were indications that the group was fragmenting. Two nuclear families were spending more and more time at other caves. Bilangan, Etut, and their five sons (see Figure 4.1) had begun to spend extended periods at new caves away from Tasaday. Mahayag and his family also established quarters elsewhere. A permanent change of residence had not yet been effected for either group; but it is conceivable that this might occur in the future, establishing two new bands, with Bilangan and Mahayag, like Fangul for the Tasaday, as their respective founders. If fission is a normal process among the Tasaday, it also helps to explain the small size of the group. (At the time Nance's book was written, plans were being made to seek out the other bands of cave-dwellers mentioned by the Tasaday. Large-scale and more intensive research among all these groups will go a long way toward answering the many questions raised by the sporadic, and in many ways superficial, contact we have so far had with the forest people.)

MAKING A LIVING

The Tasaday live in three caves in the side of the mountain from which they derive their name. These caves, which overlook a large stream, constitute their permanent dwelling place, though they occasionally stay in other nearby caves when they are out foraging and are unable to return to the main camp before nightfall. The Tasaday explain that they do not like to be in the forest at night and so try to avoid overnight foraging expeditions. Nevertheless, they do occur.

At first contact all the Tasaday, except one, were sharing a single upper cave in which they slept and ate their meals. Balayam, whose parents were dead and who was the only unmarried adult male, slept alone in a lower cave. (This changed after his marriage to Sindi, a non-Tasaday who visited the forest people with Elizalde's expeditions.) Later the Tasaday distributed themselves in two of the three caves. They gave no reason for this other than that they felt like doing it. It apparently was not due to ill feeling or conflict of any sort. (In fact, the Tasaday appear to be one of the most pacific, cooperative, nonviolent groups in the ethnographic record.)

From the caves the Tasaday go out foraging in the forest. They are simple collectors and supply their daily food requirements through only a few hours of gathering a day.[8] (More precise information concerning energy expended on food gathering must await input-output studies similar to those conducted by Richard Lee [1969] for the Bushmen.)

The staple food gathered by the Tasaday is a root they call *biking*, which is dug up with a pointed stick and is eaten either raw or cooked. They also gather various fruits and some wild yams. *Ubud* and *natek* (palm heart or pith) are also eaten by the Tasaday today. (They were introduced to *natek* by Dafal. There is some question whether *ubud* is a pre- or post-contact food, for it is extremely difficult to extract with stone tools, and the Tasaday had no metal until they met Dafal.)

The Tasaday also collect frogs, tadpoles, crabs, and fish, which are usually cooked; and grubs, which may be eaten cooked or raw (though the heads are not eaten), thereby satisfying their major protein requirements. Before contact with Dafal, the Tasaday did not hunt or trap large animals, such as deer, monkey, or pig. So, though the Tasaday are meat-eaters,[9] they are more properly classified as gatherers than as hunter-gatherers. (In addition to teaching the Tasaday to make traps, Dafal also introduced them to the bow and arrow, metal earrings to replace the rattan they formerly used, and cloth, which was less practical for them than the grass skirts the women wear and the grass genital pouches the men wear.)

The division of labor appears to be minimal among the Tasaday. The only strictly female activity is sweeping out the caves; whereas men carry the heavy loads of firewood. Men, women, and children share jointly in collecting food, both plant and animal. Men and women bear similar responsibility in child care and care of the elderly.

All food is shared among all the members of the group (but each of the nuclear families within the band must gather its own firewood). It was observed by one researcher, however, that as *ubud* grew more scarce in the area around the caves, each foraging group brought back only a small amount of food to be shared by the entire band. Apparently, each family was eating more food in private away from the caves. (The depletion of immediately available resources in the vicinity of the caves may be a factor influencing fission and, hence, population dispersion.)

POLITICAL ORGANIZATION

The Tasaday are highly egalitarian. They repeatedly expressed their disapproval of outsiders having "hard looks and big talking." The band is without a leader, without an authority structure. Decision making is a group process based on discussion, with all men and women expressing their opinions. (The Tasaday consistently claimed that, though children argued or disagreed to the point of bickering, adults never did. This assertion is difficult to accept entirely, but intragroup conflict, if not nonexistent, does appear to be minimal.)

Nevertheless, some incipient specialization is evident among the Tasaday. For example, Dul, the wife of Udelen, appears to exert more influence over the group than any other single individual. Her opinions are highly regarded, and her recommendations seem to be followed more often than are anyone else's. It is she who is usually entrusted with the task of dividing up and apportioning food, though Balayam occasionally performs this chore as well. From the evidence available, however, it is clear that Dul's influence—the reasons for which remain unknown—does not qualify her as a "leader"; she does not exercise any real authority.[10]

MARRIAGE AND INTERGROUP CONTACT

The Tasaday are strictly monogamous. Women are exchanged as wives with other bands. Etut was obtained from the Sanduka band, and Sekul, Dul, Dula, and Ginun came from the Tasafeng band. Since there are no adult, unmarried women living among the Tasaday, it may be assumed that the Tasaday also give women as wives to these other groups. (Attempts by visitors to establish this conclusively met with an indifferent response from the Tasaday.)

Marriages are said to be arranged by parents from different bands when they meet by chance in the forest and are accompanied by gifts of food. (It will strike any anthropologist as odd that so important an affair as marriage should be left to chance. There is no doubt that we need more data.) At the time of contact, the Tasaday claimed not to know any longer where the Tasafeng and

Sanduka bands were and appealed to the visitors to bring them women as wives. (The Tasaday also said they had never been outside the forest and did not know of the existence of other peoples beyond the forest.)

No elaborate ceremony surrounds marriage (nor, for that matter, any aspect of Tasaday life).[11] The group merely gathers around the newlyweds and repeats the word *mafeon* ("good" or "beautiful").

RELIGION

The Tasaday frequently refer to their ancestors in order to explain why they behave or believe as they do, but they do not appear to mean by ancestors the deified spirits of their forebears. The phrase "Our ancestors taught us to do such-and-such" is not an allusion to the supernatural but simply refers to tradition: "Those before us lived this way, so we live this way."

In fact, no terms were found among the Tasaday that could be interpreted as referring to a god or deity, nor did they have any notions of an afterlife. It is even uncertain whether they comprehend the notion of a soul. When attempting to discuss the subject with them, the phrases "inside feelings" or "that in a person which is living" were used. In response to questions regarding what happens to this "soul" at death, the Tasaday said simply that it goes out of a person, who is then dead. They did not know where it went or, for that matter, where it had come from. And it seems that they do not care to worry over the issue.[12]

When a person died, he or she was taken into the forest, covered with leaves, and left. The Tasaday then did their best to forget the person, for it "hurt them inside" to remember. This minimum ritual of covering the deceased in leaves appears to constitute the whole of the funeral rites. (Birth likewise is treated with little ritual. The placenta is taken into the forest and is either hung in a tree or buried—it is unclear which. No further ceremony is performed. It appears to follow from the incidents Nance records that an infant is not named until the next child is born.)

Though it is questionable that the Tasaday have any notion at all of spirits or supernatural beings of any kind (for there is some indication that their references to "witches," "spirits," and "fairies" derive from interaction with Dafal and subsequent visitors), they do have taboos. That is, they believe that certain acts bring supernatural retaliation. These acts are those which disturb the harmony of life near the caves. The most frequently mentioned acts are breaking off leaves or cutting trees around the caves—which would bring rain and make gathering difficult. At one point during the initial contact period several Tasaday caught cold. This was attributed to the careless behavior of some Tasaday youngsters who had been playing near the caves and had accidentally broken some small branches and leaves. This is a slim basis, however, for making generalizations about Tasaday "religion" (see Chapter 14), and obviously much more research is needed to clarify this and other aspects of Tasaday life. It may, however, be too late; for, as of this writing, the Tasaday have been subjected to a massive amount of outside influence for the past ten years.[13]

FOOTNOTES

1 Students accustomed to thinking of the civilizations of Rome or Greece as "ancient" may be surprised at my speaking of 10,000 years ago as "recent." But in terms of geological time in general or the physical evolution of human beings in particular, 10,000 years ago is barely a flickering moment.

2 The anthropological habit of speaking of primitive societies in the present tense is called the *ethnographic present.* This generally refers to such societies as they were described when first encountered by Westerners. Obviously, many of these societies have undergone extreme changes over the years, and these descriptions no longer reflect the current situation.

3 The instructor might here mention some well known exceptions, such as the net-owning rabbit-bosses among the Shoshoni (Spencer and Jennings *et al.* 1965:273ff.; Steward 1938) and the boat-owning whaling captains among the North Alaskan Eskimo (Spencer 1959).

   The classic ethnographic exceptions to the general hunter-gatherer model presented here are of course the Northwest Coast Indians (Drucker 1955). I have found it a useful exercise in my classes to have the students themselves delineate how the existence of a predictable food supply (salmon) may account for the divergence of Northwest Coast social organization from the model.

4 Speaking of one hunting-gathering group, Asen Balikci (1970:4) says, "Every Netsilik Eskimo had to look after his own equipment, make new weapons, and repair old ones. Despite the complexity of articles such as the kayak and the composite bow, every man had the skills and the tools to be technologically self-sufficient. This was an absolute necessity in the Arctic."

5 Some anthropologists prefer to distinguish religions on the basis of whether or not the notion of a high god (Chapter 14) is present, rather than employ a dichotomy between polytheism and monotheism (belief in one god)—though there is considerable disagreement over whether the concept of a high god is aboriginal or results from contact with a monotheistic society. A number of researchers argue that true monotheism is very rare, for many so-called monotheistic religions actually hold that the universe is populated by more than one supernatural personality. For simplicity, I will speak of "polytheism" and "monotheism," but the reader should bear in mind that the distinction between them is not absolute.

6 According to Webster's dictionary, an *avocation* is "a subordinate occupation pursued in addition to one's regular work," a *vocation* is "the work in which a person is regularly employed." (Quoted by permission. From *Webster's Third New International Dictionary* © 1971 by G. & C. Merriam Co., publishers of the Merriam-Webster Dictionaries.)

7 With regard to care of the ill or infirm, John Nance, in a personal communication to the author, reports that the Tasaday "do make a try now and then." And "although the botanists confirm that they have found surprisingly little use by the Tasaday of plants and herbs for medicinal purposes," he is aware of at least three uses: "(1) the snakebite treatment you have already cited; (2) the use of a plant to make a drink—perhaps a brew—which was given to Etut after she had given birth and was waiting for the placenta to separate; the drink was supposed to speed the separation; and (3) the sap of a plant stem used against

insect bites and poisonous plants; application of the sap soothes itching and stops burning. . . . Incidentally, the botanists make note also that in studying some 200 plants they did not consider their work exhaustive because inquiries on plants of suspected medicinal or 'religious' significance 'often drew evasive answers.'"

8   "One afternoon we went upstream with the Tasaday on a food-gathering foray. In less than two hours of playful collecting they had sixteen tadpoles, four crabs, three frogs, one fish about four inches long, two feet of *ubud* [palm heart], assorted edible flowers and nutty fruits" (Nance 1975:180).

9   Some writers prefer to restrict the meaning of *meat* to the flesh of mammals. I use the term in its more general sense, to refer to the flesh of any animal.

10 In this respect, Nance, in another personal communication, makes the following perceptive observation (my emphasis): "I'd tend to be a little more qualified in making Dul the most authoritative. She did indeed seem to be so in certain instances we observed, but I think Balayam, Mahayag, Sekul and perhaps others had strong influence also. I'm just not sure. I have thought sometimes that Dul's influence was enhanced by *her ability to deal successfully with Elizalde.*"

11 Nance (personal communication) comments on Tasaday ritual: "The Tasaday's description of the birth does have ritualistic aspects—the entire group gathered around, men and children back, women forward attending the mother-to-be; the elderly Sekul seeming to be in charge of labor assistance and cord-cutting, etc. Also, I think the handling of the placenta was something special to them, and that the failure to take me with them on that activity was not accidental. . . . I have thought lately that there probably was much more ritual to Tasaday life than we realized, and, in various ways, their whole life was ritualized—notably in their close relationships with plants, animals, each other and the forest."

12 Once again in a personal communication Nance offers a useful observation on religion: "As for gods, deities, soul, religion, I suspect that their expressions about the 'owner of the forest' and 'owner of the cave' hold more religious and/or supernatural connotations than we can be sure of. The power of the 'owner,' for instance, to send punishing rain, wind, lightning, sickness—and, in Lobo's case, even a sentence of death—suggests that this is a strong force in their lives. As for their concept of soul, they do refer, as you mention, to 'that in a person which is living' and that inside a person which sees the dream. And they have (at least Balayam has) expressed concern that after death this sp.rit may lure away the spirits of the still-living Tasaday; thus the dead are taken far away. Hence I'm inclined to think that they have some notion of soul or spirit."

13 For additional information, see *Further Studies on the Tasaday* (and references therein), edited by Douglas Yen and John Nance, which contains six research papers on archaeology, linguistics, and botany. It is available from the Panamin Foundation in Manila and from Bee Cross Media in Rochester, New York.

Chapter 5

Horticulturists

(Photograph by Erwin H. Epstein.)

About 9,000 to 11,000 years ago, plants and animals were first domesticated. Human beings began to produce their food independently in several areas of the world (e.g., the Middle East, Southeast Asia, northern Africa).[1] The earliest form of farming is known as horticulture.

Horticulture refers to a technique of cultivation that relies on hand tools, such as the digging stick (or dibble) and the hoe. Plows and draft animals are not employed in raising crops.

SLASH-AND-BURN HORTICULTURE

The most common type of horticulture, still in use by many of the peoples of the world today, is probably that called *slash-and-burn* or *shifting horticulture* or *swidden cultivation.* It is found today primarily, but not only, in tropical areas (such as the Amazon Basin in South America and the Congo Basin in Africa). The defining technique of this kind of cultivation is cutting down brush and trees and then burning them in order to plant. Men usually do the heavy work of cutting trees and bush cover, while women do most of the sowing and tending of crops, with men assisting for the harvest. Each plot of land is used for a time and then abandoned in order for the soil to be rejuvenated. Shifting horticulture thus requires large areas of land (or a low people-to-land ratio). The use of wide tracts of land is known as *extensive* cultivation; that is, people move periodically from plot to plot, utilizing extensive areas of land for growing crops. But where sufficient land is not available, horticulturists also practice *intensive* cultivation by means of crop rotation, fertilization, terracing, or limited irrigation. In intensive cultivation, people invest more of their labor in fewer fields. In other words, they "stay put" (are sedentary or semisedentary) and work the same land repeatedly.

Another factor that helps to account for the variable occurrence of extensive and intensive cultivation is how a group satisfies protein requirements. For example, Carneiro's work (1968) suggests that people living near rivers rich in fish are more likely to stay put and intensify their cultivation practices because they have a dependable supply of protein. Where people must hunt land animals for their major source of protein, and therefore roam over a large area, they are prevented from concentrating on developing cultivating techniques. And Meggers (1971) has shown that extensive slash-and-burn cultivation is actually more efficient in tropical environments than the intensive techniques practiced in temperate climates.

CHARACTERISTICS OF HORTICULTURISTS

It is difficult to generalize about the social organization of horticulturists, as was done for hunter-gatherers, for there is no single characteristic social organization for societies practicing horticulture. Instead, horticulturists run the gamut of social organization, ranging from a type that is very similar in many respects to the general characteristics enumerated in Chapter 4 for hunter-gatherers, through a continuum of variation, to a type like that of agriculturists in a nation-state. Yet we may still note some *very* general characteristics of horticultural peoples arising from the constraints of tilling the land.

Sedentariness

When people begin investing their labor in land to produce crops for food, they must remain sedentary for at least part of the year. Clearing the land and planting take time, and often—especially in tropical areas—these tasks must be begun and completed in one continuous stretch of time; otherwise the land will be overgrown by bush. Thus one characteristic that can be noted is the tendency toward *sedentariness* of many groups practicing horticulture. The change from a nomadic way of life to a more settled one produces other changes that ramify through social organization.

Larger Populations

Cultivation also provides a more dependable food supply than does hunting-gathering, so *larger populations* occur.

Where extensive cultivation is practiced, however, high population densities are self-defeating. A low people-to-land ratio must obtain in order for this kind of cultivation to provide adequate subsistence. Therefore, small villages, hamlets, or homesteads, which are frequently moved, are found scattered at considerable distances from each other throughout a wide area.

But with intensive cultivation, larger populations can concentrate on the land, since the same land is used and reused. People move less frequently, or not at all; consequently, larger villages or communities, perhaps closer together, are found.

Kin Groups

With more permanent communities relying on cooperative effort to produce food, affiliations to units larger than the immediate family or household usually assume an important role in social life. When groups of people begin to invest their time and energy in producing a commodity, they also begin to claim ownership over the fruits of their labor. Crops are such a commodity, and since the raising of crops normally requires the cooperation of several persons, these persons claim joint rights in the crops and the land that they worked to produce the crops. A relatively simple and common way to structure such a group is on the basis of kinship—the assertion of ties of "relatedness" among people—such as is the case with lineages and clans (see Chapter 12). Hence, horticulturists, as opposed to most hunter-gatherers, are characterized by the existence of relatively stable *descent* or *kin groups* as important elements in their social organization. (See the discussion of corporate groups in Chapter 9.)

Positions of Leadership

Greater concentrations of people more or less bound to their land because of their dependence on cultigens make necessary better defined positions of authority; and political organization becomes more complicated because of the necessity for social control and the development of a more explicit system of rights and duties regarding labor and the products of labor. Mechanisms must be devised for the adjudication of disputes over these obligations and rights. Therefore, *positions of leadership* evolve that are more stable than is usual among hunter-gatherers.

STAGES OF HORTICULTURE

Cohen (1968:49) has suggested that "there is no single horticultural pattern; instead, there are different patterns, each representing a successive stage of development, that can be distinguished in terms of different proportions of domesticated foods in the total diet." The following summary of varieties of horticultural societies is derived from Cohen (though the labels are my own).

1 Minimal Horticulture

In this first stage, a minimum of horticulture is practiced (cultivated food-stuffs providing 10 percent or less of the normal diet), and the main subsistence base is hunting-gathering. Horticulturists at this stage are highly mobile and are sedentary only periodically; "they may have permanent or semipermanent settlements and leave them for part of the year to hunt and gather wild foods, returning for the harvest" (Cohen 1968:49). They may, as shifting cultivators, periodically move their home base as well. Their social organization is similar to hunter-gatherers' in that there is little or no specialization of labor; local groups are prone to fission; and leadership, though perhaps better recognized than among hunter-gatherers, is still weak and informal and of the *primus inter pares* (first among equals) type.

2 Dependent Horticulture

For societies at this level, cultivation assumes a greater importance in subsistence, though it is equaled or surpassed by hunting-gathering as a food-getting technique. Here fixed settlements are more apparent, owing to a greater reliance on crops. The group is less likely to split up, and consequently interpersonal and interhousehold relationships become more stable. Kinship-based relations and affiliations begin to extend over a wider area, and organizations such as clans develop. But leadership roles are still rather weak, with authority limited to recommendation and persuasion. Political organization is generally not rigid. "The division of labor continues to be organized by sexual differences: the men clear the bush, hunt, fight, and tend domesticated animals while the women do the basic work in cultivation" (Cohen 1968:50). Communities are usually still well dispersed, and overall population density is still low. The more the group relies on cultivated foods at the expense of wild foods, however, the higher the population density will be.

3   Primary-Subsistence Horticulture

Subsistence in this stage is based primarily on intensive horticulture, with hunting-gathering assuming a secondary role and contributing a relatively small amount of food (perhaps up to one-third of the diet). Villages are still widely separated, but there is a slight increase in population density. The political system and authority roles become better defined. Community leaders possess more authority, arising, for example, from the need for coordination of labor activities in clearing land, the need for the division of land within the community, the need for the adjudication of disputes, and so on. Larger-order group affiliations become concomitantly more pronounced with the greater dependence on cultigens that are produced through cooperative labor.

4   Advanced Horticulture

Here hunting-gathering is insignificant as a food-getting technique and may be virtually absent. Population increases, and communities are located closer to each other. Wider group organizations become even better defined and play a pervasive role in social organization. Group affiliation generally remains based on an ideology of kinship. Political organization, according to Cohen (p. 50) "is varied and complex; political institutions range from considerable weakness and amorphousness (as . . . in highland New Guinea . . .) to highly complex state systems (as in Polynesia . . .)."[2] The failure of political complexity to correspond neatly with an increased reliance on cultigens is no doubt due to other factors, such as the amount of land available in combination with population density or the presence or absence of neighboring groups that preclude population growth. Carneiro (1970) has suggested that social or geographical circumscription of a group can lead to the development of complex political forms (what can be thought of as "vertical growth" in social organization) because the freedom to leave the group (i.e., "horizontal growth," or the spreading out of the population) has been restricted.

SUMMARY OF CHARACTERISTICS

Bearing in mind the great diversity of social organization among societies based on horticulture, we can now elaborate briefly on the basic attributes noted at the beginning of this chapter and offer a summary of characteristics that such societies tend toward, in contrast to hunter-gatherers.

Because of their greater investment in the environment, horticulturists tend toward *stable groupings* of people in *sedentary* or *semisedentary* communities. Accordingly, the *population increases,* usually with the degree of dependence on cultivated foods. If we look at human societies in cross-cultural perspective and compare collectors in general with cultivators in general (i.e., within the framework of "general evolution"), we see that this assertion is substantiated; but it may not hold for any particular society (i.e., from the viewpoint of "specific evolution"), especially when the society has only recently begun to rely primarily on cultivation. (On this and related issues, the student may wish to consult "The Transition from Hunting to Horticulture in the Amazon Basin," by Robert L. Carneiro, 1968.)

The division of labor is still primarily *based on sex and age,* and horticultural societies are basically *egalitarian,* though some specialization of labor and social stratification may develop as horticulture, as opposed to hunting-gathering, becomes more important.

The *ideology of kinship* becomes more pervasive in ordering social relations, though it is still subject to manipulation, as resources come increasingly under the control of groups. Because of the investment of time and energy in cultivating, notions of ownership and property become more pronounced. Consequently, *territoriality* (claiming proprietary rights over land) develops more or less in proportion to the intensity of cultivation and the availability of land. Notions of territoriality and the pressure of population then contribute to the occurrence of large-scale conflict or *war* among some horticulturists. Though *feuding* still exists as well, it is likely to involve larger groups, and to be less individualistic, than is usually the case among hunter-gatherers.

Religion among horticulturists is still primarily *polytheistic;* but—along with changes in investments of time and energy in the environment, the cooperative production of food, the growth and increasing formalization of power, and the emphasis on group affiliation—deities may be arranged hierarchically, with some considered more important or having greater authority than others; people may maintain more regular and formal contact with them, usually on a group (rather than an individual) basis; and they may become more involved in the welfare of the group. There may even be a high god, though this deity is often viewed as being distant or entirely removed from the affairs of human beings. Additionally, another variation of religion, called *ancestral veneration* or *ancestor worship,* is found among some horticulturists (see Chapter 14).

The following list recapitulates this summary:

Investment in the environment
Tendency toward stable groups; sedentary or semisedentary communities
Division of labor based primarily on sex and age
Basically, social equality; though social stratification may occur as reliance on cultivation increases
Pervasive ideology of kinship; kin groups become important

Development of notions of territoriality
Feuding on group level; war may occur
Polytheistic religion, with or without a high god; ancestral veneration
occurs

ETHNOGRAPHIC SKETCH: The Dugum Dani of New Guinea

The Dugum Dani are a Papuan group located in the Central Highlands of West New Guinea (properly West Irian, a province of Indonesia). In this sketch, based on Karl Heider's ethnography (1970), the ethnographic present refers to the early 1960s.[3]

SETTLEMENT AND SUBSISTENCE

The Dani live in small clusters of dwellings, called *compounds* by Heider. Each compound contains at least one men's house, several women's houses, a cookhouse, and one or more pigsties.

Men and boys gather at the men's house during the day and usually sleep there at night. It is a round structure and the largest dwelling in the compound. Women live in separate houses. These also are round, and there is usually one house for each woman living in the compound. Occasionally two women will occupy the same house; but normally cowives will not reside together, since they seldom get along well (see Chapter 13).

Each compound also contains a long rectangular cookhouse. Here residents of the compound gather to talk, cook, and eat. The cookhouse has several fires, usually one for each woman in the compound.

Every compound has at least one pigsty in which the animals are kept at night. The sty is divided into a number of stalls, and each pig (or a sow and her young) occupies a separate stall.

An inner fence connects the various structures in a compound and forms the perimeter of a central courtyard, into which opens the entrance of the compound. Beyond the courtyard, in the rear of the compound behind the men's house, are two small structures: one in which the ashes of the deceased are kept after cremation, and another called the *ghost house.* In this area there is also a small yard where bananas are grown. The entire compound is surrounded by an outer fence.

Dani subsistence is based on intensive slash-and-burn horticulture and swineherding. Their staple food is the sweet potato. Less important crops include taro and yams, as well as ginger, tobacco, bananas, and cucumbers. In all, the Dani cultivate fourteen different crops.

The Dani have three types of gardens, called by Heider *valley floor gardens, compound gardens,* and *slope gardens.* The slope gardens are located on hillsides behind the compound and are used mainly for the cultivation of taro and cucumbers, though other crops are also grown here. The compound

Table 5.1   Types of Dani Gardens

Garden Type	Location	Crops
Valley floor	Flat valley floor lying in front of compounds	Sweet potatoes, taro, yams (provide most of the food)
Compound	(a) Banana yard	(a) Mainly bananas, sugar cane, gourds
	(b) Adjacent to houses and fences in courtyard	(b) Taro, tobacco, gourds
	(c) Just outside compound entrance	(c) Mainly tobacco
Slope	Hillside behind compound	Mainly taro and cucumbers, but also sweet potatoes and yams

gardens are those situated in or just outside the compounds. A number of crops, such as bananas, taro, and tobacco, are grown in these gardens. The primary cultivated land, however, is the flat valley floor in front of the compound. These large gardens, interlaced with a labyrinth of ditches, produce most of the food—sweet potatoes, taro, yams—consumed by the Dani. (See the summary in Table 5.1).

The climate in this region is fairly uniform throughout the year; thus there are no set seasons for planting and harvesting. Several fields are in different stages of usage at any one time. The land is rich and easily worked, so that the Dani need spend comparatively little time in gardening activities. Also, because land is plentiful in the Dani area (unlike the situation in many other cultivating societies), there is little emphasis on defining property rights and land-usage rights.

To illustrate Dani cultivating practices, the following summary of the slash-and-burn cycle for the valley floor gardens is provided (based on Heider 1970:40–41):

Step 1.   Remove cover.
a Cut down trees and bushes.
b Cut grass.
c Dig out roots of trees and bushes.

Step 2.   Burn cut vegetation after it dries.

Step 3.   Clear ditches of accumulated mud and rotten vegetation and spread over garden beds.

Step 4.   Plant.
a Heap earth into small mounds and plant sweet potatoes.
b Plant taro shoots in shallow holes.
c Spread mud over mounds.

Step 5.   After mud dries, break up with digging stick.

Step 6   Continue intermittent weeding and trimming of vines throughout growing period.

Step 7.   Harvest: Dig largest tubers from mounds over a period of several months.

Step 8.   After the harvest period, allow pigs to roam through gardens and eat small tubers still remaining.

Step 9   Allow garden to lie fallow for an indeterminate period.

Though hunting is an unimportant activity, gathering provides the Dani with many of their necessities. They collect fiber for making string (which is used for making carrying nets and is essential for items of clothing and adornment), wood for building houses and fences and for making weapons and tools, vines for use in construction, and grass for making floors and roofs.

As was mentioned above, the Dani keep pigs. These not only are a source of food but are also central to Dani ceremonial life. Pigs are ritual animals, and their meat is eaten on every major Dani ceremonial occasion.

Pigs are released from the sty in the mornings. They wander about the compound, feeding on the scraps of food discarded by the residents of the compound. Later in the morning they are driven from the compound to their rooting grounds. They are usually accompanied by a child, but sometimes an adult serves as swineherd. They are brought back to the compound in the afternoon and returned to the sty by evening.

Elaborate trading networks are characteristic of the New Guinea Highlands, and trading is another major economic activity of the Dugum Dani. They are located near a relatively large brine pool from which they extract salt, a valued exchange commodity. According to Heider (1970:129–130):

Major imports into the Dugum Neighborhood are seashells, adze stones, furs, feathers, and fine woods and nets: that is, goods from the ocean, goods from a quarry one hundred kilometers to the northwest, and goods from the dense forest. (The forests in the immediate vicinity of the Dugum Neighborhood are thinned out and no longer very productive.) The exports are salt from a local brine pool, which is the best in the entire Grand Valley, and pigs. Most of the trade was between the Dugum Dani and the people of Jalemo, a densely forested area three days' walk to the northeast. The Dugum Dani exchange basic foods (salt and pork) with the Jalemo for luxuries (fur, feathers, orchid fiber, the best spear and bow woods) whose main use is in warfare and whose demand is maintained by warfare.

SOCIAL STRUCTURE

The two major principles which structure Dani society are descent and residence (or territoriality).

The two most important descent units are the moiety and the sib (or clan; see the discussion in Chapter 12). All of Dani society is divided into two categories, known anthropologically as *moieties* ("halves"). The two Dani moieties are named Wida and Waija, and everyone in the society is affiliated with one or the other. Since affiliation passes from father to child, these divisions are known as *patrimoieties* or *patrilineal* ("father's-line") *moieties.*

Each moiety is subdivided into a number of smaller descent units called *sibs* or *clans.* Since membership in a sib is also determined by a patrilineal principle, these units are called *patrisibs.* (Sibs are further divided into subunits called *lineages,* but these are unimportant in ordering Dani social relations.)

The relationship conceived to exist between moiety and sib can be illustrated by the Dani terms for them. Moiety is referred to as "the body," and sib is denoted by several terms that refer to the head or parts thereof.

Moiety membership obligates a person to participate in certain rituals (e.g., in a funeral for someone from the same moiety) and to observe certain food taboos (e.g., one kind of banana is prohibited to the members of Wida moiety, while several other kinds are prohibited to Waija members).

All sibs are associated with some environmental feature (e.g., a hill) and with a species of bird. The bird is considered a sib brother, and members of the sib are forbidden to eat it.

Neither sibs nor moieties are localized. That is, they are nonterritorial units whose members are scattered geographically.

There are, however, three territorial units recognized by name: the compound, the confederation, and the alliance. To these Heider, for purposes of description and analysis, adds a fourth: the neighborhood. Several compounds clustered in a definable area constitute what Heider calls a neighborhood; a number of neighborhoods form a confederation; and several confederations make up an alliance.

None of these may be considered a fixed or permanent unit. Membership within each is based on residence. Individuals frequently move from one compound to another, and such a change of residence may occasionally involve a change in confederation (rarely would it entail a change in alliance). Moreover, the configuration of a confederation or alliance is not stable: old ties are often broken and new allegiances formed, producing what Heider refers to as a "kaleidoscopic shifting" of associations.

So, unlike many other societies that rely almost exclusively on cultivation for subsistence, the Dani are characterized by a great deal of instability in their social groupings, from the level of the immediate family (husbands and wives or parents and children may live in separate compounds) through the most inclusive level of the alliance.

The compound is the scene of day-to-day activity, where people work their gardens, cook and eat their meals, and so on. The neighborhood is the largest area within which face-to-face contact occurs. The neighborhood in which Heider did his fieldwork covered an area of about 2 square kilometers near a hill called Dugum (thus the name Dugum Dani, applied by Heider to the residents in this area). The population in this area fluctuates at around 350. It should be remembered, however, that "neighborhood" is not a designation recognized by the Dani. The next level in Dani organization is the confederation, and it is to the confederation that individual Dani give their primary allegiance.

The confederation consists of all the compounds in a defined area and is the most important ceremonial and political unit, for it is within the boundaries of the confederation that most group activity occurs. For example, fighting—a prevalent and institutionalized activity—is carried out mostly on the confederation level. Leaders are found at this level and at the alliance level. Their position is similar to that described in Chapter 11 as "big man."

Confederations form into alliances, the largest political and ceremonial units among the Dani. It is at the alliance level, for instance, that the great pig feast—known as *ebe akho*—is held. This ceremony occurs only once every few years and is a major occasion, for it is during the *ebe akho* that all marriages take place and all funerals for persons who have died since the last *ebe akho* are finally concluded. And, although battles are fought at the level of the confederation, war is declared at the alliance level.

CONFLICT

Heider distinguishes three kinds of fighting among the Dani: the brawl, the feud, and war. Brawling is short-term fighting, usually spontaneous, between individuals within a confederation; feuding is fighting that occurs between members of different confederations within the same alliance; war is fighting between confederations in different alliances. (See Table 5.2).

All conflict originates at the individual level and may be expressed by avoidance, an exchange of insults, or actual fighting between the principals. If unresolved, it may escalate to higher levels. The major causes of conflict are disputes over pigs and women.

Neither brawling nor feuding is linked to the supernatural. Both involve "local people" (i.e., members of the same confederation or alliance) and are usually over specific issues. Warfare, however, involves "foreigners" (members of different alliances) and is a long-term affair characterized by a definite cycle and supernatural implications.

This cycle involves two kinds of fighting, having different aims. The first involves a long period of intermittent fighting, a series of one-day battles, accompanied by ritual, which may continue for ten or twenty years. During this

Table 5.2   Conflict among the Dani

Interpersonal		Brawl	Intergroup Feud	War
Tension between two individuals, expressed by avoidance or verbal insult	Fighting between two individuals	Spontaneous fighting between different groups within a confederation	Fighting between different confederations within an alliance	Fighting between alliances

Note: All conflicts originate on the individual level but may escalate into brawling, feuding, or warfare depending on the group affiliations of the original antagonists.

A Dani battle; New Guinea. *(Photograph: Carpenter Center, Harvard University.)*

time, the combatants meet in designated areas and engage in open-field fight-ing. The object is not to overrun the enemy but to engage in an almost sportive encounter in which participants can demonstrate their skill, courage, and cun-ning. These encounters are not just "fun and games," however; for despite the banter that occurs, the combatants are trying to kill or maim their opponents with spears and bows and arrows. Though Heider witnessed eight battles, he saw no one killed during these encounters (but two men subsequently died from wounds they received in battles).

When a person is killed, his or her ghost demands satisfaction: a member of the enemy group must be killed. It does not matter whether the victim is a man, woman, or child, as long as a life is taken. Raids are, in effect, killing expeditions. A group of twelve to fifty men sneak into enemy territory and surprise a lone individual, whom they spear or shoot.

A respite in the fighting then occurs while one group holds a funeral ceremony and the other holds a ceremony called *edai,* the purpose of which is to tell the ghost of their deceased that they have taken an enemy life.

The second (nonritual) phase in the cycle of war is a much more deadly one. After ten or twenty years of the kind of fighting described above, mem-bers of one side may launch a large-scale surprise attack with the aim of virtually destroying the enemy. Compounds are attacked and burned, and men, women, and children are slaughtered. The defeated group is dispersed, confederations realign themselves, and new alliances are formed. The entire cycle then begins to repeat itself.

FOOTNOTES

1 This change from collecting to producing is often referred to as the "Neolithic revolution." For some general works on hunter-gatherers, see Bicchieri (1972), Damas (1969), and Lee and DeVore (1968). A useful treatment of horticulturists, though limited to those in South America, is *Amazonia,* by Betty J. Meggers (1971).

2 Varieties of political organization are discussed in Chapter 11.

3 Appendix 3 lists other books and the major ethnographic film on the Dani of New Guinea.

Chapter 6

Agriculturists

(Photograph by Erwin H. Epstein.)

Agriculture is a system of cultivation that relies on the use of the plow and draft animals.[1] Large-scale (and often centrally controlled) irrigation which provides an adequate water supply and elaborate terracing of the land are also normally found with agriculture. Other characteristics frequently associated with this adaptive strategy are metalworking, the wheel, and larger and more substantial architecture. One anthropologist has summed up the salient characteristics of agricultural societies as follows (Bock 1969:288):

> . . . With the development of the plow and allied techniques, a fairly dependable crop surplus can be harvested in areas of moderate fertility and rainfall. This surplus makes possible both a larger population and a more extensive division of labor than do any of the other food-getting patterns. In agricultural societies, crafts can be practiced by full-time specialists, with a consequent improvement in both efficiency of technique and quality of product. With the development of metallurgy and its application to agricultural implements, food production becomes still more productive. . . .

CHARACTERISTICS OF AGRICULTURISTS

High Populations

Since agriculture is a form of *intensive cultivation* relying on the use of draft animals and a dependable water supply to work and rework a particular land area, agricultural communities are generally *permanent,* with *high population densities.* And the community is *less subject to fission* (splitting up) than any other discussed so far. Groupings are generally quite stable, with little interchange of personnel. Obviously, an adequate and dependable labor force must be available to work the land.

State Systems

Agriculture is normally found in connection with state systems. By a *state system* is meant a political system which is headed by a central authority, often one person, under which there functions a bureaucracy or, in Cohen's phrase, "a set of interlocking agencies" that carries on the business of governing the society. The central authority, the person at the head of the state, may have real power or may be only a figurehead. Nevertheless, this person is the "empirical representation of the state" (Cohen 1974:53–54). In contrast, a *stateless* society is one in which social relations are mediated on the local level (i.e., economic, political, religious, and other activities are overseen or controlled by the autonomous local community) without any overarching political institutions or supraordinate authority.

But, to repeat, agricultural societies are by and large associated with nation-states.[2] That is, almost all agricultural societies (though there are some exceptions) are state societies; but, of course, not all state societies are agricultural. For example, the Indian states of Mexico and Peru were based on intensive horticulture, not agriculture. (Plow agriculture was not found in the New World, only in the Old—Europe, North Africa, Asia, and parts of Indonesia.) And modern industrial societies are other examples of state systems.

Agricultural societies, then, generally have a well-developed system of political organization with *well-defined positions of authority.* The central authority exerts control, for example, over the allocation of water and thereby controls the labor force in the society. Political control over economic activities sets the scene, so to speak, for the rest of social organization in agricultural society.

Social Classes and Specialization of Labor
Also characteristic is a system of *social stratification* (differentiated social classes with differential access to resources and wealth), consisting, for example, of a wealthy aristocracy or nobility, commoners (craftsmen and laborers), and sometimes slaves. This nonegalitarian society develops *specialization of labor,* with various activities performed only by certain classes of people (administrators, warriors, merchants, carpenters, metalworkers, and other artisans).

Aymara Indians at market; Peru. *(Photograph by Erwin H. Epstein.)*

Ownership

In agricultural societies, the notion of *ownership* becomes more pronounced. Individuals (to some degree) and groups (to a greater degree) claim to own certain land or draft animals. But control of techniques, such as irrigation (without which the land cannot be fruitfully worked) or of trade and the distribution of produce, is claimed by the state. It is from this control of vital technological-economic activities that the state may be seen as deriving its power. (See Figure 11.3 and the accompanying text in Chapter 11.)

Decline in Importance of Kinship

Kinship, though still a referent for behavior, becomes less important in the organization of social relations, especially as regards economic activities. Instead, the state, the overarching political authority, assumes more importance; it increasingly intrudes upon, and therefore increasingly influences, the lives of individuals. It demands and receives (in return for allocating resources, adjudicating disputes, providing protection from potential invaders) tribute or *taxation* from the people in the form of currency or the products of their labor. This is another kind of specialization of labor: the state provides a political-legal service in return for economic support. Those who speak in the name of the state generally do not raise their own food; they depend on others to supply it, and they reciprocate by providing a coordinating political system.

Religion: Emergence of a Priesthood

Another form of specialization of labor that develops in conjunction with an agricultural strategy is found in the religious system: priests emerge. *Priests* are full-time religious practitioners. (In other types of societies discussed so far, except for very advanced horticulturalists, there are no priests. There are other religious practitioners, often called *shamans,* in such societies, but they perform religious functions not as full-time specialists but only as a sideline. See Chapter 14.) In agricultural states—where very often there is a contest between the officially approved deity and deities worshiped locally, reflecting the contest between the assertion of central authority over local allegiances—priests are appointed directly by political authorities or work in close concert with them, receiving support in the form of taxation (religious tithes) or from government subsidies. Hence, priests may be considered specialists within the state bureaucracy; i.e., they handle a certain political area (social control through religion). Obviously, there is in such an agricultural state system no separation of church and state. The state, in one way or another, *is* the church—and vice versa.

Religion among agriculturists may be *polytheistic,* but nearly always the deities are subordinate to a high god, a deity with power, authority, and control over the lesser deities. This more or less corresponds to the organization of the society as a whole, in which there is a central head of state. The trend in agricultural nation-states is toward *monotheism,* though monotheism is hardly ever fully achieved.

Territoriality and Warfare

The emphasis on resources and their ownership or control in agricultural societies also leads to a more strict notion of *territoriality*. This, along with population pressure, contributes to the occurrence of warfare, which is characteristic of expanding agricultural societies. But *feuding,* which has been mentioned in previous discussions as common up to this stage, is discouraged in agricultural societies. The state condemns the practice, propagating the notion that only the state has the right to use force and that it is criminal and punishable for individuals or small groups to do so. The state attempts to enforce this policy rigidly. This reaction to feuding relates to the state's concern with protecting its power and control over the organization of social relations throughout the society: if force is a permissible method of solving conflict within the society, then it is a potential threat to the security of the state; for it might some day be used against the state. (It should be noted, however, that feuding is sometimes used by a state for its own ends. The internal attrition resulting from infighting facilitates eventual dominance by the state by eliminating or dissipating potential opposition. In other words, instead of subjugating each individual subgroup in the society, it allows one or a few of these to defeat other local groups and then steps in and subjugates the victor or victors—often under the guise of "restoring order and establishing peace." This form of *divide et impera* has often been used by colonial powers upon entering a multiethnic tribal area.)

Urbanization and Peasants[3]

Before summarizing this outline of the general characteristics of agricultural societies, a few brief comments on urbanization and peasants are in order.

    Urbanization, or the growth of cities (which began between 4,000 and 6,000 years ago), is closely correlated with the rise of agricultural nation-states. Intensive cultivation and the harnessing of a relatively abundant water supply through the construction of large-scale systems of irrigation provide a more dependable food supply and, hence, allow greater concentrations of people in an area. When concentrations of people in comparatively small land areas reach a significant level—for instance, a population of 10,000 or more—we speak of cities.

    The entire population of a society, however, does not move to cities. Along with the rise of agriculture, urbanization, and state systems came the emergence of peasants. Most simply defined, **peasants** are rural farmers in a nation-state. They farm primarily for their own subsistence, but they also produce a surplus that, through a market system, provides essential support for those in positions of political authority.[4]

    Peasants may be viewed as living in two worlds: (1) their own farming communities, which are on the periphery of (2) a larger society that is usually but not always based in cities. Peasants trade in the markets of the city but remain essentially marginal to it, both geographically and socially (though they are, of course, bound by the laws of the state), while their contributions of agricultural products, taxes, and labor are crucial to the economy.

Hence, farmers in our own society, for example, are generally not thought of as peasants. Rather, they are more likely to be considered businesspeople who produce a commodity (foodstuffs) in a "factory" (the modern mechanized farm) for profit through general distribution in the society at large. American farmers typically are not subsistence cultivators. And they are not on the periphery or margin of industrial society, but fully participate in it.[5]

SUMMARY OF CHARACTERISTICS

Investment in the environment; intensive cultivation
Permanent communities; high populations; less fission of population
State systems, as a rule (in contrast to stateless societies)
Well-developed political systems with centralization of authority
Social stratification
Specialization of labor
Ownership and control of resources
Taxation (of goods, money, and labor, including military conscription)
Well-developed notions of territoriality
Discouragement of feuding; occurrence of war
Priests (full-time religious specialists)
Basically polytheistic religion, but with the notion of a high god; tendency toward monotheism
Rise of urbanization; emergence of peasants

ETHNOGRAPHIC SKETCH: The Puritans in New England in the Seventeenth Century

The Puritans (or Pilgrims) were a heterogeneous group of primarily English emigrants who first arrived in North America in 1620. By 1640 they were 20,000 strong and living in scattered villages throughout New England.

Though the overall political structure and the major religious beliefs of the Puritans were very similar, no brief description such as this can do justice to the considerable variation in local organization that characterized Puritan settlements. Not only were there differences between whole colonies such as Plymouth Colony and the Massachusetts Bay Colony (which were separate until 1691), but Puritan life often differed markedly from town to town within the same colony.

The following sketch attempts to present a general composite picture of Puritan life in seventeeth-century New England without, I hope, doing any great damage to particular cases. My authorities for this sketch are Demos (1970), Langdon (1966), and Powell (1970).[6]

The Puritans were from mixed backgrounds: well-to-do and poor, young and old, married and single; and they came from various parts of England having very different types of farming and systems of land tenure. One attribute they shared was their religious beliefs: they were unwilling to belong to an established church, which they considered had become defiled or impure (thus the name *Puritans*).

It appears that the desire to express their religious proclivities provided the rationale for their emigration from England. In 1607 they moved to Holland. There they found the religious freedom they sought; but, since they were not satisfied with their economic position, they resolved to emigrate to the New World.

Control of land in the New World had been given by the Crown of England to several chartered trading companies. The Puritans, when they did not themselves run the companies (as in the case of the Massachusetts Bay Company), entered into agreements with the companies to settle in America. The various Puritan towns that eventually grew up throughout New England, though they had considerable local autonomy, remained subject to colony-wide administrations that were offshoots of trading companies which, in turn, had received their "charters" from the Crown and were subject to its authority.

The Puritans were mainly agriculturists, though some were artisans and tradespeople as well. But, in the early years especially, there was little specialization of labor: "They were, in the first place, virtually all farmers: even the tradesman, the artisan, and the minister would spend some regular portion of time working the land" (Demos 1970:13).

Puritan life as a whole, at least for most of the seventeenth century, was characterized by a great deal of cultural consistency: social, political, and religious organization showed notable agreement. Religious doctrine served to justify the exercise of authoritarian control on all levels—colony, town, and household. Political power was used to perpetuate the religious ideology (e.g., in many towns of the colonies a man could not own land or vote unless he was a church member). And the structure of, and interpersonal relations in, the family reinforced the larger social order.

SOCIAL STRUCTURE

Each of the four New England colonies (Plymouth, Massachusetts Bay, Connecticut, and New Haven) held lands in the New World by grants from the Crown. In actuality they were virtually independent for most of the seventeenth century, though they were still technically subject to the authority of England. (It was not until the latter part of the century that England began in earnest to exert more direct control.)

Each colony was governed by a central administration, a General Court made up of a Governor, several Assistants, and deputies elected by the towns. Below these were the county courts, which had jurisdiction over several towns in an area. Taxes (called *rates*) were collected at all three levels: town, county, and colony.

Authority within the towns existed by grant from the General Court, though the form which that authority took and the manner in which it was exercised were internal matters left to the discretion of the town, so long as policies enacted were "not repugnant to the public laws of the country" (quoted in Powell 1970:87).

Affairs within the towns were managed through public meetings at which the residents gathered to decide policy regarding distribution of land, maintenance of roads, levying of local taxation, setting of wage regulations, and so on. Though town meetings were open to all members of the community, actual policy making was limited to "freemen." (The meaning of *freeman* is not entirely clear. Powell, 1970:87, says that for Sudbury in the Massachusetts Bay Colony a freeman was "an official church member who had taken an oath to uphold the colony." In Plymouth, according to Demos, 1970:7, church membership was not required, and acceptance of a person as a "freeman" depended on "general considerations of character and competence." One thing, however, seems clear enough: owning land was a prerequisite for freeman status and the right to vote. And land was granted to individuals by the town, which acted on the authority of the General Court.)

Most local officials were elected at town meetings and were recognized by the higher authorities. Some officials, however—such as the town constable in Sudbury—were appointed by the General Court and were thus the direct representatives and visible reminders of the authority of the colony's central administration.

Population growth, the desire to increase production, and local disputes were factors contributing to the proliferation of settlements in New England colonies. New towns were not founded, however, by simply striking off independently into the wilderness. Application was first made to the General Court, which alone could grant the land. (Of course, there were the native inhabitants to deal with as well. Where the Indians proved tractable, agreements were made for the transfer of land; where they were not, the land was taken by force. The colonies were organized into military contingents, and the outlying towns doubled as frontier fortresses.)

When the General Court granted land for a new settlement, it set down the conditions to be met for holding the land. For example, when a group of dissidents from Sudbury were given land by the Massachusetts Bay General Court to start a new town, the Court specified the number of families that were required to settle within a three-year period. The distribution of the land within the town, however, was left to the settlers to work out for themselves.

During the course of the seventeenth century, new towns sprang up all over New England. Speaking of Plymouth Colony, Demos (1970:11) says: "The physical aspect of Old Colony after mid-century seems to have been rather arbitrary and disorganized, with a straggling chain of settlements of varying shapes and sizes, and even some isolated homesteads, flung out over a very broad expanse of territory."

The towns themselves were what anthropologists usually refer to as "closed corporate communities." Membership was exclusive: anyone wishing to live in the town was closely scrutinized by the townsfolk. Applicants had to demonstrate their willingness to conform to the approved behavior and religious beliefs of the Puritans. The town allocated land and could repossess it.

It required all residents to contribute their time, labor, and money to many cooperative projects, though the primary productive unit was the individual family farm.

Land was divided into commons and family-owned farms. Though common land provided much of the pasturage for animals, it was the individually managed farms which formed the basis of Puritan economy.

These farms were run by the members of a single household, the core members of which constituted a nuclear family. The members of a Puritan household usually lived in a one-room structure, often with a small loft. The first dwellings were temporary thatch-roofed huts. Later came clapboard houses with thatch roofs that were soon replaced by shingles and boards. Some of these houses had a second room partitioned off in the rear. A third type of dwelling enlarged on this basic plan. It had at least two complete ground-floor rooms, perhaps a full second storey, and one or more lean-tos attached to the rear or side of the house. Windows were few and small. A chimney, with a large fireplace at its base, rose from the center of the main room.

The household was organized around a nuclear family—a husband, wife, and children. The number of children born to a couple ranged from one to ten (with a statistical average of just over three children residing in a household at any one time), though Demos (1970:68) says that "eight to nine . . . was pretty standard."

Some households also contained "servants." These might be adults, either people who had voluntarily sold their services for a specified period in order to support themselves until they could establish their own households or to learn a trade, or people who had been sentenced by the community to such servitude as a penalty for wrongdoing. The Puritans also kept Negro and Indian slaves. The majority of servants, however, were children.

Some children of poor parents went to live in well-to-do households to learn basic reading and writing. Others went to apprentice themselves to an artisan. Still others were orphans in need. But there remain a number of cases of children exchanged between households equivalent in wealth, status, and education. Morgan (1966:77–78) suggests that children were placed in other households to minimize the possibility of their being "spoiled" by their own parents. The households to which the children were assigned were in the majority of cases connected by kinship to the natal household: children were sent to live with aunts, uncles, married elder siblings, and even grandparents.

Child lending is not an uncommon practice in so-called primitive and peasant societies. Because of precarious living conditions and uncertain fortune, some of one's own children (as well as other valuable commodities, such as cattle) are distributed among one's trusted friends and relatives, at the same time that others' children are received into one's own household. Such a dispersal of assets constitutes a kind of insurance: if disease or some catastrophe should strike one household, those children (or cattle) quartered elsewhere are protected. It is unknown whether the Puritans had any such purpose in mind for their exchange of children.

It has been suggested that the "extrusion" of children serves another social function: it helps to transfer an individual's social "anchorage" and feelings of identification from the nuclear family to a wider kin group or even to the community at large (Cohen 1964a, 1964b). In other words, it weakens the child's connection with one group and strengthens the connection with another, thus shifting social orientation. Support for this interpretation in the case of the Puritans is provided by the fact that when the local community or the Court judged children to be "rude, stubborn and unruly," they could be removed from their natal household and placed "with some masters for years (boyes till they come to twenty one, and girls eighteen years of age compleat) which will more strictly look unto, and force them to submit unto government" (quoted in Morgan 1966:78). In Morgan's words, "Under the terms of this law the state compelled some parents to do what others did voluntarily."

Though the typical household consisted basically of a nuclear family, it was not uncommon to find persons attached to it other than the "servants" mentioned above. An elderly person who no longer was able to care for himself or herself might live in the household of a married child. Since the community had no homes for the aged, hospitals, poorhouses, etc., even nonrelatives who were elderly, poor, or infirm were attached to individual households. Unmarried adult women (the number of spinsters increased toward the end of the seventeenth century) lived with relatives, probably most often with a brother. (The freedom allowed to unmarried adult men varied from colony to colony. In Massachusetts Bay they were forbidden to set up independent households without express authorization. So too in Connecticut, where no single person was permitted to "keepe howse by himself, without consent of the Towne where he lives . . ."; quoted in Morgan 1966:145. Until 1669, however, Plymouth had no such law, and a man was allowed to "be for himself"; quoted in Demos 1970:77–78).

Internally, the family was organized along strict authoritarian lines. The father was the unquestioned head of the household; he was often referred to as the "family governor." By recognizing his legitimate right to govern and acceding to it, children learned to respect as well the authority of the larger society. (The legal penalty for persistent disobedience or for striking a parent was death, though this seems rarely, if ever, to have been applied.)

The Puritans, despite their town meetings and elected representatives, were no devotees of democracy. "The essence of the social order lay in the superiority of husband over wife, parents over children, and master over servants in the family, ministers and elders over congregation in the church, rulers over subjects in the state. . . . In each relationship God had ordained that one party be superior, the other inferior; for when he said, 'Honor thy father and thy mother,' he meant spiritual and political as well as natural fathers and mothers" (Morgan 1966:19; and see p. 25 for the Puritans' explicit antidemocratic stand; also, Powell 1970:117).

Women were considered lesser creatures than men and more tainted spiritually, as a result of Eve's original sin. They were charged always to be obedient to their husbands—for were not men naturally superior, according to God's will?—and to maintain a posture of "reverend subjection" toward them (quoted in Demos 1970:83).

For the Puritans, marriages were not "made in heaven"—not in any sense that we might understand to be conveyed by that phrase. First, marriage was not a sacrament. In the colonies, only a recognized magistrate of the court could perform marriages; the clergy could not. Nevertheless, marriage was a solemn and binding civil agreement, entailing numerous obligations. The main duties were cohabitation, exclusive sexual union, economic cooperation, and rearing of children, all to be carried out in an atmosphere of harmony and peace. Like other cultivating societies that rely on cooperation both within the family and within the community as a whole, the Puritans abhorred contentiousness and open hostility; and many of their laws were aimed at maintaining harmony or swiftly restoring it in the event of dispute (see Chapter 11).

Second, the marriage partners were repeatedly cautioned to restrain their affection for each other. True, husbands and wives should love each other, but such personal affection should never interfere with or stand in opposition to the higher duty: love of God and obedience to his will—and, it should be added, to political authorities who were conceived to stand in the same kind of superior relation to the family as the husband did to the wife within the family. Despite the Puritan ideology that the state rested on an agreement (or covenant) between the governed and the governors and derived its power from the family, it is apparent that the authority of the state superseded that of the family, that the family ultimately was subject to external control, and that in fact the family was a dependent arm of the central administration.

The evidence for this is abundant. Perhaps most striking is the fact that, as has been noted, town officials and the higher courts could remove children from their parents. Regular inspections were carried out to make certain that children were being raised in the prescribed manner. If they were not, parents could find themselves cited "for not attending the publique worship of God, negligence in [their] calling and not Submitting to Authority" (quoted in Morgan 1966:148).

Marriage and the establishment of a family were too important in Puritan economy, social control, and religious philosophy to be left to individual discretion. Both the courts and the town governments laid down rules specifying who was to be permitted to marry and establish households and what conditions had to be satisfied in order to do so. Once a union was solemnized, it was not easily dissolved. Nevertheless, divorces and separations were granted. The main grounds, as might be expected from the above enumeration of marital obligations, were desertion, impotence or the refusal to engage in sexual intercourse, and adultery (this last being the most common cause of divorce among the Puritans). Significantly, it was the civil government that authorized divorce and separations, since marriages were authorized by the government and performed by civil magistrates, not by ministers.

Contrary to continuing popular opinion, it is clear that the clergy did not exert a dominant influence in the civil government of the Puritans. (In a dispute over the distribution of land in the town of Sudbury, one John Ruddock told the minister, "Setting aside your office, I regard you no more than another man"; quoted in Powell 1970:127, 136.) In fact, many of the activities that were the prerogatives of religious personnel in England were denied to the church in Puritan colonies. Powell (1970:106–107) illustrates the limited role of the clergy in civil affairs in his description of the Reverend Edmund Brown's experiences in the Puritan town of Sudbury:

No longer did Brown call vestry meetings and sign vestry orders. The town ran its own meetings, granted Brown land and meadow, and elected its own officers independently. No longer did Brown visit each farmer to collect his tithes. He probably made many family visits, but he was paid a salary from the town treasury, just as the town clerk and the constable were; and the town invoice takers gathered the tax for these salaries. Brown's new church did not even have glebe land; the only perambulation was the one around the town plot. No sexton rang the bell or recorded births and deaths. A town drummer drummed for a meeting, and the town clerk was ordered to record all births, deaths, and marriages. . . .

It is not hard to understand why, after a few years, the minister began to resent the power of the town. He had few church functions left. Even the seating arrangement in the church was taken away from him and given to the town clerk, who was authorized to sell seats, but who had to sanction all sales of seats from person to person, particularly when a family left the town. The minister might consult colleagues in neighboring churches, but he could appeal to no church courts and could expect no visitation, for these had been abandoned in the Bay Colony.

The case of the Puritans provides a particular illustration of the generalization that religion is often, if not always, a political instrument that supplies a justification of, and an ideology for, the exercise of social control. Every Puritan town was also a religious congregation, and all members of the community were required by civil law to attend church meetings *even if they were not members of the church*. Failure to comply resulted in fines or corporal punishment administered by local *civil authorities,* for the church was granted no rights to punish offenders.

The church also provided reinforcement for the exercise of political authority by proffering an ideology that informed social policy. That human beings should have rulers and be subject to civil authority was ordained by God, built into the order of the universe, since the fall of Adam and Eve. It was God's "appoyntment of mankind to live in Societies" (quoted in Morgan 1966:18). Just as the rest of the animal kingdom was subject to humankind, humankind was destined to be subject to governments. A just government was one that was organized to honor the glory of God and to do justice to his precepts. And those in authority saw to it that the precepts enunciated for God's chosen were compatible with their notions and methods for maintaining social order. Those who strayed from the fold and espoused divergent religious ideologies, as Roger Williams did, either found themselves expelled from New England, or, like the four unfortunate Quakers in Boston, were hanged for their persistent deviance.

FOOTNOTES

1 Actually, and to be more precise, *agriculture* is a term that encompasses a variety of adaptive techniques and, thus, a diversity of social organization as well. For example, agriculture in a feudal society is distinguishable from nonfeudal agriculture, in its economics and the organization of social relations it entails. Plow agriculture differs from paddy agriculture, just as each of these differs from agriculture based on terracing. And, of course, large-scale agribusiness is wholly

distinct from local agriculture. To a large extent—but, I hope, an excusable one—this chapter ignores these differences in order to introduce the neophyte to the broad generalities common to most agriculturally oriented societies.

It is also more accurate to think of horticulture and agriculture not as completely discrete adaptive modes, as my heuristic emphasis on the presence or absence of the plow seems to suggest, but as representing different points on an evolutionary continuum.

2 Historians, political scientists, and anthropologists have wrangled with the problem of defining *nation-state*. The conceptualization I find most useful is, once again, one suggested by Yehudi Cohen (1974:53–54): "A nation is a society occupying a limited territory, made up of many subgroups—communities and regions, classes and sometimes castes, ethnic and sometimes linguistic groups, economic and other specialized groups, a diversity of daily cycles and life styles—all of which are centrally controlled in some measure by a set of inter-locking agencies or bureaucracies that are themselves more or less differentiated. These agencies constitute the state. . . . 'Nation' is the territorial representation of the society, and 'state' is its political representation."

It appears to hold true cross-culturally that one of the outstanding characteristics of such societies is the determination of those who speak in the name of the state to gain increasingly greater control over all other subgroups in the nation. A major way of doing this is to gain significant control over the organization of labor in the society. The least precarious way of controlling labor is to gain control of energy sources and other vital resources and to regulate the flow of goods and services in the society (thus making dependents of the other subgroups). The attempt to secure such control inevitably brings the state into conflict with other groups (such as "private industry") that are trying to maintain such control (an example is provided by the oil companies in the United States). I hypothesize that while a state's authority is still felt by its spokespersons to be insecure, what appears to be cooperation between "government and industry" will be the rule but that when those who speak in the name of the state perceive that the state's authority is secure, that it is unlikely to be seriously contested by the general populace, the state will gradually and systematically displace its rivals for control over essential resources, goods, and services. I suggest that we are witnessing the beginnings of such a changeover concerning sources of energy in the United States (See footnote 1, Chapter 8; and Figure 11.3)

3 The reader will note that I devote no space to a discussion of *civilization*. This is because (1) it is a nontechnical term without a standard definition, and (2) it often rings of ethnocentrism: the more like "us" a people are, the more "civilized" they are; the less they are like "us," the more "uncivilized" they are. When used most objectively and least objectionably, *civilization* usually refers to one or some combination of the following: (1) a particular kind of stratified political organization, usually a state system; (2) a particular kind of economic organization, usually one in which markets and trade are important; (3) a particular kind of spatial organization and settlement pattern, usually urbanization with monumental architecture; (4) a particular kind of religious organization, usually one with a monotheistic cast and a priestly bureaucracy; (5) writing.

4 Peasants, according to Wolf (1966:3–4), "are rural cultivators whose surpluses are transferred to a dominant group of rulers that uses the surpluses both to

underwrite its own standard of living and to distribute the remainder to groups in society that do not farm but must be fed for their specific goods and services in turn."

5 It might be argued, however, that some rural American farmers, such as those in Appalachia or the Ozarks, conform rather more closely than not to the definition of *peasants* given here.

6 For vivid ethnographic descriptions of present-day, local-level societies that bear striking similarities to the early Puritans in belief, behavior, and, to some extent, social organization, see Hostetler (1968) and Hostetler and Huntington (1967, 1971) on the Amish and Hutterites.

Chapter 7
Pastoralists

(Photograph by the author.)

Since herders coexist with cultivators, the question several investigators have raised is whether or not pastoralism should be treated as an entirely discrete adaptive strategy. Despite the merits of the argument that herding and cultivation are complementary enterprises and that herding exists only in conjunction with farming (though the converse is not true), I devote a separate chapter to pastoralism because it is the major way of making a living for many culturally distinct groups.

Pastoralists are people who raise and tend livestock, from which they derive their subsistence. Like agriculture, pastoralism is found only in the Old World, not in the New World.[1] Such examples of pastoralists as are found in America—the Navajo sheep herders of the Southwest and the short-lived Plains Indian horse pastoralists—were introduced to pastoralism by Europeans. Moreover, in the case of the Plains Indians, horses were used primarily to facilitate the hunting of bison (hence, I shall categorize the Plains Indians as collectors).

PASTORALISM AND NOMADISM

Pastoralism may be either *sedentary* or *nomadic*. Sedentary pastoralism occurs as an ancillary activity of people who are primarily cultivators; it need not be considered separately here. Nomadic pastoralism (or pastoral nomadism) does deserve separate treatment; it is the type that is usually meant when either "nomadism" or "pastoralism" is discussed.

But it is important to point out that the term *nomadism* does not imply pastoralism (at least in modern English, though the original Greek term did) and that the term *pastoralism* does not entail nomadism. *Nomadism* refers to a type of movement. *Pastoralism* refers to a particular type of technoeconomic system—or "resource extraction" (Salzman 1971)—based on herding. The two are not *necessarily* associated. For instance, we have already discussed nomadism as an aspect of hunting and gathering and of some types of horticulture. Both conceptually and empirically, then, we must treat these two as separate variables, and only when we find nomadic movement coupled with the herding of large herds of domesticated animals may we speak of pastoral nomadism.

Nomadic movement differs from *migration* in that in migration there is a large-scale movement or total displacement of a group from one place to another, whereas nomads often move in cycles—in more or less regular patterns or orbits—within a given area.

TRANSHUMANCE

The term *transhumance* is often applied to nomadic movement. It has been used to denote so many kinds of movement that it is becoming meaningless.

Primarily, however, transhumance has been used to designate two kinds of movement:

1 Movement from low-altitude areas to high-altitude areas; i.e., up and down mountain slopes. A better term for this kind of movement is *vertical nomadism.*

2 Movement outward from a semipermanent or permanent cluster of dwellings (e.g., a village) to the surrounding open area (for pasturage and water) and the eventual return to the original camp (this type of transhumance is often associated with a mixed cultivating-pastoral economy). A better term for this kind of movement is *fixed-reference horizontal nomadism.* When it occurs in association with movement up and down slopes, it might be termed *fixed-reference vertical nomadism.*

In any event, pastoral nomads move around. They do so in order to find pasturage and water for their animals. And since pastoralists are located mainly in *marginal, low-precipitation areas,* resources do not remain constant for a particular area throughout the year. The availability of water and pasturage fluctuates with seasonal climatic changes; therefore, pastoralists have to move periodically to go where water and pasturage are adequate.

USES OF ANIMALS

The kinds of habitats in which pastoral nomads are generally found are deserts and semideserts, grasslands (savanna and steppe), and tundra. These areas, along with the animals usually herded in them, are listed in Table 7.1.[2] An outline of the characteristics of herded animals is provided in Table 7.2.

Pastoralists make varied use of the animals they keep: (1) They consume the products of their animals: milk and milk products, blood, and meat. (2) They use animal hair and hide in manufacturing shelter, clothing, and utensils. (3) They use the animals for transport (as beasts of burden and for riding).

The *kind of animal* kept is important, for this dictates the type and amount of pasturage to be sought out, how much water must be accessible, and so on. And, as stated above, the *resources available* also influence movement, for pastoralists obviously must go where the pasturage and water are. If resources, climate, and precipitation are predictable, nomadic movement will tend to be regular. Where these factors are undependable and unpredictable, nomadic movement will take on an irregular or erratic character (Salzman 1967).

Table 7.1 Types of Environments and Animals Kept

Geographic Regions	Animals Kept	
	Primary	Ancillary
a Desert and semidesert Middle East, North Africa, eastern Central Asia (Gobi), southern Central Asia (Karakorum), parts of Southwest Asia, and southwestern Africa (Kalahari fringe)	Camel and cattle	Horse; some sheep and goats
b Steppe (short grass, relatively treeless plain) Central Asia, Southwest Asia	Sheep and goats	Camel, horse, and cattle
c Savanna (tall grass, tree-dotted) East Africa	Cattle	Sheep and goats
d Tundra (Arctic treeless plain) Northern Siberia, northern Eurasia (e.g., the Lapps in Finland)	Reindeer	

Table 7.2 Characteristics of Herded Animals

Camels	Hardy animal capable of withstanding the rigors of the desert. Rugged, mobile animal. Capable of going long periods on little or no water. Valuable for transport, as well as for hair, hide, milk, and meat. Relatively easy to herd (although camels are very easily lost if left unattended). Chief animal kept by Arabian Bedouin.
Goats	Need more water than camels but are, nevertheless, extremely tough, quick, and agile. Provide milk and milk products, meat, and hair. Need minimal herding care—unlike sheep, which are easily lost. Goats subsist on a wide variety of flora. Can exist on scanty vegetation, provided they have adequate water.
Sheep	Less hardy. Need frequent watering and are very selective grazers. Tend to keep together in flock; in this regard are easily herded. But they require more care and attention, since they are prone to getting lost.
Cattle	Need succulent growth of vegetation for pasture and need more grass per square yard than sheep. Need frequent watering.
Reindeer	Need minimal attention in herding. Durable in cold climates. Can scrape through frost on ground to get to the scrub and salt. Eat lichen and bark. Difficult to tame; not known for their manageability, though some reindeer herders do ride them.
Horses	Usually the prestige animal where found (steppe and desert) and generally pampered and protected from rigors of environment. Used for display and short-term raiding. Other animals (e.g. cattle or camels) used for heavy work.

Source: Based primarily on Johnson 1969; but also draws on Bacon 1954, Rubel 1969, and Spooner 1972.

OTHER EFFECTS ON PASTORAL NOMADIC MOVEMENT: ECONOMIC INTERESTS, SOCIAL ECOLOGY

Other economic interests aside from pastoralism may influence movement as well: whether or not and to what extent pastoralists have cultivating interests, either fields they themselves cultivate or those they rent to sedentary peoples; whether or not and the extent to which they engage in hunting and gathering; whether or not they engage in caravan trade to acquire nonpastoral products; and whether or not there are markets that they visit periodically.

The effect of *social ecology* on pastoral nomadic movement cannot be overstressed. There may be other groups in the habitat that occupy the same or similar ecological niches (i.e., that utilize the same resources) and may therefore have to be avoided to lessen the chance of undue competition (Barth 1956, 1959–1960, 1964; Bates 1972). Or movement may be restricted by an external government within whose territory the pastoralists reside (Bates 1971).

It is important to remember when discussing the social ecology of pastoral nomads that they require *contact with a sedentary group.* The pastoral products of nomads are rarely, if ever, sufficient of themselves. Pastoralists must also have cultivated foodstuffs, material equipment they cannot manufacture themselves (such as metal tools and weapons), and so forth. They obtain these from sedentary communities in a number of ways: (1) by raiding and stealing what they need; (2) by exacting tribute from sedentaries in payment for refraining from raiding—a kind of "protection racket"; (3) by establishing peaceful trade relations with sedentaries; (4) by owning plots of land in sedentary communities and receiving as rent part of the produce of the land. Lastly, pastoral nomads may own some plots of land scattered here and there which they themselves cultivate seasonally (and, hence, the locations of these plots influence the nomadic cycle). Their primary means of subsistence, however, remains pastoralism.

CHARACTERISTICS OF NOMADIC GROUPS

The Herding Group

The basic social and economic unit among pastoral nomads is the *herding group* or *camp.* This usually consists of a small group of households that camp, herd, and move together. This group, however, is unstable or flexible—as it is with hunter-gatherers. Its composition changes frequently; shifts in personnel are common. This is due to a variety of reasons: disagreement over locations of good pasturage and water; other economic interests, such as the location of privately owned garden plots (so that different individuals leave the group at various times to plant and harvest);

and social conflict, such as may arise from accusations of adultery, stealing, and the like.

Animals as Food

Pastoralists subsist mainly on the milk and milk products of their animals. Among some pastoralists there is a pervasive ideology that *they do not kill their animals for the meat.* Instead, they say, they eat the meat only when the animal dies naturally or when it is sacrificed for a ceremony. Schneider, however, has convincingly argued (1957) that, although animals are not *explicitly* killed for consumption, they are in reality many times killed to be eaten.

Division of Labor

The primary division of labor is usually *based on sex* (and, secondarily, on age), with men doing the herding and women doing the household chores. Depending on the particular pastoral group, either men or women or both milk the animals. For example, among most East African cattle herders only men may milk cattle; but among the Herero of southwestern Africa milking is done primarily by women, though men as well as young boys may also milk cows (Vivelo 1977).

In general, there is *little specialization of labor* among pastoralists—aside from the fact that pastoralism may be considered a kind of specialization in itself if it is seen as part of an overall economy which encompasses cultivation and pastoralism as two parts of a larger whole. Each household produces, manufactures, and keeps in repair what it requires. Whatever else is needed is obtained not from a fellow pastoralist who is a specialist but from someone in a sedentary community or perhaps from an itinerant merchant.

Conditions for Emergence of Leaders

Though some pastoralists—notably those few who have developed a state or statelike structure or chiefdom—exhibit social stratification, pastoralists on the whole are generally *egalitarian.* Accordingly, leadership and authority roles are usually not pronounced. But under certain conditions formal positions of authority—sometimes positions of considerable authority—may arise.

1 Mediation between Nomads and Sedentaries Pastoralists often become embroiled in disputes with sedentaries. For instance, the animals of the former are prone to trample or eat the crops of the latter. Consequently, sedentaries frequently lay claims for damages against the herders. But since it is highly detrimental to their interests to stay in one place for very long, pastoral nomads often delegate one or more of their number to represent them in such disputes while the group moves on. The payment made to these representatives and the subsequent economic interests they develop in sedentary centers, combined with the created dependence on them for purposes of litigation, can lead to a power base from which they begin to exercise authority.

2 Mediation between Nomads and the State Basically, the same process may occur in relations between nomads and the state; that is, leaders may arise originally as a result of the pastoralists' need to have a spokesperson who represents their interests in legal and other matters. Frequently, however, such leaders arise out of military encounters. State governments, whether originally foreign or indigenous, typically have difficulty exerting control over pastoralists because the pastoralists are nomadic and carry their wealth with them. They are thus difficult to tax, to conscript for military service, and so on. Consequently, nomads and the state come into conflict with each other. During the course of the ensuing war, which the nomads eventually lose, military leaders arise—men who are noted for their bravery, who are superior tacticians, who inspire loyalty and trust in others. When the war ends, it is often these erstwhile military leaders who represent the pastoralists in negotiations with the state and who become their spokesmen in most later interactions. Backed by the might of the state, which treats them not merely as spokesmen but as having real authority over their fellow pastoralists, they do indeed come to exercise real authority eventually.[3]

3 Coordination of Movement Both Barth (1959–1960) and Salzman (1967) have suggested that leaders may arise as coordinators of group movements. Barth, for instance, describes a pattern of land usage in which various pastoral groups in the same area follow different but overlapping routes of movement, or follow the same routes successively, and occupy different sections of pasturage on a basis of seasonality. He notes (p. 9) that "a prerequisite for the development of a land use pattern such as this is a political form that ensures the disciplined and coordinated migration of large populations by regular routes and schedules. This requires the development of strong and effective authorities—a feature characteristic of precisely these groups of nomads." In other, somewhat oversimplified words, someone is needed to direct traffic and to keep the groups from bumping into each other and becoming involved in conflict.

Territoriality

Another characteristic of pastoralists is that they generally do not "own" the land they use for pasturage. More precisely, land belongs to the larger group, the tribe as a whole, rather than to any of its constituent herding units. These smaller groups, however, exercise *rights of access* or *usufruct* over land. But pastoralists, individually or in small kinship groups, do own cultivating land, either plots they themselves work or those that sedentary tenants work (with the nomads as absentee landlords).

There is thus usually an absence of *particular* territoriality—i.e., a lack of a sense of territoriality for the smaller herding groups—but there is normally some sense of *general* territoriality regarding the area that the larger group as a whole occupies and exploits. (There appears to be a difference between the "general territoriality" of hunter-gatherers, mentioned in Chapter 4, and the general territoriality of pastoralists. It is fairly common to read of herders who claim, "Wherever our cattle [or camels, or sheep, etc.] graze, that is our land." That is, they seem to view the area they utilize with a proprietary sense and may even at times consider it *exclusively* theirs, expelling foreign groups or treating them as tenants on the land. Hunter-gatherers, however, appear willing enough to share the land with others, as long as they themselves continue to have adequate access to it. It is rare to find a hunter-gatherer group that claims to "own" land exclusively—in fact, hunter-gatherers are likely to declare such a notion absurd. Though this distinction between the two types of societies appears to be supported by the ethnographic evidence, it should be considered a highly tentative generalization until more pertinent evidence is available.)

Fighting

Notions of territoriality, once again, may be seen, along with extensive land use, as contributing to the occurrence of warfare; and pastoralists are notorious for their *warlike exploits* (for example, one need only mention the Mongols, the Huns, and the Hittites to substantiate this point). As the population, both human and animal, increases, new lands are required for grazing. Hence, pastoral nomads are continually expanding, and they do so at the expense of weaker groups who are unfortunate enough to happen to occupy land the pastoralists want.

But pastoralists also engage in *feuding* among themselves. Most commonly, members of different herding units raid each other for animals, or feuding may erupt over women or accusations of adultery within a group.

Kinship

The structure of a pastoral nomadic society is normally based on an *ideology of kinship,* with an original founder (called an *apical ancestor* on genealogical charts used to represent this structure) for the entire society, then his putative children as founders of subgroups (such as clans), then children of these children as founders of even smaller or more recent groups (such as lineages), down to founders of the contemporary herding units. Such an organization, called a *segmentary lineage system* (see Chapter 11), has been described by Sahlins (1961) and is found in many horticultural societies also. Descent among pastoralists with segmentary lineage structures is more often than not reckoned through males rather than through females (on descent systems, see Chapter 12).[4]

Religion

The characteristic religion of pastoral nomads is ancestral veneration (or ancestor worship). This may occur with or without notions of a high god. Many nomadic groups in the world today have embraced the Islamic version of monotheism.

SUMMARY OF CHARACTERISTICS

High mobility
Flexibility of organization of herding units
Division of labor based primarily on sex and age
Rare *explicit* killing of animals for consumption
Generally, little or no (full-time) specialization of labor
Leadership and authority usually not pronounced
Rights of access to pasture land (rather than ownership)
Sense of territoriality, usually in regard to overall tribal area
Occurrence of both war and feuding
Segmentary lineage organization; ideology of kinship
Characteristic religion: ancestral veneration, with or without a high god

---

ETHNOGRAPHIC SKETCH: The Marri Baluch of West Pakistan

The Marris are a mixed group of Baluchi-speaking pastoralists and cultivators with a total population of about 60,000 who live in northeastern Baluchistan, West Pakistan. Anthropological fieldwork was conducted among the Marri Baluch by Robert Pehrson and Jean Pehrson in 1954–1955. Robert Pehrson became ill and died in the field; but his notes were turned over to Fredrik Barth, another anthropologist, and were used as the basis for a book entitled *The Social Organization of the Marri Baluch* (Pehrson 1966). The following sketch is drawn from this report.

MAKING A LIVING

The Marri Baluch are primarily a pastoral people who also engage, to varying lesser extents, in cultivation, trade, wage labor, and collecting.

The Marris keep various domestic animals, the most important of which are sheep and goats. Other animals kept are donkeys and camels (as beasts of burden), cattle (for transport and as draft animals), dogs (for guarding camps, not for herding), and horses (as prestige items).

The large Marri herds consist mostly of sheep and goats. Their meat is eaten and is a staple in the Marri diet, and the animals are also sold for slaughter. Milk, butter, and cheese are also consumed by the Marris but are not sold

A Marri shepherd boy; Baluchistan, West Pakistan. *(Photograph,
Wenner-Gren Foundation; from Pehrson 1966:107.)*

or traded. Wool, goat hair, and meat are the primary products exported by the
Marris.

    The reliance of the Marris on small stock for subsistence in herding is in
part determined by their habitat. Since in general the Marri area does not get
more than 5 inches of rain per year, and since the better grasses necessary for
good pasturage are sparse throughout most of the year, goats and sheep can
manage adequately where heavy concentrations of large stock cannot. Cattle
are few, because available pasturage for them is too limited. Horses cannot
subsist at all on what is available and must be supplied with grains and grass
cut from areas where there is irrigation. And because of the rocky terrain,
camels cannot browse in the Marri area but must be boarded by their wealthy
owners with villagers.

    The Marri Baluch also practice plow agriculture, but this is an ancillary
activity, and the extent to which they engage in cultivation is in large part a
function of the size of their herds. All other Marri pursuits are secondary to the

maintenance of their herds. If herd size grows to 100 or more animals, the owner will neglect cultivation in favor of a more extensive nomadism to provide pasturage and water for the animals. The owner then obtains agricultural products (primarily wheat, the other staple item in the Marri diet) through other means, mainly trade, or by leasing land to a sharecropper.

Some Marris also sell their labor, performing seasonal work here and there throughout their nomadic orbit. For example, they may work in the fields of agriculturists at harvest time or clean the canals of irrigation systems.

Marris engage in various forms of trade. They haul merchandise on contract, visit Hindu trading posts, and establish special trading partnerships with residents in sedentary communities. The villager with whom the nomad develops a one-to-one relationship of trust, mutual service, and hospitality is called *bradir.*

Finally, the Marris hunt when possible, but gathering appears to be more important to their subsistence. Some of the items collected are water, firewood, honey, wild onions and fruit, dwarf palm (for tents, ropes, mats, packsaddles, and sandals), and roots and shoots.

COMMUNITIES

The type and organization of Marri Baluch communities are determined by the interaction of the various subsistence factors enumerated above, the most important of which are the need for pasturage for their animals and the need for nonpastoral products (obtained through agriculture, either directly or indirectly; through wage labor; or through trading partners or trading stores). Warfare has also been important, especially for one type of community. Before describing variations in Marri community organization, it is useful to note, as Barth does (Pehrson 1966:11), some distinctions made by the Marri:

> The Marri generally distinguish between villager and tent-dweller, subdividing the latter into *darshin*—who are structurally connected with a village and move locally within the circumference of its district—and *powindah*—who move in relation to water and seasonal pastures and whose camps are units unto themselves.

Three types of communities emerge for the Marri Baluch: (1) large permanent villages with associated *darshin,* (2) impermanent village nuclei with *darshin,* and (3) nomadic camps of *powindah.*

Permanent Villages

The permanent villages have populations ranging from 200 to 1,000 persons, most of whom are non-Marri. Nevertheless, the settlement of villages by a predominantly nomadic pastoral people deserves explanation.

First, only a small fraction of the total Marri population is organized around villages. Most important, these villages were not originally Marri settlements: they were Pathan villages conquered and occupied by the Marris. Thus these fixed settlements were not an intrinsic development of a pastoral subsistence economy but resulted from military exploits.

Second, the adoption of agriculture by the Marris in these villages (where slaves and serfs were employed as laborers) served to tie them into a fixed settlement pattern. This shifting of the major subsistence pattern meant, of course, a concomitant shift from a focus on animals to a focus on land. That is, the village Marris no longer had to be constantly on the move as a response to the needs of their animals but could instead concentrate more time and energy on developing the food-producing capacities of particular pieces of land. What animals they owned could be farmed out under contract to surrounding *darshin.* The *darshin,* whose own herds were too small to allow them to become *powindah,* thus benefited doubly: they could use part of the produce from the sedentarized herd-owner's animals for their own use and at the same time have a fixed settlement from which to obtain nonpastoral commodities.

Impermanent Village Nuclei

The second type of Marri community is based on a small sedentary nucleus (not a large village settlement) surrounded by *darshin.* The nucleus is established by a wealthy person who hires a "free-floating population of migratory labor" (p. 13) to work the land or tend the animals. Along with the leader, some of the leader's relatives (normally fewer than forty persons), and their employees, a Hindu trading post will be set up and a few artisans will be attracted to the area, scattering themselves in makeshift shelters over several square miles. The nucleus is not a permanent community, for its existence depends on the whims and fortunes of its leader-founder.

In the vicinity of the nucleus are found the camps (containing one to five tents) of *darshin.* These are Marri who, because of the small size of their herds, move in a restricted orbit around the nucleus and engage in considerable agriculture. But, as was mentioned above, such a *darshin* who can increase the size of a herd to about 100 head will shift from agriculture to pastoralism, break away from a village nucleus, and become *powindah.*

Nomadic Camps

The nomadic camps of the *powindah* constitute the third type of Marri community. The *powindah* have no fixed homesite but instead wander more or less erratically throughout northeastern Baluchistan in search of water and pasturage for their animals. These camps are discussed further in the next section. (Most of the ethnography on which this sketch is based deals with nomadic camps, for it was with the *powindah* that Pehrson lived during his research.)

SOCIAL STRUCTURE

The identification of the Marri Baluch as a discrete group is based on their political unity. They are recognized by the Pakistani government as a subordinate administrative unit within the national political structure. As a recognized unit the Marri Baluch have their own internal organization but are responsible to representatives of the national government having jurisdiction in the district.

The primary local-level Marri groups are nomadic camps. They have no standard layout, though tents tend to be placed in an arc against a hill. The camps vary in size from one to ten tents, though the normal size is three or four.

Camps tend to cohere around joint economic interests, kinship by birth and by marriage, and common defense. Each camp has a leader whose influence also helps to keep the camp together. At the same time, disagreements over camp movements, inheritance of wealth, distribution of labor, competition for leadership, and fear of adultery are divisive forces that may cause a camp to split up. The composition of a camp at any particular time is the product of a combination of fissive and unifying factors.

Camps tend to form "clusters," loose associations of separate but related camps which move in the same general area. Most males in camps constituting a cluster are related patrilineally (that is, in the "father's line"; see Chapter 12), and together they form a segment of a minimal patrilineage—individuals who claim to be descended from a common ancestor a few generations in the past.

These lineages combine, on the basis of a principle of patrilineal descent, into progressively larger aggregations: branches of subsections, subsections, and sections. Three large sections taken together constitute the Marri Baluch, who are subject to a single paramount leader called the *sardar*.

The *sardar* and the leaders (called *wadera* and *mukadam*) of the various sections and subsections form the Marri Tribal Council, which is responsible to the district authorities for local administration. Beneath the tribal council members are the leaders (*mutabar*) of the minimal lineages and the leaders (*halkwaja*) of the individual camps.

The present Marri political structure apparently arose as a consequence of war and raiding, and its basically military framework was later retained for administrative purposes, first by the British and then by the Pakistani government.

Within this structure, segments of the population were easily mustered into progressively larger units, with the heads of camps, lineages, etc., serving as commanders around whom fighting men rallied. These leaders also served as arbiters and administrators for the division of spoils. Their authority depended not only on descent and seniority but also on competence and achievement.

Under British indirect rule, this system was transformed from one which facilitated effective warfare to one which facilitated administrative control. The colonial authorities reinforced the native structure and provided support for its crystallization into a set of stable and fixed institutions. The Pakistani government then later took over administration and continued dealing with the Marris after the British manner, even adding some of its own bureaucratic machinery and innovations. Thus what began as a military expedient was retained as a governmental one.

FOOTNOTES

1 Recently, however, this assertion has been questioned; and it has been suggested that certain herders in South America may be considered pastoral nomads in the sense that this term is used here, though the evidence remains equivocal (see Browman 1974, Gade 1969, Lynch 1971, and Webster 1973).

2 For a fuller treatment, see, for example, Spooner 1973.

3 The progression from (1) a representative of the local or ethnic group to (2) a combined representative of the group to the state and of the state to the group to, finally, (3) a representative of the state to the group is one which commonly occurs when "primitive" societies are in contact with foreign national powers. For a useful treatment of "representative mediators," see Löffler 1971.

4 Without too much distortion due to generalization, we may summarize by saying that pastoralists perceive their society as based on a genealogical charter, usually with a strong patrilineal (male) bias, which approaches to a greater or lesser degree the classic segmentary lineage structure; that kinship terminology leans toward a Sudanese type, though some variation on a basic Iroquoian type is most common (see Chapter 12); and that minimal herding groups are more often constituted on a pragmatic basis rather than on strict descent criteria.

Chapter 8

Industrialists

(Photograph by Frank R. Vivelo, Sr.)

Industrialism refers to the use of energy sources other than muscular power (whether animal or human) to operate machinery for the extraction and conversion of resources. This form of adaptation first began on a large scale in Britain toward the end of the eighteenth century. Water was harnessed to provide energy to operate textile mills. The waterwheel was superseded by steam to drive machinery. The internal combustion engine, which relied on fossil fuels for its operation, soon followed. Then came electricity. This changeover from muscular power to other sources of energy is commonly known as the *industrial revolution,* and it represents the beginning of transformations in human social systems that are still occurring today. Generalizing about industrialism is difficult, partly because it is such a recent phenomenon. Nevertheless, some characteristics may be noted.

CHARACTERISTICS OF INDUSTRIAL SOCIETIES

High Populations

First, the larger number and increased productive capacity of energy sources make possible the support of greater numbers of people. Mechanized farming techniques, the use of chemical fertilizers, and so on, allow more crops to be produced. *High populations,* therefore, are characteristic of industrial societies.

Individual As Basic Labor Unit; Relative Unimportance of Kinship

More efficient techniques for the production of food also mean that fewer people participate directly in food getting. People are freed from farmland to seek a living elsewhere. The emphasis is no longer on a more or less self-sustaining group of people who cooperate in some joint endeavor, such as planting, tending, and harvesting crops, to gain a livelihood. Instead, the *basic labor unit* begins to shift from a household or several households whose members are considered kinspeople to the *individual.* A person sells his or her labor to an impersonal, machine-oriented system or factory, and then uses the payment received (money) to purchase other mechanically produced goods: food, clothing, shelter, etc. Like the hunter-gatherer who moves from place to place in search of better game, the wage-earner moves from place to place in search of a better job. What a person does for a living becomes divorced from kinship. Ties of *kinship* become *less important* for the social order in general.

This is evident in the way food is grown. Farming is no longer a "family" enterprise. Today's farm, as was mentioned in Chapter 6, is a complex factory. Modern machines do most of the work of producing a commodity—food—which is then distributed for profit.

Cities and Trade

Because most of the food grown in an industrial society is produced by a small percentage of the population, the greater percentage of the population lives in cities.

The mass production and complex technology of an industrial society require a large labor force and a diversity of skills. At the same time, the improvements in transportation resulting from the harnessing of more powerful energy sources mean that places of production need not be located near the raw materials they rely on. Thus cities develop, centers of production and, perhaps more important, of distribution of goods, to which people from rural areas migrate. And since the increased output of mass production requires a large market for the distribution of goods, *trade* increases as well. The importance of trade, in turn, influences where cities will be located (on coasts, along major waterways, etc.).

Changes in Family Organization

The decreasing importance of kinship as a referent for behavior and of kin groups in ordering society may also be seen in changes in family organization. In agrarian societies the basic unit of productive labor is a household or several related households. Economic necessity is the primary force for cohesion in these units; it is the glue that holds them together: the adaptive strategy is such that the cooperation of a larger group of people is required to clear, plant, tend, and harvest land. But in emergent industrial societies, a small household unit, the members of which form a "nuclear family" (i.e., husband, wife, and children; see Chapter 13), appears to be a workable arrangement. One partner sells labor on the outside market, while the other remains at home caring for children and performing domestic duties. *This may, however, be only a transitional stage.* With an increase in reliance on machines, and with machinery becoming more sophisticated, both partners may sell their labor outside the home. This would decrease the utility of the nuclear family as an economic unit. Since one partner is not dependent on the other for resources obtained from the outside, there is less reason for the two to remain bound to each other by formal ties such as marriage (and, incidentally, there is less basis for one partner to assert authority over the other, so that male-female relations are altered). Instead, several persons of both sexes may elect to establish and run a joint household, each person having a job outside the household and sharing in the domestic duties and the care of children (or specialists might be hired for housework and child care). This is already occurring in advanced industrial societies such as the United States. What has been erroneously called the "decline of the family" by short-sighted social commentators may simply be an attempt to adjust domestic structure to the exigencies of advanced industrialism. In other words, if we want electric toothbrushes, we may have to accept a fragile familial organization as well.

When the "family farm" was an important economic mainstay of our society, it made adaptive sense to espouse an ideology that lauded marriage, declared the sanctity of the marital bond, and admonished children to display respect and obedience to their parents. All these notions contributed to the cohesion of the economic unit and reinforced the division of labor within it. Now that there is a shift toward the individual as a separate unit of labor—a unit that sells its labor in a factory system, our dominant form of production—there is less adaptive need to promote values which contribute to the unity of the family.

In contrasting Shoshoni family organization with present-day life in America, Steward (1955:102) succinctly records some of the major characteristics of an industrial society and thus helps make the decreased importance of "the family" more understandable:

> Shoshonean culture . . . is of interest for the nature of its organization as much as for its quantitative simplicity. Virtually all cultural activities were carried out by the family in comparative isolation from other families. A contrast with modern America helps clarify this point. In the United States today, people are highly specialized workers in an economic system geared to national and international patterns; education is increasingly standardized and the community or state takes over this function from the family when the child is six years old or younger; health practices are dictated largely by research carried out on an international scale and in part administered by the state and community; recreation more and more involves the consumption of products made by national organizations; religious worship is carried on in national or international churches. These growing functions of the community, state, and nation increasingly relieve the family of functions it performed in earlier historical periods. It is perhaps difficult to imagine that a family, alone and unaided, could obtain virtually all the food it consumed; manufacture all its clothing, household goods, and other articles; rear and train its children without assistance; take care of its sick except in time of crisis; be self-sufficient in its religious activities; and, except on special occasions, manage its own recreation.

Specialization of Labor; Social Stratification; Social Mobility

Along with the diminished importance of kin groups and the emergence of a technologically complex factory system of production comes an *increase in the specialization of labor*. The sophistication of modern machinery and the diversity of uses to which it is put require specialists for efficient operation. Skilled technicians and managers must be trained. Hence, a heavy emphasis is placed on *formal education*. Persons with expertise in administration, finance, teaching, and so on, are needed to keep the overall system running more or less smoothly. Differences in skills and knowledge define access to the resources and wealth of the society; hence *social stratification* is a characteristic of industrial societies. By the same token, however, skills and knowledge can be acquired; therefore *social mobility* is also a trait of industrial societies.

State Political Organization

Specialists in the political sphere are also associated with industrial societies. Since industrial societies are invariably *state societies,* political organization and authority roles are well defined. Centralized political control of a heterogeneous society characterized by considerable division of labor serves to coordinate many economic activities in one integrated whole. Essential to this role of the state is its attempt to secure control over the major sources of energy in the society. Without such control, the state cannot exert authority over the organization of labor. And if a state cannot control labor activities, it cannot influence the organization of social relations in general.[1]

Territoriality; Warfare

Consonant with this interest in energy sources is the notable sense of *territoriality* characteristic of industrial societies. Resources within the society's own boundaries are jealously guarded at the same time that new reserves of energy outside its boundaries are sought. This in turn contributes to *warfare,* as do the need for markets to offload the results of mass production and the need for living space brought on by increasing population. And warfare, needless to say, is an activity that industrial nation-states, with their sophisticated technology, have developed to a point where the degree of potential destruction is frightening.

Religion

Lastly, *monotheistic religion* is characteristic of industrial nation-states. Once again, one deity in the supernatural realm tends to support the assertion of a single political authority in the natural realm. Full-time religious specialists, or *priests,* are the rule.[2]

SUMMARY OF CHARACTERISTICS

Extrapersonal energy; reliance on machinery
High population density; cities
Shift toward the individual as a separate unit of labor, while the factory becomes the main form of production
Money economy
Increase in impersonal relations
Insignificance of kinship and absence of large kin groups in ordering society
Increase in importance of trade
Increase in specialization of labor, social stratification, and formal education
Social, as well as geographic, mobility
Central state system
Territoriality
Warfare
Characteristic religion: monotheism

ETHNOGRAPHIC SKETCH: A Nacirema Subgroup

An anthology entitled *The Nacirema* (Spradley and Rynkiewich 1975) is a collection of forty-one articles describing a number of aspects of belief and behavior of a multifarious group of people who, until recently, have been little studied by anthropologists. These people occupy a large portion of the North American continent, as well as several islands beyond their continental coasts, and constitute a population of over 210 million. The land of the Nacirema is topographically diverse, including deserts, mountains, plains, and conifer and near-tropical forests. Large and small watercourses criss-cross the continent from coast to coast. Settlements vary from rural hamlets numbering fewer than a hundred residents to sprawling urban centers containing several million people. The natural resources of this habitat, which the Nacirema exploit by means of an advanced industrial technology, are manifold and abundant.

The people themselves are as heterogeneous as their habitat. Nacirema society is a patchwork quilt of immigrants from all parts of the world who are sewn together by mutual interest and necessity: they are dependent on a common economic system, are subject to a single centralized political system, and share—at least in broad outline—a set of cultural premises and ideals (see Garretson 1976 for a concise introduction to the major shared beliefs of the Nacirema).

Given this diversity, it is not feasible to try to present here an ethnographic sketch covering Nacirema society as a whole. What have been called *subgroups* and *subcultures* among the Nacirema often differ from one another almost as much as Pueblo Indians (incidentally, one of the Nacirema subgroups) differ from West African villagers. But it is also not practical to attempt to sample a cross-section of Nacirema subtypes; there simply is not space enough to do the job adequately. I have therefore chosen to concentrate on one subcultural variation of the Nacirema theme.

Since Nacirema society is thought to be in many ways the end product of an agglomeration of immigrants, the following sketch is based on a description of one such immigrant group.

ITALIAN-AMERICANS OF BOSTON'S WEST END

In 1957–1958 Herbert J. Gans, a sociologist, lived as a participant-observer among second-generation Italian-Americans in a low-income Boston neighborhood known as the West End. In his book *The Urban Villagers* (1965, orig. 1962), Gans describes the social organization, beliefs, and attitudes (the "subculture") of these West Enders. In the following sketch, the ethnographic present refers to the period of Gans's research.

I have selected Gans's work as the basis for the ethnographic sketch in this chapter because the West Enders' physical and social environment (including tenement dwellings, limited occupational opportunity and low income, segregation from the larger society, etc.) are comparable to those of a great many constituent subgroups of Nacirema society—at least at some point in their respective histories.³ For most of these groups, the patterns of adjustment exemplified by the West Enders represent a transitional stage, lasting one, two, or three generations, during which "Americanization" is effected. (For other groups, such as American blacks, the "transition" seems painfully long.)

The Neighborhood

The West End is a neighborhood of low-rent housing and narrow streets, whose residents are mostly poor. Physically it is separated from other parts of Boston by natural topography (a hill, a river) and by artificial features (an expressway, a park). Socially it has been a residential area for immigrants on their way from Europe to "mainstream" America, a place where they learned English, where they raised their first generation of American-born children, where they earned their first few American dollars.

In the latter part of the nineteenth century, the West End residents were predominantly Irish. By about 1900 the Irish were moving out and being succeeded in the West End by Jews, who remained the majority until about 1930. Italians and Poles were the next major groups to populate the area. By World War II most of the Jews had moved out, and the neighborhood was predominantly Italian. During Gans's fieldwork, the composition of the West End was as follows (summarized from Gans 1965:8–10): first- and second-generation Italian households, 42 percent; first-generation Jewish households, 10 percent; first- and second-generation Polish households, 9 percent; elderly Irish, 5 percent; with the remaining 34 percent being made up of small pockets of other ethnic groups (Greeks, Albanians, Ukrainians), students, artists, hospital staff (from the nearby Massachusetts General Hospital), and a scattering of individuals and families attracted by the low rents.

Gans concentrated his research on the adult population of second-generation Italian-Americans (i.e., American-born children of Italian immigrant parents). Gans calls these people *West Enders,* and so shall I.

Making a Living

The parents of the West Enders were mainly farm laborers from southern Italy (i.e., from the provinces south of Rome and from Sicily). They came to America to escape the conditions of chronic poverty under which they had lived. In the new country they found more opportunities for unskilled manual labor (most worked on construction gangs or in factories), but they also found they had to work just as hard for meager wages to support their families. They felt exploited by, and estranged from, the larger society (including the Catholic Church, whose clerics were mostly Irish). Consequently, they continued to emphasize, as they had done in Italy, the cohesion and solidarity of the family circle as a compensation for the lack of participation in the outside world. Relatives were people who could be relied on at all times, who cared about each other personally, and who shared beliefs, attitudes, and experiences. A person was either kin or was suspect.

Thus, their children—the West Enders among whom Gans worked—grew up in an atmosphere in which familial relations provided the focus of social life, the outside world was viewed with hostility and suspicion, and individuals participated in the outside world (mainly through work) only in order to meet basic material needs and to maintain interaction with relatives. Children were discouraged from continuing their education for a number of reasons: education interfered with parental authority and had the effect of weakening the child's orientation to the family group, and, most important, it prevented the children from getting a job and supplementing the family's income. But because of the child-labor laws and the scarcity of jobs for children, the West Enders' parents complied with the education laws. They allowed their children to attend elementary school but protested against their attendance at high school. Children went to work as soon as was legally possible. The kinds of work they could obtain were limited by their education and skill. Hence, West Enders grew up with an attitude toward work that is similar to their parents': one gets a job that provides money in order to allow one the means to be an active and contributing member of the family circle; but one maintains a kind of detachment from the job. A job is a necessary evil. One does not invest psychologically in, or identify with, work (the typical West Ender does not think in terms of a "career"). It is the family circle that really counts, and one evaluates one's job in terms of how much it obstructs or furthers the purposes of home life.

All the above factors contribute to Gans's identification of West Enders as "working class." Typically, the resident of the West End has a low income (although not officially poor: the average wage is about $70 a week), is an unskilled or semiskilled manual laborer, and has acquired about ten years of schooling. Most important in Gans's view is the West Enders' identification with, and reliance on, a small group of kin as opposed to outsiders. Accordingly, Gans presents his description of West End social organization in terms of relationships within three groupings: the peer group (which includes familial relationships), the community, and the outside world.

Social Organization

The basic household unit of the West Enders is the nuclear family—husband, wife, and children—although an unmarried relative (e.g., a sister, brother, or cousin) may be invited to live in the household.

The nuclear-family household is the primary economic and child-rearing unit. Duties are clearly divided between husband and wife. He works at a job to support the family and dispenses discipline to the children. She tends to the various domestic chores, does not work at an outside job (except when financial needs are pressing, as when the husband is disabled), and is responsible for the day-to-day care of the children.

This domestic division of labor is quite rigidly adhered to. For example, husbands will not help their wives with household chores. The wife cooks, cleans, sees to the needs of the children, selects the apartment furniture and even the apartment. For a man to cooperate in these tasks would throw doubt on his masculinity and render him vulnerable to criticisms about who "wears the pants" in the family.

Husband and wife are emotionally distant as well. Each relies more on same-sex relatives and friends for emotional support than on the spouse. A person takes problems to, and confides in, a sibling or cousin or childhood friend rather than a husband or wife. Between husbands and wives conversation—indeed, communication in general—is limited.

Gans (1965:52–53) explains this "absence of marital closeness" by reference to the insecurity—mainly economic—of West End life. Until recent years, because of limited occupational opportunities, the risk of layoffs, disability, and death, chances were high that one spouse would find himself or herself alone. The lack of intimacy with a spouse and a habit of reliance on other relatives helped to see the survivor through hard times.

There is, likewise, a good deal of segregation in parent-child relationships. Gans describes the West End family as *adult-centered,* i.e., "run by adults for adults, where the role of children is to behave as much as possible like miniature adults" (1965:54). Policies are established by parents, mainly the father, and children are expected to conform to them without protest. They are not to disturb adults with demands or noisy play or introduce any disruption in household routine. As soon as possible (about age seven or eight) girls begin to help their mothers with household chores, though boys are allowed more freedom to wander the neighborhood.

Though children are closely supervised at home, they (especially boys) are free to act as they like away from home among their peers, provided they do not make trouble for their parents.

Boys are not encouraged to obtain more education than is necessary to get a skilled blue-collar job or a simple white-collar one. Girls are not encouraged to obtain more education than is required by law, since they are expected to spend their lives as housewives. College is generally discouraged as sissified and as no guarantee of a better job. In part, extensive education is disapproved because it draws individuals away from the peer group and the family circle.

The family circle, as opposed to the nuclear family, is the social unit in which most valued interaction occurs and with which the individual identifies psychologically. It is the primary reference group and point of social anchorage for the West Ender. In order to understand the family circle, it is necessary to appreciate something of the importance of peer groups generally among West Enders.

West Enders of all ages direct most of their social energy toward interaction with peers, persons of roughly the same age, the same sex, and the same economic level.

During childhood these peers are mainly friends from school and the streets with whom one "hangs out" on street corners, in candy stores, and so on. It is with members of this group that children are most intimate, since their relations with their parents and with other adults are restrained and ordered according to a formal authority structure.

These peer groups demand a strict allegiance from their individual members. For instance, they are sexually segregated,and even in late adolescence contact with the opposite sex is subordinate to ingroup relationships. Boys and girls rarely date as individuals. Instead, whole groups attend recreational affairs, such as dances, at which the boys tend to congregate in one area and the girls in another.

At marriage, both the husband and wife leave these peer groups but soon join another. The new group is called by Gans (1965:39) the *family circle.* It consists mainly of relatives (siblings and cousins by birth and by marriage) and a few close friends of both the husband and wife. The closeness of the kinship connection is secondary to other factors: similar age and income level, shared beliefs and interests. Persons in senior generations (parents, aunts, uncles, etc.) are often excluded. An individual may belong to several such groups; thus throughout the West End a network of interconnected social ties and communication links is created.

The groups meet informally several times each week at the homes of members. Though the gathering occurs after supper, food is consumed in large quantities during the course of the evening. For the most part, the meetings are sexually segregated: men talk to men, women to women; the sexes may even gather in separate rooms.

Any attempts by individuals to lead the group are discouraged, though each member has the opportunity during an evening for self-display through conversation, by telling anecdotes and expressing opinions. West Enders, however, avoid disagreements and arguments during meetings of the family circle. Opinions expressed are usually those generally held within the group, and anecdotes and conversation function to reinforce attitudes and beliefs already established in the group. If a matter comes up about which different opinions are held, the subject is quickly changed so as to avoid any conflict.

The family circle provides each individual with a group of sympathetic contacts to whom he or she can turn in times of crisis and from whom advice on mundane matters is received. The extensive network of family circles and the psychological and social (including, occasionally, economic) support it provides its members reduces their reliance on outside agencies, either in the community or in the larger society.

The family circle also functions as a mechanism for social control. Anyone who exhibits behavior or expresses attitudes disapproved by the group is subject to open criticism. Because of physical proximity and the interwoven kinship and friendship patterns of West Enders, there are few secrets. A person cannot long continue habits considered deviant by his or her peers without their knowing about it and exerting pressure for change. West Enders worry considerably about others' opinions of them and, consequently, strive for a high degree of self-control.

It is within the family circle that attitudes toward the outside world are most strenuously reinforced, for it is recognized that the greater a person's participation in the larger society, the more likely that person is to become estranged from the group. This reluctance to endanger the home-based group is apparent in the West Enders' relationships with the community and with the outside world.

Within the community, West Enders limit their involvement almost entirely to activities that reaffirm the importance of the family circle. For example, men of a peer group belong to a church organization because it provides them with the chance to engage *as a group* in recreational activities, such as bowling. The only other regular community-based participation is attendance at religious services. But even in this regard their involvement is restricted, for, as

Gans (1965:111) points out, West Enders "identify with the [Catholic] religion, but not with the church. . . ."

Gans (1965:106) summarizes as follows:

> In the middle class, people are viewed as participating in community activities. That is, they enter organizations because they share the values and aims fostered by them; or because they find organizational activities—such as the acquisition of prestige, leadership experience, or social and business contacts—useful for their own purposes. Since for the West Ender, parallel functions can be satisfied within the peer group, participation in the community is ancillary.

There is more involvement with the world outside the local community, but this is fraught with suspicion and hostility where the West Enders have little choice in the relationship and is highly selective where it is more voluntary. In Table 8.1 the West Enders' orientation toward aspects of the outside world[4] are summarized. For the sake of brevity, I will touch lightly on only two of these: work and government.

West Enders work to earn money to meet their material needs, to buy clothes and other personal and household items so as to assert their individuality, and to meet expenditures required by participation in peer groups (for example, a large chunk of a West Ender's budget is spent on entertaining the family circle).

Most West Enders do not save their money, for money is considered important only for the purposes to which it can immediately be put. And the main purpose, as far as West Enders are concerned, is the maintenance of satisfactory peer-group relations. For the same reason, work itself is not important: one's occupation should not become a preoccupation. Gans (1965:124) comments:

> Even when work is well paid and satisfying, the West Ender will try to minimize any involvement in it beyond that required of him. Work is a means to an end, never an end in itself. At best, single-minded dedication to work is thought to be strange,

Table 8.1 West Enders' Attitudes toward the Outside World

Accepted as Vital Necessities, Usefulness Recognized	Accepted as Inevitable, but Usefulness Doubted	Welcomed, but on a Highly Selective Basis	Viewed with Suspicion and Curiosity, though Mainly Ignored	Viewed with Hostility, Considered Exploitative
Work	Education beyond elementary school	Consumer goods	Social services	Law
Health care		Entertainment through mass media, especially television	Welfare agencies	Police
				Government

Source: Gans 1965: 120—121.

and, at worst, likely to produce ulcers, heart trouble, and the possibility of early death.

. . . The idea that work can be a central purpose in life, and that it should be organized into a series of related jobs that make a career, is virtually nonexistent among the second generation.

This attitude relates to a general characteristic of West Enders that Gans calls *person-orientation*, as opposed to *object-orientation*. An individual who is object-oriented strives "toward the achievement of an 'object.' This may be a moral object, for example, a principle; an ideological object, such as 'understanding'; a material object, such as level of income; a cultural object, such as a style of life; or a social object, such as a career or a status position." For an individual who is person-oriented, "the overriding aspiration is the desire to be a person within a group; to be liked and noticed by members of a group whom one likes and notices in turn" (Gans 1965:90).

Person-oriented individuals also tend to personalize all aspects of society. They think not in terms of structures, bureaucracies, institutions, and so on, but in terms of individual persons acting for their own private interests. The West Enders' attitude toward government provides an example.

Government is considered inherently exploitative and politicians are considered to be corrupt. West Enders attempt to have little direct contact with government agencies (though they can hardly avoid it altogether) and leave as much as possible in the hands of the local politician. West Enders think that he is corrupt, too, or he would not be a politician; but they feel that he is more likely than other officials to act in their behalf because by so doing he furthers his own interests, since he needs their votes to stay in office. In statewide and national political processes the West Enders take little interest.

West Enders do not conceive of government as an "it" but as a collection of individuals who more often than not pursue selfish goals and attempt to enrich themselves at the public's expense. "The personalization of government operations," says Gans (1965:164–165), "stems in part from the West Enders' inability to recognize the existence of object-oriented bureaucracies. The idea that individual officials follow rules and regulations based not on personal morality but on concepts of efficiency, order, administrative hierarchy, and the like, is difficult to accept."

The Passing of the West End
In order to complete this sketch and, in passing, to locate the West Enders within the context of a modern, industrialized, state society, the ethnographic present will be dropped.

Between 1958 and 1960 the West End, considered by those in authority to be a "slum" area, was torn down and replaced by high-rise apartment complexes to be occupied by middle- and high-income families. The former residents were dispersed throughout the Boston area. The decision to "redevelop" the area was made in the outside world over the protests of the West Enders.

The clearing of the old West End and the relocation of its residents hastened *acculturation* (the process whereby a group assumes many of the major sociocultural characteristics of a different group with which it is in contact). Relocation caused abrupt and immediate change, but signs had already appeared that the former ways were losing their hold on the third generation and that change would have been effected eventually, albeit more slowly and less painfully.

For example, members of the third generation were staying in school longer and moving into more technical white-collar jobs. Increased occupational opportunities and attendant upward mobility probably would have weakened the bonds among members of the family circle while strengthening those in the nuclear family. Better jobs and more money would probably have induced some nuclear families to move out of the West End, thus increasing social distance with physical distance. All this would have tended to increase participation in the outside world, to foster a shift in identification to new reference groups, and to stimulate the adoption of "mainstream" American patterns of behavior and beliefs.

In short, even without the destruction of their old neighborhood, the Italian-Americans of the West End probably would have followed a typical pattern of "Americanization," according to which they very likely would have progressed from marginal, low-income, immigrants to middle-class surburbanites or the equivalent. But they did not. They were unwillingly wrenched from the West End, and *that* may be seen as a notable by-product of modern, industrial, state systems.[5]

FOOTNOTES

1   This line of reasoning may help to explain why the federal government of the United States overwhelmingly supports, financially and technologically, the shift to nuclear power over the development of solar energy systems. The control of nuclear power plants will be primarily in the hands of the state; thus reliance on this energy source represents a major advance in political power wielded by the state, for the more people are dependent on a centrally controlled energy system, the more they are subject to the authority of those who maintain control of that system. An efficient solar energy system, through which each household can supply much of its own energy needs, threatens to lessen the influence of an external authority. (Of course, a solar energy complex that can be overseen by the government is, however, a different matter.)

As was mentioned in footnote 2, Chapter 6, the state views as threats any active competitors for the control of crucial resources. Since any individual or group who controls the flow of vital resources, goods, and services upon which the society is dependent exerts a concomitant degree of power within the society, those who speak in the name of the state attempt either to transfer control of the commodity to the state (for example, through gradual legislation during peacetime or more abrupt takeover in times of war or other national crises, whether real or fabricated) or to stimulate the development of replacement commodities and to foster public dependence on them. It is because of this that I see the United States government and the oil companies coming increasingly into conflict. The surreptitious power afforded by control over oil resources represents a challenge to the licit authority vested in the state. Hence, we are exhorted by the spokespersons for the state to lower our levels of consumption while "alternative sources of energy" are sought out.

2   This characteristic, monotheism, needs qualification in addition to the comments made in Chapter 4. Industrial societies are typically heterogeneous in composition, and, along with occupational, physical, linguistic, and "ethnic" diversity, religious diversity is also found. And, coincidental with a variety of religious groups, beliefs, and practices, there occurs in industrial societies an increasing secularization of ideologies, both public and private.

3   Though particular responses to these conditions vary, the patterns of adjustment in the West End are similar in many respects to those of other immigrants. In Chapter 11 of his book, Gans outlines the similarities and differences between the West Enders and other immigrant and low-income groups in the United States (e.g., Irish, Polish, Jewish, Puerto Rican, black) and in other parts of the world (e.g., Mexico, Britain, the Middle East) and provides a variety of bibliographic references on these groups.

4   In Gans's terminology, *the outside world* refers to "the world beyond the peer group society and the community: the world of employers, professionals, the middle class, city government, and—with some exceptions—the national society. . . . It consists of those agencies and individuals who interfere with the life of the peer group society" (p. 120).

5   Gans, however, disagrees. In a personal communication to the author, he suggests: "The villain here is capitalism, to some extent, although the socialist countries in Europe bulldoze neighborhoods the same way." I do not accept Gans's suggestion, because one of the characteristics of states seems to be that, despite their accompanying "isms," they try to break down local (including ethnic) allegiances, for these are interpreted as conflicting with broader loyalty to the state and acceptance of its authority. Seen in this light, "capitalism" and "socialism" are almost incidental to the general policy of eroding local attachments: they merely provide the legitimating ideologies. Certainly the destruction of the West End and the dispersal of its residents served to weaken local attachments. (See Chapter 11 for my remarks on "capitalism," "socialism," and the use of power in nation-states.)

Part Three

Institutional Overview

Preliminaries: Ordering
Social Relations

(Photograph by the author.)

Having completed our brief overview of ecological types, we are now in a position to deal more specifically with the organization of social relations in regard to specific institutions: kinship, marriage, economic organization, political systems, and so on. That is, in Chapters 3 through 8 the focus was on what I have called—loosely and with qualifications—an evolutionary overview, which only characterized in passing how social relations are generally organized at each of the levels. In Chapters 10 through 14 I will concentrate on social relations in particular by dividing them up into arbitrary spheres (economics, political organization, religion, etc.) and attempt to present an overview or general picture of the various ways people structure their activities in these spheres. In other words, the question will be asked, "What is the range of variation in types of economies (or in types of political systems, or in types of religious orientations) in human societies?" As was mentioned in Chapter 3, this is called an *institutional approach.*

At this point, it is wise to recall our earlier discussion concerning the distinction between the social realm and the cultural realm. When I speak of "the social," I refer to actual behavior patterns (what people do); when I speak of "the cultural," I refer to rules or ideas *about* behavior. I will use this distinction to formulate definitions for some preliminary terms that will be of use in subsequent discussions.

ROLE AND STATUS

The literature on these concepts is vast, and a number of new contributions to the proposed relationships of role and status have appeared in the last few years. The relevant arguments and theories have indeed grown increasingly complex and subtle (see, for example, Goodenough 1965 and Keesing 1973). Since my aim in this handbook, however, is to keep discussions uncomplicated, I will make a distinction between the two that many, but by no means all, anthropologists make.

A *role* is a set of appropriate behaviors, expected or conventional behavior which is culturally acceptable. It is a guide to behavior expected from a person in a particular social position. One "plays" a role, that is, one acts out the appropriate behavior.

Status is a position or place occupied by a person within a society. A status is ascribed to a person, or the person achieves it. The appropriate concomitant behavior, the expected behavior associated with that status, is called the *role.*

Ascribed status, or *assigned status,* is status a person is born to, one in which membership is involuntary (e.g., sex, age, caste). *Achieved status* is one in which membership is voluntary or competitively attained (e.g., doctor, lawyer, teacher). (Once again, I am simplifying in order to introduce these concepts. It is not always so easy to categorize a status as ascribed or achieved. For example, some analysts may consider "draft dodger" to be an assigned status, while others see it as achieved.)

Every society has a kind of blueprint of social positions called a **status system,** an arrangement of statuses in the social structure. Statuses may be ranked relative to each other according to the value or prestige attached to them. Thus, male and female, old and young, or hunter and shaman, doctor and carpenter, are more or less prestigious in a society, depending on the degree to which they are valued by people.

Male, female, child, teacher, policeman, doctor—these are all statuses, identified positions or places in the social order. And the roles of teacher, of doctor, of policeman, and so on, are those sets of culturally appropriate or expected behaviors associated with the statuses. A role is not the position itself, not the person in it, and not the actual behavior of the person. The role is, rather, composed of the ideas about what that behavior is *supposed* to be. In short, applying the definitions of *norm* (footnote 1, Chapter 2), a role is constituted by the ideal norms attached to a particular status. Thus, we can think of *roles* as being in the cultural realm and *statuses* as being in the social realm.

CATEGORY AND GROUP

As Keesing and Keesing point out (1971:149), "the distinction between social and cultural also enables us to see a contrast between *cultural categories* and *social groups.*"

A **category** is a collectivity of things, people, events—"a set of entities in the world" (Keesing and Keesing 1971:149)—the members of which are perceived to share certain attributes. Flowers, left-handed people, automobiles, and so on, are all *categories.* They are things classed or categorized together. All categories, then, may be seen as part of the cultural realm and may be taken, on the whole, as contrasting with *groups.*

A **group** is a collectivity whose members do something together. People who get together to do things form a group. We may therefore distinguish between categories and groups on the basis of whether or not the members act together for some purpose as members of these units. A category is a classificatory device: i.e., it is a way of classifying individuals together and does not imply that these individuals interact. But the term *group* designates precisely that the members interact as members of the unit for the attainment of some end.

Gatherings or **aggregations,** as opposed to groups, are simply collectivities of people thrown together without any internal structure or organization, who happen to come together for some incidental purpose, and who are not interacting to accomplish some common goal. Rather, in this case, each person is pursuing an individual goal which just happens to bring him into contact with other persons who are pursuing their individual goals. Even though their goals may possibly be the same, they are not forming together as a unit to achieve them. People in a train car constitute such an aggregation, as does an audience at some performance.

Formal and informal groups

We may further distinguish between *formal* and *informal* groups.

An **informal group** is one in which the members simply do something together—nothing else. That is, they are organized for a specific (usually short-term) objective and have no sense of unity aside from that necessary to accomplish the objective. Such an informal group is often called an *action group* or *task group.* It may be four hunters who join together to bag a large animal seen in their area; or it may be some cultivators who get together to clear a plot of land; or it may be a neighborhood group which gets together to see that a traffic light is installed at a dangerous intersection.

A **formal group** possesses the same characteristics as an informal one—specifically, people getting together to do something—but the members of a formal group also share some common symbol or symbols which represent that group and provide a sense of unity beyond particular tasks. We are all familiar with such symbols: emblems, banners, jacket patches, and the like.

Primary and Secondary Groups

Another distinction is to be made between *primary* and *secondary* groups. Very simply, **primary groups** are groups in which the members interact face-to-face. A household is a primary group, as is a college class. A **secondary group** is one in which not all members interact face-to-face—some members interact with others, and these in turn interact with still others. Keesing and Keesing (1971:150) mention stockholders in a business corporation as an example. Not all stockholders interact with each other, but they all interact with the management.

Corporate Groups

Finally, the term **corporate group** should be discussed, since it occurs throughout the anthropological literature. The most commonly accepted (though not unchallenged) description of a corporate group is as follows (based on Fortes 1953 and Cohen 1968:50):

1 It appears as a single legal personality—"one person"—from the outside. Correlatively, when viewed from the outside, all members of a corporate group are seen as jurally (or "legally") equivalent. That is, one member's action in regard to outsiders is seen as the action of the corporation. Each of the members represents the corporate group when interacting with society at large.

2 Internally, the corporate group is a face-to-face (i.e., a primary) group "in which the individual is responsible to and for the other members of the group and the latter are responsible to and for him" (Cohen 1968:50).

3 It exists in perpetuity over time. That is, though its members continually change, through the death of some and the birth (or other means of recruitment) of others, the unit as a whole remains intact, a continuing entity.

4 Most important, a corporate group is one which controls some re-source or property, often land. A group cannot be corporate unless it has something to incorporate about (Lee and DeVore 1968). There is thus al-ways some valued commodity over which the group exercises proprietary rights.[1]

There has been much controversy over just what a "corporate group" is, considered anthropologically. The above description is the one that has been used most, but it is falling somewhat into disfavor. It has been crit-icized as being an overlegalistic view applicable only to modern Western societies and to some primitive societies, especially some in Africa. The argument has been made that *corporate group* is a poor anthropological term because it is not valid cross-culturally. In the main, this criticism appears valid: "corporateness" is something that differs from society to society. And so the argument has gone that we should either abandon the term completely or define it each time we use it, the definition being based on context. I have brought the matter up here because you are going to run across it again and again if you continue in anthropology. Also, as you read back through the older literature, you will encounter this term without de-finition; and you should have some idea what writers mean by it.

I have noted four characteristics of a corporate group. These consti-tute, generally speaking, the older version. To modernize this somewhat, but to retain simplicity as well, we can consider for our purposes that char-acteristic 4—the control by the group of some valued commodity—is the defining characteristic of "corporateness" and that the other three chracter-istics are secondary and may or may not be present in any particular case. I emphasize characteristic 4 because, as was mentioned above, if there is nothing to incorporate about—no valued commodity—then there is no need for a "corporation."[2]

With these considerations behind us, we can proceed to a discussion of ways in which human groups order social relations. Before taking up specif-ic institutions, I will briefly consider in the remainder of this chapter some aspects of social organization that cross-cut institutional divisions.

LIFE CYCLE

In all societies, the processes of birth, maturation, reproduction, and death—known collectively as the *life cycle*—are socially marked and cultur-ally elaborated. The attention paid to these "life crises" may be minimal, or they may be surrounded by much pomp and ceremony; but in no society are they totally ignored.

The life cycle is based generally on biological processes of devel-opment; persons move from stage to stage as maturation progresses. This movement from stage to stage is often marked by special ceremony. By emphasizing the transition or passage from one state to another, the group impresses upon the individual the significance of the change.

The special rituals accompanying these changes are called *rites of passage;* they mark the transition from one status to another within the life cycle (see Van Gennep 1960).

Rites of passage center on individual life crises. They may be contrasted with *rites of intensification.* These are rites which intensify group ties: "rituals and ceremonies that mark occasions or crises in the life of the community as a whole, such as the need for rain, defense against epidemic or pestilence, preparations for planting, harvests, the initiation of communal hunting or fishing activities, and the return of a successful war party" (Beals and Hoijer 1965:594).

Rites of passage have been described by Van Gennep as comprising three stages: (1) separation, (2) transition, (3) incorporation.

Separation refers to the removal of the subject from his or her former status identification, i.e., "the individual first is (physically or symbolically) separated from his present position" (Bock 1969:71).

Transition is the stage wherein the individual is placed in "an external suspended state, cut off from regular contact" (Keesing and Keesing 1971:214). That is, it is a transitional state in which the individual no longer occupies his or her former position but has yet to move into a new position.

Incorporation is the final stage, in which the subject leaves the suspended state and is ritually incorporated into a new social position. The individual once more has a defined place in society.

Rites of passage, though primarily associated with transitions in the life cycle, are also in evidence in other contexts. For example, in societies whose members have strong notions of sacredness and pollution, passage between these states and ordinary activity will probably be marked by ritual.

A person in such a society who becomes defiled or polluted—perhaps a man who has killed an enemy in battle, or has eaten tabooed food, or has been contaminated by a menstruating woman[3]—may have to go through a ritual which cleanses and brings the person back into ordinary society. Such rituals are called *rites of purification.*

A person who has been in close personal contact with the supernatural may also need to go through a rite in order to pass back into mundane society. In this case, the rites are called *rites of desacralization.* In some societies, the power that emanates from the supernatural realm is considered so strong that contact with it might have disastrous consequences for any ordinary mortal and for any third parties who subsequently associate with such a person. Rites of desacralization are, in essence, ways of neutralizing this power.

But, to repeat, rites of passage are chiefly concerned with movement through the life cycle. It is to a consideration of this cycle that I now turn.

Birth

Prenatal Taboos   Pregnancy is a time of uncertainty. Will the fetus develop satisfactorily? Will there be a miscarriage? Will the birth be easy or difficult? Will the child be healthy? The greater the ignorance concerning the physiology of gestation and birth, the greater the anxiety. And the greater the anxiety, the greater the need for reassurance in the form of magical precautions, taboos, and ritual protections. Thus we find prenatal behavioral restrictions to be common cross-culturally. A pregnant woman should not eat this kind of food but should eat that kind. She should not walk backwards through a doorway. She should not tie or untie knots. And so on. Very often such restrictions apply to her husband as well and even to other near relatives.

Parturition   Parturition usually takes place in the presence of women, either relatives of the mother or a midwife, though in some societies the husband may be present and may even assist at the birth. Modern industrial societies are atypical in that birth usually takes place among strangers and in unfamiliar surroundings.

Postnatal Practices   Postnatal practices vary widely cross-culturally. In some societies, a woman resumes her normal activities almost immediately; in others, she and her child must remain confined for a specified period of time, and she may be required to observe many taboos. A practice that Westerners often find striking is the **couvade:** the father retires, rests, and is subject to strict taboos, while the mother resumes her regular activities. (In some societies, the father may even simulate giving birth.) Another fairly common postnatal custom involves *postpartum sex taboos,* in which the woman (and perhaps her husband also) is enjoined from having sexual relations for a specified amount of time after the birth of a child.

Often birth in itself is not sufficient for the child to be accepted as a full member of the society. After birth there may follow at designated periods a series of rituals that incorporate the child into the group, such as *naming ceremonies* and the formal *presentation of the child* to the group and its deities. For example, before recent changes in their social organization, the Herero cattle herders of southern Africa used to hold a brief ceremony about a month after the birth of a child. The child's forehead was touched to that of a male calf, and the child was given two names, a common one and a sacred one. The child was then held up and formally introduced to the ancestors as one of their descendants (Gibson 1952:170, Vivelo 1977:132). Similar practices are found in other societies, and they illustrate that becoming a member of society is usually a process, not a state which occurs at birth.

Childhood

Childhood, the time between birth and puberty, may be treated in one society as a single continuous phase, while in another it is subdivided into different periods, each marked by ritual. Childhood is often the time when the rules do not apply, at least not all of them. For example, since children are in a sense "precultural beings," they may be permitted to eat some foods denied to adults and normally are not bound by the same rules for sexual behavior as adults are. Nevertheless, despite current popular notions regarding primitive "permissiveness," childhood is nowhere a wholly care-free time of life. Children learn the proper control of their bodily functions; they are taught basic etiquette; they begin to master the correct behavior to show toward relatives, neighbors, and strangers; they learn to assume standard attitudes toward their deities; they learn which personality characterisitics are valued and which are not. In short, they learn to become social beings. And sociality means constraint and conformity.

Socialization

Socialization (or *enculturation*)[4] is the process whereby the individual learns to behave as a member of his or her society, to become a social being. The person learns what society expects of him or her—that is, learns the cultural rules that are the references and guides for appropriate social participation. He or she learns how to fit in with the patterned processes of social interaction in the group. In short, socialization refers to the "transformation from an infant organism to an adult participant in society" (LeVine 1973:61).

Socialization begins at birth and never really ends until death, for one is continually adjusting behavior to take into account the presence of others and one's interaction with them. This may be illustrated by a brief mention of three sources of influence on a person's behavior: (1) caretakers, (2) peers, and (3) self.

Socializing Agents

Caretakers   During infancy and early childhood, the primary socializing agents are the child's *caretakers* (parents, other adults, elder siblings, etc.). It is these individuals who see to the child's physical and emotional needs. They provide the child with food, protection, shelter, companionship, and so forth. They also begin to modify his or her behavior. The child learns to behave in certain ways in order to obtain satisfaction of wants and needs.

Peers   As the child grows, interaction with playmates assumes a socialization function. Behavior must be modified—i.e., the child must exhibit a certain amount of conformity—if the child is to be accepted among peers. Thus, this mechanism for inducing conformity is known as *peer group pressure.* We are used to talking about this process in our own society mainly in reference to children and adolescents; but it is an important pressure for conformity among adults, too. In fact, in many nonliterate societies, it is the primary means of imposing conformity.

Three-year-old Herero girl (foreground); southern Africa. *(Photograph by the author.)*

Ridicule; gossip; exclusion Ridicule, gossip, and social exclusion are very powerful weapons in a small face-to-face local group. In addition, three other mechanisms should be mentioned: supernatural sanctions, accusations of witchcraft, and blood feud.

Supernatural sanctions Supernatural sanctions are a common force for conformity. Frequently it is believed that transgressions of the rules for behavior disturb the moral order, since they disturb the social order and the social order is intimately bound up with the moral order. And the moral order is usually overseen by supernatural beings: spirits, ghosts of ancestors, deities, etc., (see Chapter 14). Thus the person who breaks the rules is in danger of supernatural retaliation—in the form of sickness, accident, "bad luck," or even death—as a consequence of wrongdoing.

Witchcraft In some societies, persons who continually break the rules may be in danger of being accused as witches and punished accordingly. Punishment may be as light as a small fine or as severe as death (or ostracism from the group, which may amount to a death sentence). Accusations of witchcraft are a good way to chasten or get rid of someone who cheats or steals or breaks too many rules too often. They are also a good way to get rid of someone who is too successful, has too much "good luck," or has accumulated a noticeable amount of wealth. (Anyone so rich must be a

witch.) The threat of an accusation of witchcraft, therefore, helps to maintain conformity, to lessen the chance that someone will "step out of line"
and flout community standards.

Determining the guilt of someone who has been accused as a witch—
or, for that matter, of any wrongdoing—may take several forms. One common way is through **trial by ordeal.** This may be defined as the practice of
putting someone through a physical ordeal or trial or forcing the person to
perform some feat in order to ascertain guilt or innocence or to test the
person's veracity. For example, the subject may be bound and tossed into a
river. A subject who does not drown is innocent. (Sometimes, however, one
can lose both ways: a subject who survives must be guilty because obviously a person could not survive without help; and so the forces of evil must be
taking a hand. But a person who drowns is innocent—but is, alas, dead.)
Sometimes both the accuser and the accused undergo the ordeal. The one
who survives is telling the truth.

Blood feud   The threat of blood feud and bloodwealth (damages paid
in compensation for injuring or killing a member of another group) can also
be a pressure for keeping order. It promotes social conformity by acting as
a deterrent to the would-be perpetrator of a crime, especially the wounding
or killing of another person, because if a person does take the life of someone in another group, that other group can retaliate by taking the life of
someone (usually anyone) in the killer's group. Thus the group itself puts
pressure on its individual members to keep the peace lest they become
involved in a feud or have to pay bloodwealth. (Feuding is further discussed
Chapter 11.)

Self   Lastly, the *individual* may be seen as a socializing agent. As a
result of **internalization**—the process whereby a person makes his or her
own the values, attitudes, goals, etc., that have been communicated as appropriate in the society—the individual may become his or her own watch-
dog. One develops a "conscience" (or, to use Freudian terminology, a "su-
perego"), a set of standards used to monitor and evaluate one's own
thoughts and behavior. A person who perceives that his or her behavior is
at odds with internalized cultural norms (and this perception need not be
conscious) may experience the tension this produces as guilt or anxiety and
attempt to modify behavior in order to lessen the tension. But even an
individual who has not internalized to any great extent the rules of the
society may closely monitor his or her behavior as a result of a sense of
pragmatism or *reasoned self-interest.* In other words, an individual may recognize that getting along in a society means cooperation with, and adjustment to, other people. One realizes that in order to achieve one's goals—to
win the game—the best bet is to learn the rules and how to use them. In the
long run, this is in one's own interest, though at times it may not seem so.
A person who continually breaks the rules not only will not win the game

but may even be prevented by others from playing at all. (It should be noted that such motivations for self-control may not be common cross-culturally. They seem to be increasingly evident in our own and other industrial societies, but little documentation is available to support a contention that they are widespread in "primitive" societies.)

Puberty

"Puberty marks the twilight of youth and the dawn of adulthood" (Hoebel 1972:380). In many societies, the onset of puberty is surrounded by ritual. It represents a turning point at which individuals formerly considered children must begin increasingly to assume the identities and roles of adults in their society. It is thus puberty as a social marker, and not as a physiological change, that is our proper focus.

The time when puberty ceremonies—more commonly called *initiation ceremonies*—are performed need not correspond to actual physiological puberty. As Keesing and Keesing (1971:215) point out, in those societies in which persons pass through the life cycle as individual personalities, initiation ceremonies more or less correspond to physical signs of puberty; but they may also depend on additional factors, such as being visited by a spirit in a dream. In those societies in which persons pass through major stages collectively (i.e., in groups), the time an initiation ceremony is held may have little to do with actual puberty. For example, among the Herero of southern Africa, initiation ceremonies were held at irregular intervals, whenever a sufficient number of uninitiated boys were present in a community. At that time *all* uninitiated males, regardless of age, underwent the ceremony. Hence, historical records show a one-year-old infant undergoing a "puberty" ceremony, as well as a seventeen-year-old man.

Some societies have initiation ceremonies for boys, some for girls, some for both, and some for neither. In a sample of fifty-four societies, Frank Young (1965a:14–15) found that 40 percent had initiation rites for males and 57 percent had them for females. He also found that the rites for males were more severe or elaborate than those for females.

For boys, initiation often involves circumcision, and some Australian Aborigines practice subincision (an operation which exposes the urethra). There is usually less mutilation of females, though it occurs; in a few societies clitoridectomy is even practiced. Cicatrization; scarification; filing of teeth; piercing of ears, nose, or lips; and tattooing are some other practices frequently associated with initiation ceremonies.[5]

Adulthood

In a great many societies, full adulthood is not achieved until the individual is married or has gained a certain standing or prestige in the society—and this may be delayed until what we would call middle age. Frequently, one is not considered an adult until he or she is a parent.

In some societies, marriage follows soon after initiation; in others it is delayed a number of years. For example, in some East African societies, a young man enters a warrior class after initiation (see the discussion of age grades below); and so long as he remains in this class, he may not marry. In fact, he may be expected to remain sexually continent during this period. In neighboring societies with similar warrior classes, however, this may be a time of relative sexual freedom.

Old age, too, is treated in various ways. In some societies, old people may be accorded the status of elders and treated with respect and deference. In others, old people may be considered an unavoidable evil and are cared for as dependent members of the group similar to children. In still others, old people may be too much of a burden on the active members of society and so are left to their own devices, to care for themselves or die or commit suicide; or they may be killed by their younger relatives (this is sometimes referred to as *senilicide*). It is probably safe to say that the way the elderly (and other unproductive members of the group) are treated reflects to a large extent the precariousness or security of the group's adaptive strategy. Where resources are severely limited, technology simple, labor investment high and return on labor low, economically unproductive members of the group cannot easily be tolerated. They threaten the existence of the entire group. Where the environment is more hospitable and the tools and techniques for the extraction and conversion of resources are adequate to produce a surplus, the old and infirm can be supported. (Meggers 1971 has applied a similar argument to account for a high incidence of *infanticide,* the killing of newborn children.)

Death

Death is disruption. It alters social relationships in which the deceased was a participant and which therefore have to be rearranged to allow for his or her absence. The complexities of inheritance and succession have to be dealt with. Death confronts people with profound and disturbing philosophical questions concerning the nature and meaning of existence. And death puts a severe psychological strain on those whose emotional lives were bound up with the deceased.

Where uncertainty, fear, disruption, emotional strain, and so on, are found, ritual is also found. And death is in all societies surrounded by ritual. Precisely what the content of the ritual is varies from society to society, but funeral ceremonies themselves are universal. The deceased may be buried, cremated, abandoned in the bush, laid out on stands, exposed to the elements, or wrapped in a protective covering. An individual's membership in society may cease with finality upon his or her death, or it may not. Death may not end an individual's participation in the affairs of the group; it may simply represent a change in the way this participation is viewed. In such a case, as where ancestral veneration is practiced (Chapter 14), it makes sense to view the funeral ceremony as a rite of passage from one status (living member) to another (deceased member, or spirit).

AGE GRADES AND AGE SETS

Age, usually socially defined rather than being based on strict chronology, plays an important part in the organization of social relations. This has been indicated somewhat by the preceding characterization of the life cycle. But societies may use a more formalized approach to age to inject order, stability, and predictability into social organization. One common cross-institutional way of structuring social relations on the basis of age is through a system of age grades.

Here let me repeat the distinction made earlier between *category* and *group*. A category is a classification together of entities on the basis of something they are perceived to have in common, whereas a group is a collectivity of persons who do things together. On the basis of this distinction, we may say that age grades are categories and age sets are groups.

Specifically, **age grades** are categories which order people according to age criteria; i.e., people are classified into these categories based on how old they are. Age grades are a fixed (unchanging) set of conceptual categories through which people pass as they mature.

Age sets are the groups of people who together occupy the age grades. Age sets are given a name and have a group identity. All the members of a single age set pass through the various age grades together as a unit. Coevals (age-mates, members of the same age set) share certain rights and duties toward each other (e.g., they may be expected to take each other's side in disputes, to fight together, to provide economic aid when needed, to show each other hospitality). At the same time, each age set as a unit has certain rights and duties in relation to senior age sets (e.g., they must show a certain amount of deference or obedience to their elders, and they may expect certain favors from them as well) and to junior age sets (e.g., they can exert a certain amount of control over their juniors, but they are also charged with giving them proper models of behavior to emulate).

Cyclical and Progressive Age-set Systems

Two types of age-set systems have been distinguished, based on naming customs: cyclical and progressive.

Cyclical age-set systems are those in which the name used for an age-set in the past may be used again for a new age set at a later date. In other words, the same name appears periodically.

Progressive age-set systems are those in which the name for an age set is used only once; when the last member of an age set dies, the name is retired and may never be used again.

Ethnographic Example

Perhaps an ethnographic example will help make age grades and age sets clearer.[6]

The Tiriki are a Bantu-speaking tribe in western Kenya, Africa. The foundation on which their organization of social relations is built is their age-grade system (which, however, is not an indigenous part of their culture but was borrowed from a neighboring group).

The Tiriki traditional system (as opposed to the newer Christian-influenced system) consists of four age grades: warriors, elder warriors, judicial elders, and ritual elders. In addition, there are seven age-set names. When the senior age-set becomes extinct, its name is given to a new group entering the age system at the most junior level (a name is reused about every 105 years). It is thus a cyclical age-set system.

Adolescent boys are admitted to the formal age categories through a series of initiation ceremonies that lasts about six months and includes circumcision; seclusion; and intensive instruction in ritual, hunting, singing, dancing, warfare, and weaving of ceremonial costumes.

Initiations are performed every four or five years, but each age set remains in a particular age grade for about fifteen years. At the end of each fifteen-year period, each age set moves as a unit into the next higher grade, while at the lowest level new initiates are admitted to the system.

Sangree (1965), from whom this account is taken, makes the following comments (excerpted from pp. 66–69):

The . . . Tiriki initiation rites, in the six months of dramatic and rigorous instruction during seclusion following circumcision, teach the initiates how to behave as members of the highly formalized graded age groups that traditionally regulated Tiriki traditional military, political, and ritual activity. . . .

. . . The initiation rites, apparently with marked effectiveness, do give the initiate a sense of belonging to a special tribal brotherhood, and do much to teach him what kinds of social attitudes are appropriate for and expected of members of that brotherhood.

. . . Very likely the shock the initiates receive because of the contrast the Tiriki initiation cycle presents to all their previous socialization procedures is probably just as significant to their effectiveness as their actual content. The relentless and dramatic intensity of the initiation is a radical departure from the casual on-again-off-again tutelage and supervision of near peers, women, and old people that guide a youth before his initiation. The principal agents of socialization during initiation . . . are initiated men still in their physical prime—the very group with whom youths, before initiation, have virtually no contact. . . .

Prior to initiation a youth has very little contact with initiated men outside his own homestead; his peers are drawn from different clans all over the neighborhood, but his main loyalties are to those in his homestead, clan and kin group. After initiation, however, all these loyalties are in most circumstances subordinated to his age group ties, and to the judicial and ritual authority of the elder age groups. Thus the Tiriki initiation rites quickly orient the initiates to their new status of manhood, indoctrinate them in the intricacies of the graded age group organization, and effectively shift their primary bonds of loyalty and social reference from their extended family to their age group and the graded hierarchy of more senior age groups.

Adjacent and Alternate Generations; Primogeniture and Ultimogenture

Age is of course used more informally in all societies for ordering social interaction. In this regard, two pairs of terms should be introduced here, since the student will come upon them in the anthropological literature.

It is not uncommon cross-culturally to find that there exists a certain amount of tension, even hostility, between *adjacent generations* (those generations, the parents' and child's, which follow each other in consecutive order). This is probably due to the fact that it is the members of the senior adjacent generation who exercise direct authority over the junior, and to the resentment this may engender in the members of the latter. It may also be attributed to the fact that the elder generation sees the junior as its usurpers, while the junior generation views the elder one that it will replace as an obstacle to its ambitions.

On the other hand, the relationship between *alternate generations* (every other generation, grandparents' and grandchildren's) is likely to be warm and friendly. This may be because they are too far apart in age to consider each other rivals and because the elder generation is not so directly involved in asserting authority over the younger.

The other pair of terms deserving mention pertains to inheritance practices based on age distinctions. *Primogeniture* refers to inheritance by the firstborn (or oldest child). *Ultimogeniture* refers to inheritance by the lastborn (or the youngest child).

In some societies, the oldest child inherits most or all property, and younger siblings are either dependent on the oldest or are left to seek their fortunes on their own. In other societies, as children grow and marry, they leave the household to make their own way in the world; but the youngest (usually male) child remains in the household after marriage to care for the parents in their old age. In such a case, it is the youngest who inherits. (Needless to say, there are other societies in which inheritance is divided among a number of heirs.)

NONKIN ASSOCIATIONS

Age-grade systems, where they are well delineated, provide for the same kind of solidarity, references for behavior, and structuring of social interaction that kinship provides in many other nonliterate societies (kinship is discussed in Chapter 12). Age grades, however, are not the only such devices. Associations (or sodalities) are another.

Voluntary and Involuntary Associations

Voluntary associations are groups formed on an elective basis (they may be as small as a dyad—two persons—or they may be very large, including literally thousands of members). One anthropologist (Bock 1969:151) defines voluntary associations simply as "any group of persons who act together by choice to attain a particular end."

We are all familiar with such groups in our own society (clubs, lodges, street gangs, veterans' associations, fraternities, sororities, consumer-interest groups, and so on, *ad infinitum*). The proliferation of associations in industrial societies is usually attributed to the diminished importance of kinship as a principle of social organization and as a major means of social affiliation for individuals in societies based on an industrial adaptive strategy. Associations in such societies are seen as providing anchorage or a sense of belonging for individuals, as promoting social integration and solidarity in a community or throughout the society, and as facilitating the achievement of individual and group goals.

Not all associations are voluntary, however. *Involuntary associations* are those in which membership is ascribed or compulsory. Labor unions for certain occupations in our society are an example of involuntary associations.

Associations also occur in nonindustrial societies. But as a general rule, it is safe to say that the probability of associations' existing in a society is greater the more complex its technoeconomic base is; for as a society grows more "modernized," kinship decreases as a primary basis for ordering social relations.

Varieties of Associations

Viewed cross-culturally, associations occur in so many different varieties that all cannot be covered in a handbook such as this. I will mention a few that you are likely to happen across in your reading.

First, what are often referred to as *tribal fraternities* and *tribal sororities* are fairly common. These are involuntary associations based on sex; that is, all adult males or all adult females are required to become members. (They are therefore referred to as *inclusive* groups.) Though male associations seem to be statistically predominant cross-culturally, both types are found in some societies, and female associations only are found in a few.

Military societies are another type of association, one in which membership is voluntary and therefore *exclusive* (i.e., only some individuals become members). Many North American Indians, especially those of the Great Plains, had strong military societies.

Secret societies are also an example of voluntary and exclusive associations. Members of these groups possess secret or esoteric knowledge denied to nonmembers. Though every group probably has some sort of "secret" its members share, the term *secret society* is usually reserved for groups whose power or social influence is seen as deriving from the "secret" or those in which the "secret" is used for certain ends or renders its possessors particularly adept in certain activities, such as healing or warfare. An example is provided by the associations of curers among the Indians of Sia Pueblo in the American Southwest, about which White says (1962:136): "The societies were endowed with supernatural power and were provided with songs, paraphernalia, rituals, and in some instances dances, through which this power was expressed or used for certain purposes such as curing sickness, hunting or warfare."

Finally, **special-interest groups** are a type of association. They are groups formed by persons who seek to achieve the same goal or who share a particular interest.[7] For example, the NAACP, the National Rifle Association, the Audubon Society, and various "liberationist" groups are examples from our own society. Two common special-interest associations in other societies are bond friendships and trading partnerships.

Trading partners will be mentioned in Chapter 10 as an example of a kind of economic exchange relationship often established between a pastoral nomad and a resident of a sedentary community. Nothing, therefore, need be said here about this form of association.

Bond friendship (or a **multi-purpose association**) is another type of reciprocal relationship, one established between two social equals who are usually about the same age and the same sex. It involves mutual obligations and rights, e.g., gift giving and hospitality (which may include wife lending), legal, economic, and emotional support, and so on. An individual may have several bond friends, and one's relationships with these serve as a reliable network of persons to whom one can turn in time of need. They thus extend the range of dependable social relations beyond the realm of kinship.

INEQUALITY OR SOCIAL STRATIFICATION

Some societies, especially those based on advanced cultivation or industrialism, use a principle of inequality in their social organization. Hence, another nonkinship method of ordering social relations is **social stratification,** which may be described as a system of classifying persons in a hierarchically arranged series of social strata (classes or castes) having differential access to the resources, goods, and skills (in short, what is valued as good or desirable) available to the society as a whole. Or, as Collins (1975:349) phrases it, "individuals or groups of individuals are conceived of as occupying higher or lower social levels or strata" and "higher levels reflect more of the 'goodies' available in the society."

Another author (Haviland 1975:222) has listed some common elements in an accepted definition of stratification:

> hierarchically ranked groups that maintain relatively permanent positions, have differential control of the sources of power relative to their ranking, are separated by cultural and individual distinctions, and have an overreaching ideology that provides the rationale for the entire system. Such societies can be distinguished by a relative degree of inequality of rewards and privileges.

Regardless of the specific attributes that can be listed in a definition of stratification (over and above the basic element of differential access to resources within the population), it seems clear that, before stratification can occur in a society, two conditions must be filled: (1) there must be some vital commodity (resources, goods) that can be controlled or monopolized by some members of the group; (2) a surplus must be possible.

As is evident from Part Two of this handbook, social stratification emerges in human society as a correlate of technoeconomic complexity. The more advanced the adaptive strategy (i.e., the more sophisticated the extractive techniques, so that more and more resources can be tapped), the greater the likelihood of surplus, occupational specialization, monopolization of valued commodities, strong political systems, and social stratification. Thus, though ranking based on individual characteristics (such as ability, personality traits, etc.) occurs in hunting-gathering societies, social stratification is normally absent. In the few collecting societies that *are* stratified, such as the Northwest Coast Indians, this characteristic is correlated with the presence of surpluses and monopolizable resources. Social stratification is much more characteristic of food-producing societies and is found in varying degrees among horticulturists, pastoralists, agriculturists, and industrialists. The presence of stratification and the widespread use of kinship to order social relations are not *necessarily* mutually exclusive, as my remarks above might imply. In parts of Africa and Polynesia, for instance, kinship groups (such as clans and lineages; see Chapter 12) are ranked relative to each other. Sometimes this ranking involves differential access to resources, and sometimes it does not.

Caste Systems and Class Systems

Two major types of stratification are usually distinguished: class systems and caste systems.

A *caste system* is one in which the society is divided into a hierarchically arranged number of fixed groups, and membership in these groups is ascribed by birth (i.e., membership is hereditary). Membership in a caste determines a person's occupation; the kind of work he or she will do is decided by accident of birth. Castes are endogamous; i.e., one must marry someone who is a member of the same caste (see Chapter 13). But for distinguishing a caste system from a class system, the most important characteristic is that in a caste system membership in the caste is fixed at birth and cannot be changed. Put another way, there is theoretically little or no social mobility in a caste system.

A *class system,* on the other hand, is usually distinguished by the characteristic of social mobility (if not in fact, at least in ideology); a person may theoretically move up and down in the class structure. Thus we may define a class system as a division or ordering of society into a series of hierarchically arranged strata or levels called *classes,* in which membership, though initially determined by birth, may be changed through personal achievement. An individual is not tied to any particular occupation ascribed at birth and there is no formal rule requiring marriage within one's class.

In brief, a caste system may be described as *closed,* while a class system may be termed *open.*

Outcasts and Slaves

While on the subject of inequality, two additional designations should be mentioned: outcasts (or outcastes) and slaves.

Outcasts (or *pariahs*) are persons excluded from normal social intercourse with other members of society. They are "untouchables," polluted and polluting persons who are "cast out" of the system. The pariah group often performs work that is useful or even vital to the society as a whole, but, because such work is considered defiling, no one else will perform it.

Slaves, by contrast, are persons who have a place within the society; they are not cast outside it. The characteristics usually used to define slavery are the lack of reciprocal relations between slaves and masters and the exercise by the master of rights of proprietorship and disposition over the person of the slave. Slavery is not an equitable contractual relationship. It is a relationship in which the bulk of the rights resides with the master and the duties with the slave. Despite these defining characteristics, however, slavery is a variable institution. In some societies, slaves hold a lowly, degraded position and are treated as chattel. In others, as in much of Africa, the slave becomes a member of a household and is treated like a kinsperson, with many of the prerogatives kinship entails. Bohannan (1964:105–108) comments on the differences between slavery in Africa and slavery in Europe (and America) during the European "age of exploration":

> Both the Europeans and the Africans at the time . . . had a tradition of slavery, but the two traditions were of very different sorts. African slavery (usually called benign, domestic, or household slavery) was a domestic institution—there were only a few exceptions on the continent. Domestic slaves are interesting because their economic value was not the most important thing about them (although they may, like housewives, be of economic value). It was rather their value as political followers and as indicators of prestige that was dominant.
>
> . . . The word "slave" in this sense refers to people who are attached to domestic groups by non-kinship links of a sort that contain elements of servility. . . .
>
> A slave was, thus, a kind of kinsman—with different rights from other kinsmen, but nevertheless a kind of kinsman. . . .
>
> In Europe slavery was a very different institution. . . . European slavery was, from the beginning, primarily economic—perhaps it would be better to say that domestic slavery was the exception. . . .
>
> Particularly in the medieval world, the form of subservience or servility was scarcely "slavery" in the African sense at all, because it consisted of the institution that European history knows as the "bond servant." . . .
>
> What happened in the slave trade is that the economically dominated

feudal version of servility from the European area met the basically benign, family-dominated slavery from Africa. Like many other aspects of culture, they met first in the market place. Africans saw nothing wrong in selling slaves. Europeans found nothing wrong in buying them—indeed, many of the Negroes in the earliest importations were treated as bond slaves, their bondage limited by contract to a period of years. But the idea that each had about the role of the slave in the world's work was totally different from that of the other. Supply of slaves became expensive, and the "bond" became permanent. From the meeting of the two and the establishment of new nations and new economies, a new institution—New World slavery—emerged.

Though by no means exhaustive, the variety of topics covered in this preliminary chapter should indicate that social relations are ordered through a diversity of mechanisms. They do not fall neatly into confined spheres— religion, kinship, economics, and other institutional categories—as the remaining chapter headings might suggest. A society is more fruitfully conceived of as a complicated network of mutually dependent, interlocking activity systems. The interconnections among these activity systems are still poorly understood by social scientists, though a staggering body of theory exists on the subject. In Chapters 10 through 14, therefore, I will be concerned primarily with cross-cultural variation within these institutions and only secondarily with their complex relationships to each other.

FOOTNOTES

1 Exogamy as a primary characteristic of corporate groups is omitted here, since it appears to be the one feature which is most often disputed by theorists. (Exogamy is covered in Chapter 13).

2 Here the instructor might want to raise the question of whether units controlling nonproductive property, such as ritual items or ceremonial knowledge, are "corporate" or not.

3 Cross-culturally there is a widespread, though by no means universal, belief in the impurity of women, a belief that women are a source of pollution or defilement. Frequently associated with this is the notion that menstrual blood is vile and contaminating. For instance, very often girls are isolated from the community at menarche (first menstruation) and are required to observe a number of restrictions (especially regarding food). Not uncommon also is the seclusion or semiseclusion of women, regardless of age, during their monthly menstrual periods. During this time they may not be permitted to cook or handle food, to assume certain physical postures, to engage in sexual intercourse, or even to be seen by the community at large. (Three useful studies on this topic are Stephens 1961, Young 1965b, and Paige and Paige 1973.)

4 Following Mead (1963), Williams, in a comprehensive introduction to the study of socialization (1972:1), differentiates *enculturation* (which he defines as "the process of transmitting a particular culture") from *socialization* ("the process of transmitting human culture"). Yet a review of the literature indicates that most anthropologists use the two terms interchangeably. Hence, I shall do so as well.

The reader should bear in mind, however, that the point Williams is making is a valid one. (It is similar to the distinction that is made between the general human capacity to learn language and the learning of a particular language.) No serious anthropologist would argue against it, even one who chooses to use terms differently.

5 An interesting discussion on the "functions of initiation ceremonies" has occurred in the literature. See the following (listed in order of publication): Whiting, Kluckhohn, and Anthony 1958; Whiting 1961; Burton and Whiting 1961; Norbeck, Walker, and Cohen 1962; Stephens 1962; Young 1962; Brown 1963; Cohen 1964a, 1964b; Whiting 1964; Young 1965a, 1965b; and Cohen 1966.

6 There are a number of good ethnographic accounts of such systems. See, for example, Gulliver 1953, 1958, and 1968. Legesse (1973) has written a provocative book which uses a particular age-grade system as an ethnographic focus in illustrating three anthropological approaches to the study of society.

7 Some authors have distinguished between associations that are *instrumental* and those that are *expressive*. The former are those in which the achievement of some objective or objectives is the primary reason for the group's existence. The latter are those in which membership in the group is its own reward, individuals receiving their primary satisfaction simply from belonging. Since probably all groups have both instrumental and expressive aspects, and since it is often difficult or impossible to disentangle these, I have not chosen to focus on this distinction. (For a succinct description of associations in which both aspects are apparent, see Little 1957.)

Chapter 10

Economic Organization

(Photograph by Nelson A. Ossorio.)

Economics, broadly defined for our purposes, is concerned with the allocation of resources, goods, and services among alternative ends. Economic anthropology deals with how potential energy in the habitat and in the human population is utilized; how goods and services are produced, distributed, and consumed; and the social relationships and behavior patterns these systems of activity entail, along with the conceptual framework associated with them.

Hence, in studying the economic organization of any society, we may ask questions concerning three general areas: production, distribution, and consumption.

PRODUCTION

How are goods and services produced? What natural resources from the environment are utilized by the human population, and how does the population employ its energy in extracting these resources and converting them into goods? "Economic anthropology seeks to discover how the work of production is divided among the members of human societies and whether or not individuals or groups within a society specialize in particular occupations" (Beals and Hoijer 1965:451).

Our main interests when dealing with the study of production in a society are its *technology* and *organization of labor.*

Technology consists of the tools and techniques used to extract resources from the habitat and to produce goods and services. Technology was mentioned in the previous discussions of levels in sociocultural evolution. The **organization of labor**—or how people organize themselves for purposes of work—was also covered in broad outline. We found that a *division of labor based on sex and age* is common among nonindustrial, nonstate societies; for in such societies, with their relatively simple subsistence techniques, there is little or no occupational specialization: each household or small kin group is capable of performing the various tasks necessary for survival. But as we move along the evolutionary continuum and examine other ecological types or adaptive strategies, we find that a sexual division of labor is gradually replaced by, or absorbed within, an ever-increasing *specialization of labor,* as urbanization, state systems, and industrialism are approached, since the subsistence techniques become more varied and more complicated. Because these new techniques are complex and require skills that take time to learn, they become the occupation of specialists—people who perform one task or set of related tasks full time.

DISTRIBUTION

How are goods and services allocated? Here we are asking how the products of technology and labor are distributed throughout the society. But first we must ascertain which products are intended for public distribution,

Kibbutz children during a harvest ceremony on the eve of Passover; Israel. *(Photograph by Jacques Zakin.)*

for some goods are intended only for the use of the producer and his or her household. For example, plant foods collected in hunting-gathering societies are usually not publicly distributed but remain within the household; whereas meat from a kill is distributed throughout the camp. If the society's economic base is horticulture and the people are primarily subsistence cultivators, only a small portion of the food grown may be distributed, while the bulk of the crop is consumed by the household.

Once we have determined what is intended for distribution and what is not, we can then study the mechanisms for distribution, the associated patterns of social interaction, and the system of rules concerning distribution. Is distribution based on general sharing within the community, rather informally executed; or is there a formal ceremony during which goods that have been stored for the purpose are brought out and distributed; or is there an exchange system based on individual, personal trading relationships, or on a market system?

Distribution within a Society

Karl Polanyi, an economic historian, has identified three modes for the allocation or movement of goods and services within a society (Polanyi 1959): (1) reciprocity, (2) redistribution, (3) market exchange.

Reciprocity Reciprocity is often referred to as gift giving. It is an exchange which usually occurs between individuals of equivalent social status. Or, as Otterbein (1972:28) has phrased it, reciprocity "is the exchange of goods and services between units of the same kind, such as individuals, households, kinship groups." These exchanges usually follow preexisting networks of social relationships, those based on kinship and friendship. Material gain or profit does not seem to be the object of reciprocal exchange. One party to the exchange is not trying to get the better of the other. Rather, the main function of reciprocal exchanges appears to be the reaffirmation of the relationship already existing between the parties. Reciprocity does not create ties but serves to maintain them.

Sahlins (1965) has gone on to distinguish subtypes of reciprocity.

Balanced (direct) reciprocity Balanced reciprocity is a form of direct exchange in which goods flow two ways. One party gives a gift to another party, and this second party is expected to return a gift of equivalent value within a specified period of time. If an item of commensurate value is not returned, the relationship is damaged.

Generalized (delayed) reciprocity Generalized reciprocity is a predominantly one-way exchange. No return gift of equal value is required to balance any particular gift. Instead, the donor gains prestige and respect in return for generosity. The sharing of meat depicted in the well-known ethnographic film *The Hunters* (see the References for Appendix 3, page 233) is an example of generalized reciprocity. There was no immediate return of anything of commensurate material value for the meat that was distributed. In the long run, however, things do balance out, for the successful hunter this time may be unlucky some other time, but he will receive meat if someone else makes a kill.

Negative reciprocity According to Sahlins (1965:148–149), negative reciprocity "is the attempt to get something for nothing with impunity." It refers to "the most impersonal sort of exchange" in which "participants confront each other as opposed interests, each looking to maximize utility at the other's expense." The objective of negative reciprocity is the "unearned increment." Self-interest and profit making inform negative reciprocity. Hence, it is more likely to be the kind of economic interaction in which strangers engage (and the form in which much of intersocietal trade is cast), as opposed to balanced or generalized reciprocity, which are more predominant among kin and friends. (Thus, the nature of negative reciprocity is such that it falls outside the common use of *reciprocity* as that term was described generically above.)

Redistribution Redistribution refers to a mode of exchange in which goods and services are sent to an administrative center and are reallotted by authorities. For example, in taxation, which may be considered a kind of tribute, members of the population send a percentage of the products of their labor (for example, money) to a governmental agency. The funds are pooled and then redistributed throughout the population. In moneyless economies, the goods may be in the form of cultivated crops, such as yams, which are given to a village headman and are later redistributed during a communal ceremony.

Market Exchange This mode of exchange refers to "the organizational process of purchase and sale at money price which is the mechanism of transacting material products, labor and natural resources" (Dalton 1968:144). In other words, it is a form of exchange based on the principle of "supply and demand." Strictly speaking, market exchange exists only where there is a standard monetary system—something that can represent the value of an object or service—and an authority system that is able to enforce the fulfillment of contractual obligations—in other words, a state or near-state system (see Chapter 11).

These three modes of exchange are not mutually exclusive. All of them may be found in the same society, with one kind applied in certain transactions and another in a different type of transaction. To oversimplify, and to put exchange in some kind of evolutionary perspective, we may say that reciprocity is the predominant mode of exchange among hunter-gatherers and simple cultivators, though redistribution is also found to varying degrees. Redistributive exchange tends to predominate among more advanced cultivators and pastoralists, while market exchange begins to appear and reciprocity continues to govern various lesser transactions. In agricultural and industrial societies, the market principle becomes predominant, with redistribution an important complementary form of exchange and reciprocity assuming a minor position.

Intersocietal Exchange

These three modes of distribution are used to characterize the movement of goods within a society, what can be labeled *intrasocietal exchange* or *internal trade.* But movement of goods also occurs between societies; this is *intersocietal exchange* or *external trade.* Unfortunately, no one has offered a neat classification of intersocietal exchange that is comparable to Polanyi's classification of intrasocietal exchange. It is possible, however, to employ Polanyi's three modes of exchange to order a presentation of intersocietal exchange—even though one has to squeeze the data a bit to make them fit the categories, a dangerous practice at any time.

Reciprocity between Societies: Simple Trade This is trading that occurs between individuals from one society and those from another, in the absence of a market system having a monetary standard. It involves the exchange of one kind of goods for another. "Because the goods exchanged are usually few in number and no great quantities of material are involved, neither markets nor other elaborate trading procedures are necessary. Trading contacts usually occur between individuals who meet at irregular intervals for this purpose . . ." (Beals and Hoijer 1965:461). Such trade can occur because the resources of an area are not equally available to all people living in the region or because one society specializes in one type of food-getting technique and another society specializes in a different technique. Thus hunter-gatherers may exchange goods with horticulturalists, and pastoral nomads may exchange goods with farmers along the nomadic circuit. The Plains Indians, for example, exchanged meat for the grain products of Pueblo Indian cultivators.

Dumb barter, or *silent trade,* is a form of exchange in which the trading partners do not meet face to face. A well-known example is the Mbuti Pygmies of the Ituri Forest in central Africa. These people maintain a trade relationship with their Bantu-speaking neighbors. The Pygmies are hunter-gatherers and the Bantu are horticulturists. The Pygmies supply the Bantu with meat, hides, wild fruit, and other goods; and the Bantu in return provide the Pygmies with domesticated crops and iron tools. This is merely an example of a simple trading relationship, but it is called *dumb barter* because the manner of exchange involves a minimum of contact, or no contact, between the exchanging parties. Goods are left in designated locations near the Bantu settlements; the Pygmies come from the forest (sometimes at night), collect the goods, and leave goods of commensurate value which the Bantu then retrieve when the Pygmies have returned to the forest.

Trading partners is a term referring to a personal but formal exchange relationship between two individuals from different societies. It occurs commonly between nomads and sedentaries. A nomadic herder, whom we shall call individual A, is unable to satisfy all needs solely from pastoralism and so enters into an institutionalized special friendship with B, who lives in a permanent village that is located along the herder's nomadic orbit. Once or twice a year A is fairly certain to be in B's vicinity, at which time A can leave the herding camp and take milk and milk products (such as cheese), hides, and even an occasional live animal and exchange them with B for grain, metal for weapons, possibly woven material, etc. Each party, then, receives products made by the other. A may have several trading partners at various settlements located throughout the herding orbit; B will maintain a similar exchange relationship with several other herders who regularly pass the village. Thus, each is assured of a fairly dependable supply of "foreign" goods. Moreover, such partnerships are continued in succeeding generations: that is, A's children will very likely enter into such a friendship with B's children.

We might even extend the analogy to include Sahlins' elaborations concerning balanced and generalized reciprocity. Sometimes the herder and sedentary engage in an immediate direct exchange of goods, but often the exchange is delayed (even for several years) because one party (usually the herder) cannot reciprocate immediately.

"Redistribution" between Societies   I am stretching a point by calling this second mode *redistribution,* for there is really no parallel in intersocietal trade for redistribution within a society. *Raiding* and *tribute for protection* are the forms of intersocietal exchange that come closest to this mode, though actually they are more nearly forms of negative reciprocity.

Pastoral nomads or hunter-gatherers, such as the Indians of the Great Plains, may raid horticultural communities for goods instead of entering into peaceful exchange relations. Or the raiders may exact tribute from the farming community in exchange for abstaining from raiding and for protecting the community from other raiders.

Market Exchange   Finally, societies may engage in trade based on a market principle in which exchanges of goods and services are conducted through the medium of a money economy. This, of course, is the predominant mode of exchange among modern industrial nation-states.

CONSUMPTION

How are goods and services consumed? That is, how are the products that are distributed eventually used, what are the behavior patterns through which these uses are effected, and what are the rules or cultural principles regarding use or consumption of products?

"In many societies, in which the techniques of production and distribution are extremely simple, production, distribution, and consumption take place within one small group, the members of which live in daily face-to-face contact with each other" (Beals and Hoijer 1965:452). Unfortunately, anthropologists have devoted considerably less attention to consumption than to production and distribution. The generalizations that can be proffered are therefore few. To quote Beals and Hoijer again (p. 475): "In societies lacking true division of labor [i.e., specialization] and any considerable internal and external trade [e.g., many hunter-gatherers and simple horticulturists], patterns of consumption are ordinarily uniform throughout the society." Since there is very little, if any, surplus produced, "each unit of the society has about as much as its neighbors, and no group achieves either material wealth or any patterns of conspicuous consumption."

With the development of complex technology and specialization of labor, and the growth of both internal and external trade, however, social stratification also develops, the strata being characterized by different patterns of consumption. Commodities consumed, the amount and manner of consumption, and so on, serve to underscore status, to differentiate the "haves" from the "have-nots." This general picture of practices of consumption should be no surprise to anyone who has read this far, for it accords with our previous outline from usually egalitarian hunter-gatherers to inequality in state systems and parallels the accumulation of surplus.[1]

FOOTNOTES

1 This is another appropriate juncture for the instructor to raise the issue of the potlatch among Northwest Coast Indians and to have students attempt to account for this form of conspicuous consumption in a hunting-gathering-fishing society. Harris's comments in this regard (1975a:111–130) are particularly useful.

Chapter 11

Political Organization

(Photograph by the author.)

Political organization refers to the means of maintaining order and conformity in a society.[1] It concerns the allocation of power and authority[2] to make decisions beyond the personal level, i.e., decisions which affect the group (the "social body") as a whole. It provides the structure through which decisions about social policy, and the implementation of social policy, are effected. In addition to dealing with these matters *within* the society, political organization also concerns the way a society orders its affairs in relation to other groups, i.e., its intersocietal or external affairs.

The easiest way to present a brief, general overview of variation in political systems is in an evolutionary framework. The following taxonomy is based on that suggested by Elman Service (1962, 1966).

BANDS

Band organization (Figure 11.1*a*) is characteristic of most hunting-gathering societies. The band is a simple, flexible grouping of people without a permanent office of leadership. Instead, leadership is of the first-among-equals type (see the discussion of *primus inter pares* in Chapter 4). No one gives orders by virtue of holding an established office; rather, the members of the group—which is usually small (the figure normally given is fifty or fewer individuals)—congregate and discuss a problem with each person free to offer an opinion, and decision is reached through group consensus. Since warfare is rare among hunter-gatherers, positions of authority are not established through leadership in the activities of war.

In general, we may characterize band societies as those in which decision making is theoretically open to all and there is little or no stratification. Within the group, leadership roles tend to be informal and based primarily on personality characteristics. Moreover, there is no overarching political form uniting the several bands in a larger structure; each band is politically autonomous. The society is knit together through networks of interpersonal relationships—ties of kinship, marriage, friendship, trade, notions of hospitality. Beals and Hoijer note (1971:198), "Food gatherers are organized primarily as self-sufficient family groups or, more often, as loose confederations of families or bands. Accordingly, their mechanisms of social control and interaction are based more on kinship [and friendship and proximity] than on political organization [i.e., a formal political structure]."

The absence of large-scale political organization, coercive authority, formal leadership, and social stratification is related to the lack of control over productive resources. Foraging for naturally occurring foods and the nomadism this entails make the monopolization of resources difficult. Theoretically, all members of the group have equal access to resources. Hence, the idea of private ownership of important resources is absent. If productive and socially valued resources cannot be monopolized and controlled, or if the means (such as bows and arrows or digging sticks) for tapping these

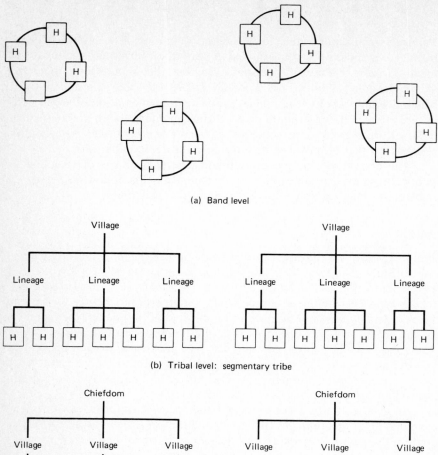

(a) Band level

(b) Tribal level: segmentary tribe

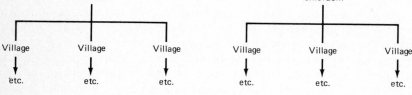

(c) Tribal level: chiefdoms

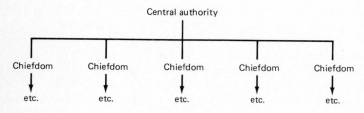

(d) State level

Figure 11.1 Political structures. (*a*) Band level; politically autonomous nomadic camps composed of several households (H) each. (*b*) Tribal level: segmentary tribe. (*c*) Tribal level: chiefdoms. (*d*) State level; another major subdivision could be substituted for the chiefdoms.

resources cannot be controlled, then there is little basis for the exercise of power. An individual who is not able to control a valued commodity, so as to create dependence in others, and cannot threaten to withhold that commodity, is in no position to give orders and to be obeyed. The growth of increasingly complex and pervasive forms of political organization and coercive authority systems is tied in with greater investments in land and labor and with reliance on resources and extractive techniques that can be controlled by some members of the society.

TRIBES

Tribal organization is characteristic of most horticulturists and pastoral nomads. Tribes are like bands in that in tribal societies there is no overall centralized political authority having jurisdiction over the several tribal sections. Thus, tribes are referred to as *acephalous,* meaning "without a head." Tribes are also characterized by their commingling of institutions: economics, politics, kinship, religion, and so on, are not separately organized. In tribes, "these are not so much different institutions as they are different *functions* of the same institutions: [they are] different things a [kinship group], for instance, may do" (Sahlins 1968:15). But a tribe is like a state in that the problems tribal organization must solve are similar to those in state societies; because populations are larger and more dense, problems concerning the maintenance of order and conformity are more complex.

The structure of a tribe is a kind of building-block arrangement. Small units are combined to form progressively larger, more inclusive units, until the level of the tribe as a whole is reached. For instance, at the lowest level the units may be composed of individual households. Several related households taken together may form a lineage. (A lineage is a group of people who consider themselves descended from a common ancestor. Lineages will be discussed more fully in Chapter 12.) Several lineages may then constitute a village. All the villages in a defined area constitute a district or ward. And all the districts or wards taken together constitute the tribe.[3] (This ideal structure of a tribe is diagramed in Figure 11.2.) But it is important to remember that there is *no central authority* at the maximal tribal level.

This is the general plan for tribal societies as a class. Now let us look briefly at two major types of tribes: *segmentary tribes* and *chiefdoms.*

Segmentary Tribes

The segmentary tribe (Figure 11.1*b*) is divided into a number of independent local communities called *primary segments.* These may be villages or homesteads but are often, especially in Africa, lineages (thus the name *segmentary lineage system* for this type of organization). Primary segments, as the name implies, are the smallest significant units in the segmentary structure and constitute the focal units in economic, political, and religious activity. In other words, most of the business of social life is taken care of at the primary level.

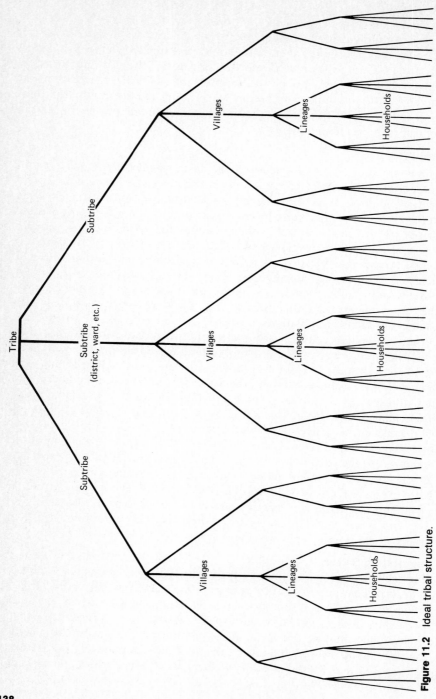

Figure 11.2 Ideal tribal structure.

In Sahlins' terminology (1968), the primary segments—in fact, all units on any one level—in a segmentary tribe are *structurally equivalent* and *functionally equivalent* as well as being *politically equal.*

Structural equivalence simply means that in a blueprint of the society's organization, or a diagram of the arrangement of its parts, the same-level units in the scheme are interchangeable as structures or as building blocks constituting the whole.

Functional equivalence means that each unit or primary segment "does for itself, economically and in other ways, what the others do for themselves" (Sahlins 1968:21). That is, all units perform the same *functions* for themselves.

Political equality is manifest in the notion that no segment of a level is better than any other segment on that level; none is superior or politically dominant. No segment holds authority over any other like segment; each is politically independent of the others. As Sahlins (1968:21) says: "Jealous of their own sovereignty, they recognize no greater political cause standing over and against their separate interests. Certain groups may ally for a time and a purpose, as for a military venture, but the collective spirit is episodic. When the objective for which it was called into being is accomplished, the alliance lapses and the tribe returns to its normal state of disunity."

Nevertheless, in the background, behind the notions of jealous separatism, there is a feeling of ethnic or cultural connection. Some measure of tribal identity is given by the similarities of language and custom that link the various segments into a loose whole and distinguish them from other peoples with different languages and customs. There is some notion of their all being alike, of being "one people, " and there is usually some idea of historic identity.

Leaders in Segmentary Tribes   There are two basic leadership roles associated with segmentary tribes that anthropologists designate by name: the *headman* (sometimes called *petty chieftain*) and the *big man.* Both are found, of course, at the local level of the primary segment, since it is at this level that whatever power there is occurs. I repeat: tribal organization is acephalous, i.e., there is no central authority.

Headman   The headman (or petty chieftain) is the head of a local community—the head of a lineage or homestead or village. Headmanship is a recognized status within the group; it is an official position. In this it differs from the *primus-inter-pares* leadership found in band societies. It also differs from *primus-inter-pares* leadership in that the position of headman is an office governed by some rules of succession—even though these rules may be minimal or vague and can usually be superseded by other considerations. For example, the ideal line of succession may be from father to son, or from brother to brother, or from oldest male in the group to oldest male.

Whatever the particulars of ideal succession may be, it is important to remember that, though descent or the like may be significant in qualifying a person for the position, personal characteristics are usually decisive. Thus, headmanship is similar to *primus-inter-pares* leadership in that the headman must distinguish himself by being successful at what he does, by having some measure of wealth, by being fair in his adjudications, by not being too aggressive, by being able to inspire loyalty, and so on. In other words, though a man may be the legitimate successor to headmanship, he must validate his occupying the position by exhibiting the admired personal qualities; for bear in mind that he does not "rule" the group but stands at its head as spokesman and advisor, leader of ceremonies, coordinator of economic activities, and perhaps as war leader. He does not order people about; he does not have that kind of authority. As Sahlins (1968:21) puts it, "One word from him and everyone does as he pleases."[4]

(A summary of the characteristics of different types of leaders and the political levels with which they are associated is provided in Table 11.1, below.)

Big man   We get the term *big man* from studies conducted in Melanesia, where this kind of informal leadership is common. It differs from headmanship in that it is not an official position. Being a big man depends solely on personality and personal achievement. Because he is a persuasive talker, is wealthy, is usually successful in his ventures, has a dominating personality that inspires trust, confidence, and loyalty, and perhaps because he is a good warrior or magician, people follow his lead. To retain his leadership, he must continue to manifest these valued characteristics. If he turns out to be a disappointment to his adherents, he will no longer be considered a big

Table 11.1   Types of Political Organization and Leaders

Level	Leadership	Basis
Band	*Primus inter pares*	Personal
Tribe		
(1) Segmentary	(a) Headman	(a) Official position. Ideals of succession. Personality and personal achievement.
	(b) Big man	(b) Personality and personal achievement.
(2) Chiefdom	Chief	Official position. Hereditary order of succession.
State	Central authority (king, president, etc.)	Official position. Hereditary or elected office.

man and will lose his leadership. Moreover, one does not inherit a position of big man, for it is not an official position governed by a defined order of succession. Each big man must make it on his own merits. Finally, a big man has no formal authority; he cannot enforce rigid compliance to his wishes. In the words of Keesing and Keesing (1971:273), "He is simply a man who leads because people follow, who decides because others defer to him."

Chiefdoms

With these descriptions behind us, that form of tribal organization known as a *chiefdom* (Figure 11.1c) is fairly easy to understand. In chiefdoms, the locus of authority has moved farther up in the tribal structure, beyond the small local communities (or primary segments), which have lost their autonomy and are now reduced to interdependent political subdivisions. In other words, in the diagram of tribal structure in Figure 11.2, the centers of power have moved to a position intermediate between the level of local communities and the level of the tribe as a whole—for chiefdoms are still tribes and as such lack an overall central authority. The tribe is composed of several chiefdoms that are politically independent of each other.

For example, in a chiefdom, descent groups, such as clans, are ranked in a hierarchical order, with one of the groups considered the chiefly or noble group. From this group comes the chief, who holds authority over all the groups in a particular area. A chiefdom, then, is composed of a number of descent groups occupying a defined territory and under the leadership of a chief who is a member of the senior descent group. A number of these chiefdoms, to repeat, make up the entire tribe.

The position of *chief* is an official one, a fixed office, governed by an order of succession that is based on heredity. The authority of a chief is greater than any of the others so far discussed. Usually the chief has the power of life and death over subjects. But you must remember, once again, that the chief and the chiefly lineage or clan only stay in power as long as they are strong enough to hold it. It is always a possibility—and not uncommon—that another group will gather enough strength to overthrow and supplant them.

STATES

Once you have grasped the idea of a chiefdom, it is an easy step from there to understanding a state system (Figure 11.1d). Earlier we defined a state system (on the basis of Cohen's suggestions) as one headed by a central authority (often one person), under which there functions a bureaucracy or set of interlocking agencies that carry on the business of governing the society. The key feature is the presence of a central authority. Add this to a tribal structure, and the result is a state.

Imagine, for instance, a geographically dispersed tribe made up of politically independent chiefdoms. Chief A is ill-disposed toward chief B because the latter stole some of A's horses. A raiding party is formed by A, who attacks B. Instead of just retrieving the horses, though, A decides to teach B a lesson by taking all B's animals and reducing the target camp to ashes. A manages to do just that and as a result amasses considerably more wealth and power. B's people now look to A as their chief. A, adding these new followers to the original fighting forces, then mounts a campaign against C. After defeating C and subjugating C's people, A refuses to stop but goes on to defeat chiefs D, E, and so on. In the end, A has become the paramount central authority of the tribe; the other chiefdoms in the tribe have been reduced to political subdivisions under A's control. Thus a state has been created.[5] (In essence, this is the process that resulted in Genghis Khan's establishment of the Mongol state in the twelfth and thirteenth centuries.)[6]

States, which are characteristic of agricultural and industrial societies, arise under various conditions. Not all result from conquest, and, of course, not all state societies were at one time tribal societies. The question of the origins of states is an issue still under intensive investigation; and we as yet have no really satisfactory answers. It would defeat our present purposes, however, to list the many hypotheses and counterhypotheses surrounding the debate. The important point to note here is the distinguishing characteristic of state societies: the presence of a single central authority.

But perhaps a word or two on a familiar theme would not be too out of place here. Ever since the time of Karl Marx, there have been a growing number of observers who ascribe to "capitalism" per se the various socioeconomic problems they choose to identify. Yet the primary social source is probably the general type of political system defined above as a nation-state (with "capitalism," "socialism," "communism," etc., being only particular attributes, or variants, of a common political form). Consider the following alternative interpretation. *Postulate:* Those who speak in the name of the state enact policies and pursue courses of action that tend to increase the security of the state—i.e., they tend to increase power and authority, thus rendering the state less susceptible to challenge from the populace—despite self-depreciatory postures of the state to the contrary.

Power

Power (the ability to manipulate people, to compel or prevent behavior) rests in the ability to control technology and the organization of labor—i.e., in control of "economy," primarily the means of production and distribution. It is through its control over the vital resources, goods, and services in a society that the state creates dependency on itself. Dependence lays the groundwork for control. The controllers simply threaten to withhold vital resources, goods, and services in order to gain compliance with their policies. To the degree to which the state controls the tools and techniques, and the labor organized to use these tools and techniques for the extraction and conversion of resources and the distribution of goods and services, to that same degree it exercises social control over the population. *This interpretation applies whether the "economic system" is "capitalist" or "socialist."*

Authority

Authority is determined by the extent to which those in power are able to convince the population that they have the "right" to exercise their power; authority concerns the *legitimation* of power. All states appeal to an ideology to justify their use of power and, thus, to validate their authority. The aim is to secure the emotional allegiance of the population, so as to minimize the possibility of threats or challenges to the power of the state. Once again, *this interpretation applies whether the supporting ideology is "capitalist" or "socialist."* (There are, of course, innumerable devices used by states to propagate the values, beliefs, and attitudes that help to reinforce political power and authority. One of these is the system of formal education. It is, among other things, a mechanism for social control that perpetuates key elements of the legitimating ideology and helps to foster dependence on the state. Again, *this interpretation applies whether the society as a whole is characterized as "capitalist" or "socialist."*)

An attempt to summarize this position is provided in Figure 11.3.

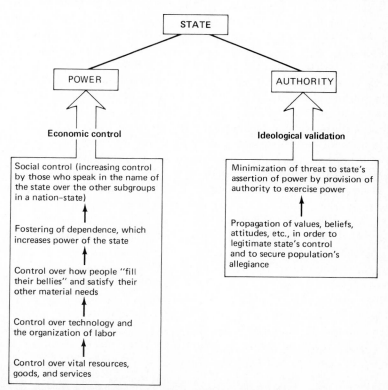

Figure 11.3 Marshaling of power and authority by the state.

LAW AND WARFARE

It is usually at this juncture that the subjects of war and law are mentioned, and I shall not depart from tradition. Both operate as ordering devices: law functions as a regulatory mechanism within a group, while war serves to regulate intergroup relations.

Law

Though controversy has raged for years over just what "law" is, we can define it for our purposes as follows: *law* refers to the way disputes are habitually resolved in a society and the way transgressions of publicly recognized rules of behavior are handled. (Implied in this definition, of course, is a specification usually assigned to the legal sphere—namely, the clarification of the rights and duties of individuals and groups within the society.)

It is difficult to discuss the subject of law without citing numerous ethnographic cases. In lieu of such a procedure, the following summary is provided.

Among hunter-gatherers, disputes and transgressions of appropriate behavior are dealt with by the principals involved and their friends and relatives in such a way as to minimize intragroup tension. There are no formal courts or judges, no police, no strict "legal" procedures as Westerners would understand them. If someone's behavior is disruptive to camp life, social pressure will be brought to bear to correct his or her ways (e.g., a man may be shunned as a hunting partner, or a woman may find that her visits to neighbors' homes are unwelcome). More drastic measures may be taken with a habitual offender, including ostracism from the group. Disputes on the band level—since there is little or no competition over productive resources and no private ownership—are usually of a personal nature. Accusations of adultery, for example, may flare into violence between the accuser and his or her allies (often close kin) and the accused and his or her allies. Resolution may be achieved in several ways. The two parties may settle the issue immediately through physical conflict, or they may be persuaded by relatives to resolve the matter in peaceful discussion. If the dispute is not settled immediately and it threatens to disrupt the cooperation and social cohesion of the group, the entire camp may be drawn into the issue. Each party airs his or her grievance, and resolution is attempted through group consensus. If this fails, the group may split up, or the dissident faction may break away and join another camp. There are also institutionalized ways to settle differences. For instance, among some Eskimo groups men meet each other in singing duels. Each composes songs aimed at wittily insulting and humiliating his opponent. The singing is performed publicly, and the audience judges the event. Thus, the singers are provided with a way of releasing their hostility and anger without endangering the harmony of camp life. After the singing bout, the singers exchange gifts, signifying an end to the dispute and the dissipation of animosity.

As we move along the evolutionary continuum, from bands to tribes to states, we find that legal activity becomes increasingly formalized and institutionalized. In tribal societies, the emphasis is still by and large on effecting reconciliation between the disputing parties and on reaching consensus for the adjudication of disputes. Consonant with the greater populations in tribal societies and with the greater importance of larger-scale kin groups, techniques for the resolution of disputes and for dealing with transgressions of rules involve a larger number of people and a more formal procedure. The aim is not punishment, however, but the restoration of amicable relations within the community. A headman and council of advisors, for instance, may preside during litigation procedures, but the final settlement must satisfy the community as a whole. Otherwise the purpose of adjudication—the maintenance of order—will not be served. So, though courts are found in tribal societies, their decisions are subject to community approval and are not imposed on the community. (Other mechanisms that aid social control, such as accusations of witchcraft, were mentioned in Chapter 9.)

In tribal societies organized on the basis of chiefdoms, however, legal procedures become less amorphous, more rigid, and less reliant on sentiments of kinship. Disputants may be totally subject to the final decision of a judge (the chief, or a representative of the chief). Fines are levied, hands and noses may be chopped off, or capital punishment may be administered.

The culmination of authoritarian legal systems is found, of course, in state societies. Legal institutions increase in number and importance. The settlement of differences no longer occurs in the context of kinship and friendship. Legal mechanisms take on an impersonal tone. Courts and judges proliferate, and they operate on extracommunity standards. Laws are codified in innumerable volumes of law books that are read and interpreted by specialists. All this is geared to maintaining order in a complex, heterogeneous, densely populated society based on a market economy.

War

If *law* refers to a form of resolving conflicts *within* a group, *warfare* may be used to refer to a method of resolving conflicts *between* groups. Relations between groups can be mediated by peaceful negotiations or diplomacy and by the use of force, of which three main types are often distinguished: warfare, feuding, and raiding.

Warfare *Warfare* may be described as large-scale armed combat between political communities. It concerns comparatively long-term hostilities between whole communities as units. Large fighting forces are mobilized, and the fighting is an organized affair.

Feuding   *Feuding* is small-scale armed combat, either between factions within a community or between structurally equivalent communities. It involves a smaller number of participants than warfare, and the combatants on each side in a feud are often allied by bonds other than the immediate military ones—for example, they are usually related by kinship. Feuding takes place when one small group is in conflict with another small group like it, and there is a relationship of attack and retaliation between them. For instance, a feud may begin as a result of a homicide. The relatives of the victim may form a retaliatory party that attacks the killer's group (the killer's village or relatives) and takes a life from that group (not necessarily the life of the killer; anyone from the killer's group will serve the purpose). The second group then retaliates against the first, and so on. In this way, feuds can continue for generations. But it is important to remember that feuding does not involve the entire community, only a small faction which forms around the principals.

Raiding   *Raiding* is usually a more organized use of force than feuding. It involves short-term attacks, like feuding, but it is often aimed at the acquisition of goods or resources and not at revenge over personal injuries. As was pointed out in Chapter 7, raiding is characteristic of pastoral nomads. Herders raid each other for livestock and raid sedentary communities for goods they themselves do not produce (such as grain crops). Thus, raiding can be seen as a particular kind of economic adjustment through which goods and resources are distributed throughout a large or widely dispersed population.

It should be emphasized that even though such definitions as the foregoing are necessary in an introductory presentation, they are of limited value otherwise. The actual fighting in which people engage is difficult to place into neat categories. For example, there is a classic ethnographic film called *Dead Birds* (see the References for Appendix 3, page 233) in which fighting in New Guinea is depicted. This fighting involves whole political communities and even several allied communities (warfare?), which have an attack-retaliation relationship (feuding?). It is well organized and involves all able-bodied men (warfare?), but fighting ceases with one death on either side (feuding?).

An additional difficulty is that not all anthropologists would agree with the above descriptions of feuding, raiding, and warfare. But, as Keesing and Keesing say (1971:283), "Quibbling over definitions is usually a waste of time. It is clear from the evidence that [armed conflict] takes widely varying forms in different societies." Let us turn now to a broad, cross-cultural characterization of fighting within an evolutionary framework.

Fighting in Cross-Cultural Perspective   *The band level*   Fighting at the band level is usually not common (though a few hunting-gathering societies, such as those of the Plains Indians, are noted for their bellicosity). When fighting occurs, "combat [is] sporadic, often minimally planned, individualistic, relatively disorganized, and lacking elaborate weaponry and tactics" (Keesing and Keesing 1971:284). This is not surprising in light of what has already been said regarding hunting-gathering societies. In general, fighting at the band level is mostly of the sort we described as feuding, for it occurs within or between camps and more often than not concerns personal animosities. Hunter-gatherers usually do not mount large-scale military campaigns unless they are in conflict with a technologically superior group.

The tribal level   At the tribal level, fighting is more common. Feuding, raiding, and warfare occur. Hostilities between kin groups may erupt into a feud, touched off, for instance, by an individual aggressive act or by an accusation of wrongdoing. Cultivators may raid other cultivators for heads, territory, or women. Pastoralists may raid each other for animals, or pastoralists may raid cultivators for crops. Tribes, especially those with a segmentary lineage organization, often expand over large territories at the expense of weaker neighbors (Sahlins 1961) and may even engage in large-scale warfare for conquest. Tribal fighting can be a "vicious and deadly business" resulting in the loss of a great number of lives, or it may simply involve "elaborate posturing and even pageantry" (Keesing and Keesing 1971:284). The latter aspect—that of "ritual combat"—is exemplified in the film *Dead Birds,* mentioned above. At one point, the fighting ceases because of rain, and both sides return home; the combatants were afraid that the rain would spoil their hairdos. This illustrates that an important function of such fighting is display (of strength, of ferocity, etc., often in order to validate territorial claims). The rainy weather threatened to undermine the display, and so the game was called.

The state level   States, especially modern industrial states, with their elaborate weaponry and sophisticated technology, have developed war to its deadliest form. Moreover, in both agricultural and industrial states, the central authority and its representatives assert sole right to the use of force. Feuding within the society is not tolerated—for this threatens the state's claim to authority—and unofficial attacks against other societies, such as occur in raiding, are also forbidden—for this leaves the state open to retaliation. Armed aggression has become a highly organized activity supported by official approval and executed by trained specialists.

FOOTNOTES

1   Obviously, such a description can extend to almost all structured activities in a society: principles of kinship function to maintain order and conformity; religion functions similarly, as do child-rearing and socialization practices. In fact, it is almost impossible—especially in primitive societies—to distinguish clearly among spheres of behavior and to label one *economics,* another *politics,* and another *religion.* We in modern industrial state societies are accustomed to think-

ing compartmentally, and we even take a certain amount of pride in segregating our various activities (we avoid "mixing business with pleasure," or "bringing our problems home from the office"; we extol the idea of the "separation of church and state"). The practice of sectioning off activity into separate areas has been called *differentiation.* When one is speaking of this practice on a societal level, it is called the *differentiation of institutions;* when referring to individual behavior, it is called the *differentiation of roles.*

But in nonindustrial, nonstate societies, the people who work together, eat together, play together, and worship together constitute the same collectivity—or at least overlapping collectivities; and it is difficult to label an activity *economic* when it is as much *political* or *religious* as it is anything else. All these spheres of behavior are interdependent and intermingled. Anthropologists refer to this phenomenon as the *commingling of institutions.*

I mention this to make the reader aware that the division of this book into chapters called "Economic Organization," "Religion," etc., is merely a device to aid discussion and that the divisions, though customary, are based on arbitrary criteria.

2   It is useful that I make explicit at the outset of this chapter the gross distinction I make between power and authority. **Power,** basically, concerns the ability to manipulate people, whereas **authority** is the recognized "right" to exercise power, the "legitimate" use of power. Thomas Gordon, a psychologist, notes (1970: 191–192), "Power does not 'influence' in the sense of persuading, convincing, educating, or motivating a [person] to behave in a particular way. Rather, power *compels* or *prevents* behavior." If the power of a person or group to manipulate others' behavior is socially recognized as "proper" or "appropriate," we say that that person or group has "authority." To illustrate, I can probably force you to behave as I want by pointing a loaded gun at your face. That is power. But unless I am, for instance, a legally recognized peace officer and you are violating a law, it is not authority. (For a systematic discussion of the concepts of power and authority, along with a breakdown of subtypes, see Manicas 1974:1–31.)

3   Political alliances may extend beyond the tribe itself to other tribes to form an intertribal *confederacy* (as was the case with the League of the Iroquois in North America).

4   I have used the standard anthropological term *headman,* as opposed to *head-person,* because the latter would be a misleading label for this kind of petty chieftaincy. According to the ethnographic literature on segmentary tribes having this type of leadership, the formal position of headship virtually always devolves upon males. (This holds as well for *big man.*)

5   When a state goes on to conquer other states or other independent societies and reduces them to political subdivisions, the resultant entity is called an *empire.*

6   This is certainly not intended to be an adequate "explanation" of the emergence of the Mongol state, nor do I mean to suggest a psychological or "great man" basis for the origin of states. (On the social and economic bases for Genghis Khan's success, see Lattimore 1963. Students wishing to gain an acquaintance with theories of the state might begin by consulting Carneiro 1968 and Fried 1967, 1968.)

Chapter 12

Kinship, Descent, Residence

(Photograph by Ingrid Deich.)

KINSHIP

Kinship (according to Keesing and Keesing 1971:157) is a kind of relationship modeled on the relationship conceived to exist between parents and children. That is, the notion of kinship is based on the biology of reproduction, but *biology interpreted through culture.* It is important to remember that kinship is only *modeled* somewhat on biology and only to a greater or lesser degree. **Kinship** is that part of a conceptual system or a culture which deals with notions of, or ideas about, "relatedness"—or relationship through birth and (more broadly) through marriage.

Hence, we must be careful in using familiar terms when we speak about kinship relations in other cultures. As an example, let us take *father.* (I will give one version here; these terms may be used somewhat differently—e.g., see Bock 1969:88–89.) Three kinds of "fathers" may be distinguished:

1   *Genitor.* This is the actual biological father, the male whose sperm has fertilized the ovum of a female.

2   *Pater.* This is the sociological father, the socially and legally recognized father, whether or not actual conception was produced by him. He is the individual through whom the child traces relationship and the individual who is socially recognized as responsible for the child. Actually, this person need not be a male, or even be alive; the Nuer have "female fathers" and "ghost fathers" (Evans-Pritchard 1951).

3   *Vir.* This simply refers to a husband, whether or not he is a "father."

Parallel terms exist for the concept of "mother": *genetrix, mater,* and *uxor.*

Symbols and Basic Terms

Before we deal with types of kinship terminologies, descent, and residence it is necessary that we establish meanings for some fundamental terms and notational symbols.

Seven basic symbols are used by anthropologists in constructing kinship diagrams:

1   A male is indicated by a triangle: △

2   A female is indicated by a circle: ○

3   A person whose sex is unspecified is indicated by a square: □

4   Descent (as from parent to child) is indicated by a vertical line: |

5   Codescent (as in the case of siblings) is indicated by a horizontal line with descending vertical lines: ⊓

6 Marriage is indicated by (*a*) a horizontal line with ascending vertical lines: ⌇

Or by (*b*) an equals sign: =

Thus, to indicate a married pair with two children, one of each sex, either of the diagrams shown in Figure 12.1 would suffice.

In addition, anthropologists use shorthand symbols to indicate genealogical positions. There are nine basic symbols:

F or Fa: *father*
M or Mo: *mother*
S or So: *son*
D or Da: *daughter*
B or Br: *brother*
Z or Si: *sister*
(*Note;*   Elder and younger siblings are indicated by "e" and "y," as in eB and yZ.)
H or Hu: *husband*
W or Wi: *wife*
C or Ch: *child*

Other terms are usually combinations of these, such as FF (*father's father* and MF (*mother's father*) for an individual we in our kinship system would call *grandfather.*

It may seem to the reader an unnecessary complication to use these symbols. Why not call FF a *grandfather* and be done with it? There are two primary reasons why these symbols are used. First of all, *grandfather* is a term in *our* kinship system. We distort our understanding if we try to translate another people's system into our own. We want to understand their system as *they* understand it. The symbol FF does not mean *grandfather;* it refers to an individual who occupies a particular position in a genealogical diagram. (Such a diagram is shown in Figure 12.2.)

Second, some kinship systems are a good deal more complicated than we in Western societies are used to dealing with. If we find out that the appropriate marriage partner for a male Australian Aborigine is his mother's mother's brother's daughter's daughter, it is much more convenient to note this as MMBDD than to write out the entire phrase.

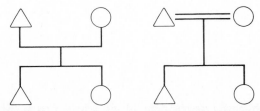

Figure 12.1   Alternative ways of depicting a married pair with offspring.

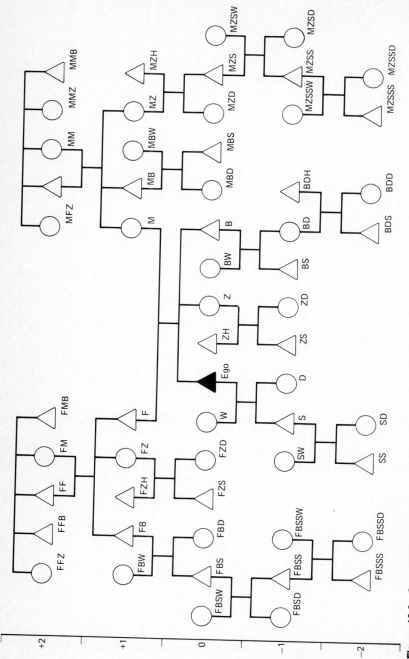

Figure 12.2 Genealogical chart.

In examining Figure 12.2, you will note that one individual (indicated by the shaded triangle) is designated *ego*. **Ego** refers to the individual from whose point of view we are looking at some kinship relationship; ego is the point of reference for tracing relationships. All the other individuals in the diagram are labeled in reference to their relationship to the one designated as *ego*. Thus, the male individual shown immediately to the right of ego is ego's ZH (sister's husband). If we focused on another individual as ego—i.e., if we changed our reference point—the other designations would have to be changed.

In order to illustrate how anthropologists use kinship diagrams, I have provided in Figure 12.3 an attenuated diagram showing the genealogical designations of some Herero relationship terms. (The Herero are a group of Bantu-speaking cattle herders in Africa among whom I conducted field-work in 1973.)

Alter, in contrast to ego, is the individual to whom the relationship is being traced. Thus, in the above example, ZH is alter.

A **linking relative** is any individual through whom a relationship is traced to another person. For example, in order to trace the relationship from the individual labeled *ego* to the one labeled ZH in Figure 12.2, we have to go through the individual labeled Z. So ego's sister (Z) is a linking relative.

Any relationship traced through ego's father is called a **patrilateral relationship** (*patrilateral* meaning "father's side"). In other words, when ego's F is the linking relative, alter is a patrilateral relative. Similarly, a **matrilateral relationship** is one on the "mother's side."

A **cross-cousin** (XCu) is a child of ego's parent's sibling, when that sibling is a different sex from that of the parent; i.e., a cross-cousin is ego's parent's cross-sex sibling's child. For example, your FZC is your cross-cousin because your father and his sister are of different sexes.

A **parallel cousin** (//Cu) is a child of ego's parent's sibling, when that sibling is the same sex as the parent; i.e., a parallel cousin is ego's parent's same-sex sibling's child. For example, your FBC is your parallel cousin because your father and his brother are the same sex.

Putting some of these terms together, we see that:

FBD and FBS are ego's patrilateral parallel cousins.
MZD and MZS are ego's matrilateral parallel cousins.
FZD and FZS are ego's patrilateral cross-cousins.
MBD and MBS are ego's matrilateral cross-cousins.

These terms have not been introduced gratuitously, for they will be useful in later discussions (especially in regard to marriage).

Another set of symbols needs mention here. You will note five num-

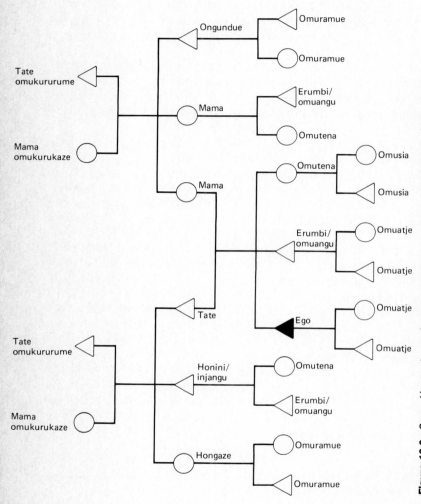

Figure 12.3 Some Herero terms for consanguineal relationships, and their genealogical referents. (*Note*: Where two terms, separated by a slash, are shown, which term is applied depends on relative age: FeB = *honini*, whereas FyB = *injangu*; eB = *erumbi* whereas yB = *injangu*; whereas FyB = *injangu*; eB = *erumbi* whereas yB = *omuangu* for a male ego, and *omuangu* for a male ego; and eZ = *erumbi* whereas yZ = *omuangu* for a female ego.)

bers on the left-hand side of Figure 12.2. These refer to generation: +2 refers to the *second ascending generation* (i.e., two generations up from ego), +1 refers to the *first ascending generation,* 0 refers to *ego's generation,* −1 refers to the *first descending generation,* and −2 refers to the *second descending generation.*

All these terms I have mentioned are in the realm of what is called *kinship studies.* Returning to the distinction between culture (or ideational rules or conceptual organization) and the social (or actual behavior), it can be readily understood that anthropologists have been interested in kinship mainly from two perspectives: (1) what different cultures define as kinship categories or how they classify "relatives" and conceptually organize their kinship systems; and (2) what behavioral correlates are associated with which kinship systems, i.e., how people in different societies behave toward each other on the basis of their kin relationships.[1]

I will not in this handbook go into either of these subjects in detail; they require their own books. I shall instead adhere to the policy of presenting generalities.

Types of Kinship Terminologies

I do not pretend to cover all possible types of kinship systems (or their variants)—for a number of reasons, the primary one being that no exhaustive typology exists. Moreover, anthropologists are beginning to doubt the utility of such typologies. We need not worry about this, however, for if typologies have any utility at all, it is in an introduction like this. I will cover, therefore, some general types of *kinship terminologies* (or relationship terminologies)—i.e., some ways of classifying "relatives" in terminological systems. (The classification I offer is based primarily on Murdock 1947 and Schusky 1965, though it is not identical with either.)

If we are going to designate different types of something, we have to decide on a set of characteristics which vary from one type to another, so that we have a basis for distinguishing one from another. Various typologies for relationship terminologies have been advanced. Some have distinguished between kinds on the basis of behavioral correlates (e.g., the prevalent form of marriage in the society); others have used inherent cultural criteria (e.g., a componential analysis of kinship terms). We shall be unsophisticated and take a very simple system: the types of cousin terms (in ego's generation) used and the terms for the first ascending (parental) generation as distinguishing characteristics.

Hawaiian or Generational Type   Cousin: sibling terms and cousin terms are the same:

   Z = FBD = FZD = MBD = MZD
   B = FBS = FZS = MBS = MZS[2]

First ascending generation: terms for "aunts" and mother are the same, as are those for "uncles" and father:

M = MZ = FZ
F = FB = MB

All the Hawaiian terminology does is distinguish generation (and sometimes sex). Everybody in ego's generation (XCu, //Cu, sibling) is called by the same term. Everyone in the first ascending generation is called by the same term, and so on.

Hawaiian is the "simplest" terminology because it makes the fewest distinctions: (1) generation, and (2) kin and nonkin (those to whom terms are applied and those to whom they are not applied).

Eskimo or Lineal Type   Cousin: all "cousins" are equated terminologically but differentiated from siblings:

B ≠ FBS = MBS = FZS = MZS
Z ≠ FBD = MBD = FZD = MZD

First ascending generation: both matrilateral and patrilateral "aunts" are equated but differentiated from mother:

M ≠ FZ = MZ
F ≠ FB = MB
(FB = MB; thus FBS = MBS)

Iroquois or Bifurcate Merging Type   Cousin: same terms used for siblings and parallel cousins; but separate terms used for cross-cousins (yet matrilateral and patrilateral XCu are equated):

(Z = FBD = MZD) ≠ (MBD = FZD)
(B = FBS = MZS) ≠ (MBS = FZS)

First ascending generation: the term for mother and mother's sister is the same, but father's sister is differentiated:

M = MZ ≠ FZ
F = FB ≠ MB

Crow and Omaha Types   Cousin: same terms are used for siblings and parallel cousins but distinguished from cross-cousins; and patrilateral cross-cousins are distinguished from matrilateral:

$$(Z = FBD = MZD) \neq MBD \neq FZD$$
$$(B = FBS = MZS) \neq MBS \neq FZS$$

First ascending generation: same as the Iroquois type.

Crow and Omaha, when other factors are considered more specifically—especially whether the system exhibits an agnatic or uterine bias (see below)—are separated into distinct types. But for our purposes here, we can consider them similar variants of an Iroquois type.

Sudanese or Bifurcate Collateral Type Cousin: all cousins are given distinct terms based on individual relationship to ego:

$Z \neq FBD \neq MZD$, and so on
$B \neq FBS \neq MZS$, and so on

First ascending generation: all distinguished:

$M \neq MZ \neq FZ$
$F \neq FB \neq MB$

The Sudanese type, in contrast to the Hawaiian, distinguishes every relative. It makes the *most* distinctions. (The Sudanese type is often found in conjunction with segmentary lineage systems; see Chapter 11.)

The above is just a short sketch to introduce you to variations in kinship systems. Very few anthropologists would be willing to accept it if a claim were made that it is anything more than a first introduction to relationship terminologies.[3]

To put these terminological systems in an evolutionary framework, we may say the following. Eskimo terminology tends to emphasize a distinction between the nuclear family group (Chapter 13), its lineal progenitors and descendants, and collateral relatives on both sides (patrilateral and matrilateral); and this probably reflects the socioeconomic discreteness of this group. Hence, Eskimo terminologies are most often found at the two ends of the evolutionary continuum, i.e., in hunting-gathering band societies and in industrial state societies. It is between these two that the other types of relationship terminologies are more often found. It is in cultivating and herding societies that the greatest diversity of terminologies seems to occur, with some variation of a basic Iroquoian type being statistically predominant. In Iroquoian systems, relatives on one "side" are distinguished from those on the other "side," once again reflecting the alignments of personnel in cooperative activities and, often, corporate control over some valued commodity.

Real and Classificatory Kin; Consanguineal and Affinal Kin

In discussing kinship systems, anthropologists often speak of *real* and *classificatory* kin.

Real kin are those who the investigator concludes are actually biologically related. *Classificatory kin* are those who are classified as kin (i.e., those to whom a kin term is applied) but who are not really biologically related.

Another distinction you will encounter often is that between *consanguineal* and *affinal* relatives.

Consanguines are related by birth ("blood" relatives). *Affines* are related by marriage ("in-laws").

Descent

Types of Descent

Kinship organization also involves *descent*. Simply speaking, **descent** concerns the tracing of relationships through succeeding generations, i.e., who is *descended* from whom.[4] There are many different ways of tracing descent.

Unilineal Descent   Unilineal, or "one-line," descent is that form of descent in which relationship is traced through one sex or line, i.e., through one parent as the linking relative between ego and ego's forebears, either all males or all females.

Agnatic or patrilineal descent   This is a form of unilineal descent traced through males only. (It is important to remember that ego, the person calculating descent, may be either male or female. Females in a patrilineal system trace descent just as males do.) See Figure 12.4*a*.

Uterine or matrilineal descent   This is a form of unilineal descent traced through females only. (Once again, it should be pointed out that both females and males trace descent in this way.) See Figure 12.4*b*.

Double descent   Double descent is also called *double unilineal, duolineal,* or *bilineal* descent. It is a form of unilineal descent which combines both patrilines and matrilines. Descent is *separately* traced through males *and* through females. For example, an individual (who, again, may be male or female) may trace descent patrilineally for some purposes (e.g., to claim inheritance rights to "sacred" cattle or rights of succession to formal office) and may also trace descent at the same time matrilineally for other purposes (e.g., to claim inheritance rights to "secular" cattle or to farmland). See Figure 12.4*c*.

Parallel descent   This is a form of unilineal descent in which women trace descent through females only and men trace descent through males only. See Figure 12.4*d*.

Ambilineal or optative descent   This is a form of unilineal descent in which an individual may choose to trace descent patrilineally *or* matrilineally. Normally, though a society may recognize both types, an individual may choose only one and must stick to the choice. In some societies, how-

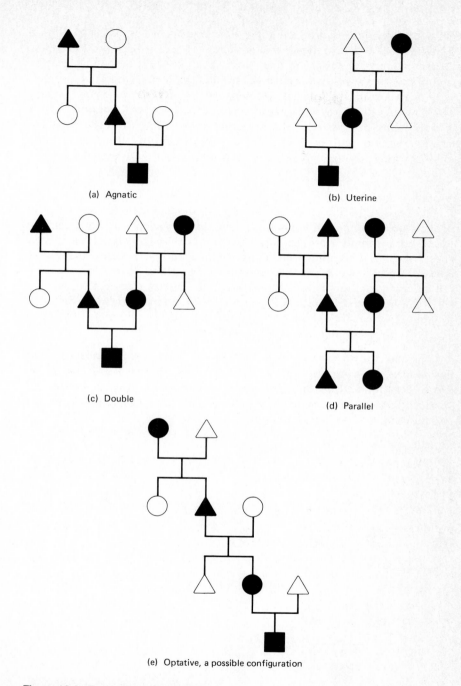

(a) Agnatic

(b) Uterine

(c) Double

(d) Parallel

(e) Optative, a possible configuration

Figure 12.4 Types of unilineal descent.

ever, the individual reserves the right to change his or her affiliation (Otter-bein 1972:52). In an optative or ambilineal system it may occur that descent, though traced through one parent, may not be traced through progenitors of only one sex. Because of the elective element in optative systems, a person's significant forebears may be both male and female. Thus, in this case it may be more accurate to speak of "filiation" rather than of "descent" (Scheffler 1966, Shapiro 1967). Ego, through identification (or filiation) with one of his or her parents, accepts the same progenitors for social purposes accepted by that parent. See Figure 12.4e.

A pattern similar to that characteristic for terminological systems emerges for the cross-cultural distribution of types of descent systems: cognatic descent is most common in hunting-gathering band societies and in industrial states, while some form of unilineal descent is characteristic of tribal societies. This is not surprising, since the technoeconomic systems of foraging and industrial societies tend to emphasize individual labor and the near self-sufficiency of small households based on "nuclear families" (husband, wife, children), and tribal societies utilize affiliation to larger kinship units in their adaptive strategies (which require dependable and relatively stable groupings for economic cooperation, defense, and so on).

   Cognatic or Bilateral Descent   Cognatic descent is often referred to as *nonunilineal* or *multilineal* descent to distinguish it from all the preceding types. Descent is not restricted to any particular line or sex; rather, descent is traced through *all* progenitors, male and female, through both the mother *and* the father. See Figure 12.5.

Agnatic and Uterine Kin
Before going on to consider some of the kinds of units people form on the basis of their notions of descent, it is necessary to provide a note about the terms *agnatic* and *uterine* used above.

   Agnatic kin are persons (of either sex) related through males. Male

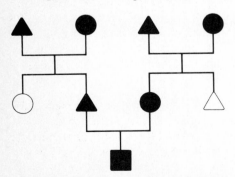

Figure 12.5   Cognatic or bilateral descent.

agnates are males related through males, and female agnates are females related through males. Thus, for example, a brother and sister with the same pater may be termed *agnatic siblings* because they are related through a male.

Uterine kin are persons (of either sex) related through females. Male uterine kin are males related through females, and female uterine kin are females related through females. For example, a brother and sister with the same mater may be called *uterine siblings* because they are related through a female. (Incidentally, siblings who have both parents in common are usually referred to as *full siblings*.)

Thus an agnatic or uterine relationship can exist regardless of whether or not there is agnatic (patrilineal) or uterine (matrilineal) descent.

Sociocentric Units

Descent Categories and Descent Groups   People can use the ideas (concepts, constructs) of descent they have to classify people into categories. Such categories we call, for obvious reasons, *descent categories*. Simply, descent categories include all those people who, by using the notions of descent prevalent in their culture, trace their relationship to a common ancestor. These are descent *categories*, remember, because they are collectivities of individuals who share a common characteristic (descent from the same ancestor), but they do not form together on the basis of their common descent to *do* something. This latter kind of collectivity would constitute a *descent group*. Thus, people of common descent who use that descent as a basis of eligibility or recruitment for membership in a group form a descent group. A number of people can be in the same descent category, but only some of them may invoke the notion of descent to form groups. Obviously, then, a descent group and a descent category need by no means be coterminous. That is, the descent group may include only some of the people classified in a descent category. (This should become clear below, through a discussion of lineage and clan.)

Local or Residence Group   One kind of group that can be found using descent as a criterion of membership is a *local group* or *residence group*, i.e., a group of people who live together. A local group can be formed on many different bases, but people who reside together and who use descent as the basis for grouping themselves residentially form what is called, not unsurprisingly, a *descent-based local group*.

Lineage and Clan   A *lineage*, especially in tribal Africa, is such a descent-based group. A **lineage** is usually defined (though the definition is sometimes challenged) as a descent group consisting of persons unilineally descended from a known ancestor through a series of genealogical links or relationships they can trace. That is, it is usually considered that the members of a lineage can demonstrate their descent relationship to the claimed ancestor genealogically, either patrilineally or matrilineally, and that the number of generations counted to link ego to the ancestor is relatively few.[5]

Lineage is often contrasted in definition to *clan* or *sib*.[6] A clan (or sib) can be a group or category; i.e., it can be a collectivity of people who get together, based on some notion of descent, to do things; or it may only be a way of classifying individuals on the basis of their descent. In either event, the characteristic usually used to distinguish a lineage from a clan is that in a lineage individual members can demonstrate their descent from an ancestor, while in a clan they cannot. There is the notion of common descent among clan members, but they cannot actually trace or demonstrate it. We may therefore define a **clan** or **sib** as a group or category of persons of both sexes, membership in which is determined by unilineal descent, but in which the members cannot trace their descent back to the apical ancestor (cf. R.A.I. 1956:89).[7]

Lineages and clans, *as types of groups,* though they differ in the ability of the members to trace their ancestry, share a number of characteristics:

1 Both are based on unilineal descent. They are often referred to as *unilineal descent groups.*

2 From both may be, and often are, formed local or residence groups.

3 Both may be corporate groups, i.e., they may control some valued commodity.

4 Both may be exogamous—i.e., the members may be prohibited from marrying within the group. (*Exogamy* is the rule which states that marriage cannot occur between two members of the the same group; or, positively stated, it is the rule which requires that individuals must seek a marriage partner outside the group.)

5 Both often have group *taboos.* Simply, a taboo is a proscription, a "don't," which, usually, carries with it supernatural sanctions. For example, members of the group may be prohibited from eating a certain food or killing a certain animal. Related to this is a phenomenon called *totemism,* which pertains mainly to some clans. Totemism refers to a characteristic of clan organization in which the clan is named after some object in nature— usually a plant or animal—and the clan members are forbidden to kill or eat that object. Sometimes associated with this is the belief that the clan members are descended from this object or that the founder of the clan was somehow closely associated with it, as related in myth or legend. The totem, the natural object after which the group is named, represents the group, becomes its symbol.

6 Both lineage and clan groups contain members of both sexes originally. That is, in a society with lineage or clan organization every child is a member of the group at birth (or shortly thereafter) by virtue of descent. But when exogamy is associated with this type of organization, one sex must leave the group upon marriage. For example, let us suppose we are dealing with a *patrilineage* or *agnatic lineage,* i.e., a situation where people are affiliated with the lineage on the basis of patrilineal or agnatic descent.

Then let us couple this descent principle with a rule of lineage exogamy. Now each man, when he wants to marry, must find a mate outside the group. And let us suppose there is a rule that a wife must live where her husband lives (we will deal with residence rules shortly). The man, therefore, goes outside the group, finds a wife, and brings her back to live with him. Now we have someone in the group who is not related by descent. In the meantime, our hero's sister is old enough to marry. She, too, must obey the rule of exogamy. And she finds a husband outside the group and then leaves the group because, remember, the residence rule states a wife must live where her husband lives. What we have now is a local group (people living together) the core members of which (the term *core members* refers to those who are born in the group and who remain in the group) are related by patrilineal descent. The group is still a descent-based local group, but descent is not the only criterion of membership. Marriage into the group also provides members, while marriage out of the group results in loss of active membership. I say *active* membership because the woman who married out is still a member of the descent *category* from which this descent *group* is formed, but she no longer is a member of the *group*. Should her husband die or she get divorced (and provided she does not remarry), she can, in all likelihood, come back and live in the group again.[8]

Phratry; Moiety I have now brought into our discussion another subject, residence, which deserves fuller treatment. But before doing so, there are a few additional matters that must be mentioned.

A **phratry** is a classificatory unit larger than a clan. It is based on some notion or recognition of relationship between two or more clans. Phratries are usually categories; but if the member clans do get together for some purpose, we would have to call such a phratry a *group*.

So far we have been talking about descent groups and categories. The last term to discuss in this section is **moiety.** Moieties may or may not be based on descent and may be either groups or categories. *Moiety* simply means "half," and a society which is divided into two halves has what is called a *moiety division* or *dual organization.* The moieties may simply be a classificatory device which places people in one category or another. Or it may be a group division, with the society divided into two groups for some purpose or purposes. The division may be based on descent or on something else (e.g., "winter and summer" people, "east and west" people, "red and black" people).

Egocentric Units

From each individual ego's point of view there is a circle of people regarded as kin. To just which people this relationship is extended varies from society to society. In different societies, different sets of people are considered kin. They make up a *cultural category* to ego, a category of kin. Ego has certain obligations to them, and they to ego, by nature of their being classed as kin.

Such a category of kin, seen from ego's point of view, is called a **kindred.** And as Keesing and Keesing point out (1971:158), "kindreds are not separate and enduring social groups, though action groups are recruited from them; any one person is included in the kindreds of many different people." (In other words, your uncle is somebody else's brother or someone else's nephew, etc.) Thus, kindreds are different for different individuals in the same society. Only full siblings have the same kindred. A simple way to think of kindreds is as many overlapping circles, with an individual (ego) at the center of each.

RESIDENCE

Residence Rules and Patterns

Residence rules are norms which govern where people should live. They are that part of the conceptual system of a culture which deals with appropriate residence behavior: who should live where and with whom. Actual *patterns of residence* are a statistical summary of what people are actually doing, where people are actually living and with whom. Thus, residence rules are a part of culture, and residence patterns are in the social realm.

There are so many different kinds and combinations of residence rules

A Herero house; southern Africa. *(Photograph by the author.)*

that to attempt a definitive presentation here would be confusing and beyond what is needed. As always, I will try to keep it simple, while still
covering the area adequately.

First of all, when we speak of *residence rules*, we should always make
clear what class of people in the society we are talking about. Residence
rules for a single man may be different from those for a married man.
Residence rules for a man are different from those for a woman. Those for
a child are different from those for an adult. Therefore, we must be explicit
regarding whom we are speaking about.

Most of the time, anthropologists are interested in postmarital residence, and that in two respects: (1) which of the partners, the husband or
the wife, moves upon marriage; and (2) where do the newly married couple
set up their residence?

Bearing this in mind, let us go on to the terms used to describe residence.[9] (The suffix -*local* is used in all these terms to indicate location.)

Types of Residence

When the husband and wife are regarded as separate individuals, the follow
types may occur:

Virilocal ("man's place"). The wife removes to[10] the husband's residence.

Uxorilocal ("wife's place"). The husband removes to the wife's place of
residence.

Natolocal ("place of birth"). This term, suggested by Robin Fox
(1967:85), refers to the practice by which neither partner moves. In other
words, they do not reside together at all but remain in their natal groups,
visiting with each other for only short periods.

When the couple is regarded as a unit, the following types of residence
may occur:

Patrilocal. This term literally means "father's place," and as such does
not tell us whose father, the wife's or the husband's, the couple resides with;
but it is commonly used in reference to residence with the husband's father.
Because of this imprecision, the terms *patrivirilocal* or *viripatrilocal* ("man's
father's place") are usually preferred. (*Patrilocal,* to add to the confusion,
has also been used at times in place of *virilocal.*)

Matrilocal. Since this term means "mother's place," it can, like *patrilocal,* be confusing because it does not in itself indicate whether the move is
to the man's mother or to the woman's mother. Actually, it usually refers to
the couple's move to the wife's mother's place of residence, and this is how
it will be defined here. (Unfortunately, *matrilocal* has also often been used
when *uxorilocal* is meant.)

Avunculocal. The couple resides with the husband's mother's brother
(the husband's maternal uncle), rather than with either spouse's parents.

The term *viriavunculocal* ("man's mother's brother's place") is sometimes used. Avunculocal residence also refers to the practice, common in matrilineal societies, by which a male child (often around puberty) leaves his parents' household and goes to live with his MB. If, after marriage, he continues to reside with his MB, we call this *avunculocal residence* too.

Ambilocal or **bilocal.** The couple has the choice of residing with the parents of either spouse.

Neolocal ("new place"). The couple removes to an entirely new residence, apart from others. A pattern of neolocal residence is prevalent in our own society.

Commonlocal. Keith Otterbein (1972:37) has suggested this term for the practice by which couples establish their residences in a group in which both the husband's parents and the wife's parents live.

FOOTNOTES

1 An example of how kinship is used to order social relations is provided by the complementary customs known as *avoidance* and *joking relationships.*

   Avoidance relationships are those governed by formal rules that restrict interaction between classes of relatives or even impose complete avoidance between them. For example, an avoidance relationship between a man and his mother-in-law is one that is not uncommon cross-culturally. Among some Australian Aborigine societies, for instance, a man may not converse with, or even speak the name of, his wife's mother. The Trobriand Islanders in the Pacific are famous for their brother-sister avoidance rules which forbid the two to be alone together or to have private conversations.

   Joking relationships are just the opposite. They allow joking, teasing, free access to personal belongings, and perhaps sexual license between certain classes of relatives. Such a relation frequently exists, for example, between a man's wife and his younger brother (especially in cases where the levirate is practiced; see Chapter 13).

2 The equals sign here indicates that the same term is applied. Thus FBD = FZD may be read: "The relationship term applied to a relative genealogically designated FBD is the same term applied to one designated FZD." (When the terms are not equivalent, i.e., when different terms are applied, this is indicated by ÷.)

3 The instructor may wish at this point to present to the students our own relationship terminology. It may be pedagogically useful, also, to contrast our terminology with a non-Western type.

4 Individuals who are related "vertically" or in a "line"—i.e., descended one from the other, as FF, F, ego, S, SS—are called *lineal* relatives. Codescended individuals—i.e., those related "horizontally," as ego, B, FBS, MBS—are called *collateral* relatives.

5 A lineage based on patrilineal descent is usually called a *patrilineage,* one based on matrilineal descent a *matrilineage,* and one based on ambilineal or optative descent an *ambilineage* or *ramage* or *optative descent group.* Groups based on cognatic or bilateral descent have been called *cognatic* or *bilateral* or *unrestricted descent groups.*

6 Formerly *clan* and *sib* were distinguished, as were other units called *gens, demes,* and so on. Since such distinctions are no longer common in the current anthropological literature, they are not dealt with here (but see, e.g., Murdock 1949, as well as the Glossary to this handbook, page 235).

7 It should be pointed out that in an actual ethnographic situation it is sometimes difficult to distinguish clearly between a "lineage" and a "clan." Consequently, many ethnographers have chosen to write of "minimal," "minor," "major," and "maximal" lineages. The student should remember that in ethnographic fieldwork the object is not to fit the discovered reality to textbook terms but to find usable terms that help to describe the reality.

8 I have found it helpful in making this example clear to students to contrast it with its matrilineal counterparts: (a) matrilineage + lineage exogamy + uxorilocal residence, and (b) matrilineage + lineage exogamy + virilocal residence for the wife and avunculocal residence for the couple as a unit.

9 These terms have been used to denote particular residence rules (cultural norms about who should live where) and to describe patterns of residence (statistical descriptions of who is actually living where).

10 The terms *resides with, removes to,* and so on, can be read as "takes up residence at or near." The above types of residence need not refer to actual coresidence within the same household, although this may occur, but can also indicate residence in the same general vicinity.

Chapter 13

Marriage and Family

(Photograph: Tony Howarth, Woodfin Company and Associates.)

Note on Incest   It is customary (and logical enough) to discuss the subject of incest in any introductory treatment of marriage. Incest is a favored topic in anthropological circles; it has been defined, redefined, debated, and analyzed *ad nauseam*.

Why? What makes incest so important a subject? Basically, there are two reasons, one deriving from the other. The incest taboo has been called *universal*, which means that it is found in every known human society. That is, according to most authors, all societies have rules which prohibit mating (sexual intercourse) between parents and children and between siblings; hence, the "incest taboo" is viewed as a universal characteristic. Because of this it has been focused on as *the* cultural rule, the rule which marked the emergence of the human being as a cultural animal, set apart from other animals.

It follows, then, that if the "incest taboo" can be shown *not* to be universal, or at least if there is enough evidence that seriously questions the claim to universality, it loses its central importance in anthropological theory. In fact, if one reviews the ethnographic literature on the topic, this is precisely what one finds. A number of societies allow some or all forms of mating behavior which we think of as "incestuous," so that one wonders why most writers, especially the authors of virtually all introductory texts, persist in their assertion of universality for the "incest taboo."

Because the ethnographic facts do not seem to justify the inordinate amount of attention the subject of incest has received, I will not deal with it within this chapter. But because the topic has been so influential in cultural anthropology, and because this handbook is meant as an introduction to cultural anthropology, the "incest taboo" cannot be totally ignored. Hence, I am forced into a paradoxical position: incest does not deserve the amount of space it has received in the past; yet, in order for me to support this claim, I must myself devote an excessive amount of space to the subject. I have tried to resolve this predicament by including at the end of this handbook an appendix on incest theories (Appendix 2, Evaluating Incest Theories). This appendix defines the subject and the various terms employed in discussions of it, challenges the claim to universality, outlines the major theories proposed regarding it (which spring from a belief in its universality), and suggests a framework (which is derived from several authors' suggestions) for evaluating incest theories. It also proposes that even though the "incest taboo" is not universal, it can still be studied. The student is therefore advised to consult Appendix 2 after reading this chapter, for nothing further on the subject will be said here.

MARRIAGE

Ideally, a preliminary step in any discussion should be a definition of the subject. Thus we should first define marriage and then go on to discuss its cross-cultural variations. Unfortunately, however, there is no one accepted definition of marriage that applies to all societies. The best definition we can find is probably something like the following: **marriage** is a socially recognized and normatively prescribed relationship between at least two persons that defines economic and sexual rights and other duties each owes the other or others and provides the *primary* mechanism in a society by which offspring are recognized as legitimate and "accorded full birth-status rights common to normal members of [their] society or social stratum" (Gough 1959:32).[1]

But any definition of marriage (including the above) may be found wanting when we try to apply it to a particular society. It is probably more useful to try to provide some general cross-cultural characteristics of marriage than to try to define it rigidly. Below, I list four generalizations relevant to a discussion of marriage, some of which are borrowed from Keesing and Keesing (1971:181–182).

Characteristics of Marriage

1 More often than not, when marriage is viewed in cross-cultural perspective, it turns out to be a *relationship between groups* rather than just a relationship between individuals. Keesing and Keesing suggest that a marriage system which at first seems odd to us will often make more sense if we view it as a contract between corporate groups. This is emphasized by the fact that in many societies the contract established by marriage *does not necessarily end with the death or withdrawal (e.g., through divorce) of either partner* (see the discussion of the levirate and sororate below).

2 Marriage is *not only a sexual relationship;* it is a *form of exchange* involving a transfer of rights and obligations between the contracting parties. For example, a man often gains economic rights over a woman's labor when he marries her. He reciprocates by giving the woman's group gifts to compensate them for the loss of her labor (bridewealth is discussed below). In most cases marriage establishes an economic cooperative unit, with each partner contributing his or her labor and the products of that labor. It may also be considered a political mechanism by which groups exchange spouses and thereby set up an alliance.

3 No society allows indiscriminate marriage or mating among its members (even if it lacks a recognizable "incest taboo"). There is always some group or category one may not marry into. And there is always some specifiable entity in which most marriages occur in that society (even though there may be no formal rules specifying whom one should or must marry). In other words, all societies are both exogamous and endogamous (see the definitions below).

4 Comparatively few societies limit their members to one spouse apiece; in most societies it is considered desirable to have more than one.

Definition of Terms

Exogamy refers to marriage (not mating) outside one's own social unit (for instance, a group, such as a lineage; or a category, such as a moiety). *Endogamy* refers to marriage to someone within one's own social unit (for instance, within the phratry, the tribe, or the nation-state).

Monogamy is the marriage of one man to one woman; *polygamy* is the marriage of one person to two or more spouses at the same time.[2] There are two principal types of polygamy: *polygyny* and *polyandry.*

Polygyny is the marriage of one man to two or more women at the same time. (*Sororal polygyny* refers to the marriage of one man to sisters.) *Polyandry* is the marriage of one woman to two or more men at the same time. (*Adelphic* or *fraternal polyandry* refers to the marriage of one woman to brothers.)

Group marriage is a form of marriage that has been postulated in which an entire group of men is married to an entire group of women, so that all the wives are shared by all the men and all the husbands are shared by all the women. Most anthropologists aver that no society has been found in which true group marriage is the standard arrangement (if, that is, they acknowledge that it occurs at all).[3]

There are two terms that sound as if they belong with monogamy and polygamy but refer to quite a different kind of marriage practice: *hypogamy* and *hypergamy.* Both refer to marriage between social levels (classes or castes) in societies characterized by social stratification.

Hypogamy is marriage between strata, where the *woman* is a member of the higher stratum.

Hypergamy is marriage between strata, where the *man* is a member of the higher stratum.

Hypogamy is more likely to be found in association with a matrilineal descent system (since in such systems children receive their social affiliation from the mother), while hypergamy is more likely to be associated with a patrilineal system (where children are socially affiliated with their father).

I said in Chapter 9 that castes are usually endogamous. How then can marriage between strata occur? The answer is that castes are often internally stratified, and hypogamous or hypergamous marriages take place between individuals at different levels within the caste.

Types of Marriage Systems

Claude Lévi-Strauss, a very influential French anthropologist, has developed a view of social interaction as exchange, a view according to which reciprocity in behavior is a key principle in social relations (1969).[4] One aspect of this view is that marriage, too, is a system of exchange—an exchange, between groups, of women as marriage partners. Although Lévi-Strauss's theories are hotly disputed by anthropologists, I will use his framework to discuss types of marriage systems—not because I think the framework is beyond reproach (not by any means) but because a presentation

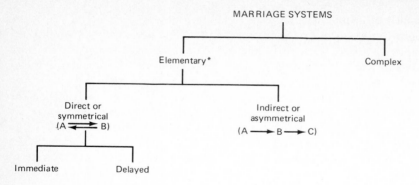

*Synonyms for elementary systems:

(1) Direct or restricted exchange, symmetric system,
    reciprocal marriage pattern
    (a) Immediate exchange, sister exchange,
        bilateral cross-cousin (MBD/FZD) marriage
    (b) Delayed exchange,
        patrilateral cross-cousin (FZD) marriage
(2) Indirect or generalized exchange, asymmetric system,
    circulating connubium, one-way wife flow,
    matrilateral cross-cousin (MBD) marriage

Figure 13.1 Types of marriage systems. *(Based on Fox, 1967:222.)*

based on Lévi-Strauss's suggestions is the most economical way that I know to introduce the subject.

The first distinction to be made is that between elementary and complex systems of marriage. (Figure 13.1 diagrams types of marriage systems and, since usage is far from uniform, lists synonyms for the types of elementary systems.)

Elementary systems are those in which the rules specify whom (i.e., into which category or group of persons) one should or must marry.[5] Thus, the rules in elementary systems are positive ones.

Complex systems are those in which the rules state whom one *cannot* marry, but they do not specify whom one should or must marry. The rules in complex systems, then, are negative ones.

Elementary Marriage Systems   *Direct exchange*   The simplest system of exchange is *direct* or *symmetrical exchange* (also called *restricted exchange*). It simply means that group A gives its women as wives to group B, and in return group B gives its women as wives to group A.

When the entire exchange takes place in the same generation, it is called *immediate* direct exchange or *sister exchange* (Figure 13.2*a*). It is also

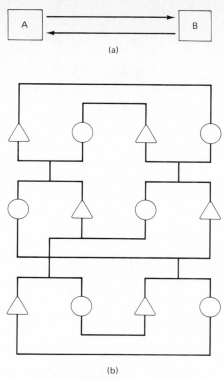

(a)

(b)

Figure 13.2 Immediate direct exchange.

called *bilateral cross-cousin marriage* because when this system is shown in ideal form on a genealogical diagram, each man is seen to marry a woman who is related to him as MBD/FZD (see Figure 13.2*b*).

A second type of direct exchange is *delayed direct exchange* (Figure 13.3*a*). In this type, group A gives wives to group B in one generation, and group B then reciprocates in the *next* generation. In other words, there is a delay before wives flow back the other way (from B to A). Often this marriage system is depicted as a chain (Figure 13.3*b*) or a circle (Figure 13.3*c*). It is also called *patrilateral cross-cousin marriage* because ideally a man marries his FZD—or a woman in the same kinship category as his FZD (Figure 13.3*d*).

Indirect exchange In *indirect* or *asymmetric* systems (also called *generalized exchange*), women move in one direction only. In this type of marriage system, a group that gives women as wives to some other group or groups can never receive wives in return from the same group or groups but must get wives elsewhere. One group cannot be both "wife givers" and

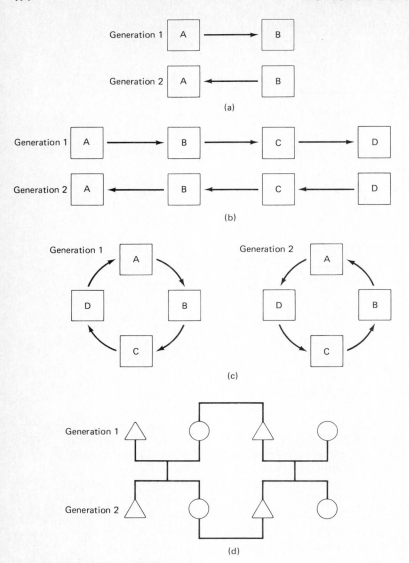

Figure 13.3 Delayed direct exchange.

"wife takers" in respect to any other single group. Instead, it is a wife-giving group in respect to some groups and a wife-taking group in respect to a different set of groups.

In other words, in Figure 13.4a the members of group B are "wife givers" to group C and "wife takers" to group A; and these relationships can never be reversed.

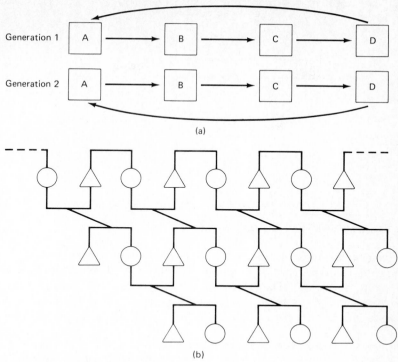

(a)

(b)

Figure 13.4 Indirect exchange.

This is also called *matrilateral cross-cousin marriage* because when rendered ideally in a genealogical diagram (Figure 13.4*b*) it results in each man's marrying his MBD.

Bint 'amm In Chapter 12, I said that lineages are usually exogamous. A classic exception to this generalization is provided by many Arab and other Islamic societies that are divided into a number of patrilineages. In these societies a man's preferred marriage partner is his FBD (his *bint 'amm*, to use the kinship term)—a woman in the same lineage as he. No one else, in theory at least, may marry her without first obtaining the permission of her FBS. This type of marriage is called *bint 'amm marriage, FBD marriage*, and *patrilateral parallel cousin marriage* (Figure 13.5).

Since this kind of marriage specifies appropriate marriage partners (has positive rules), it qualifies as an elementary system in Lévi-Strauss's terms. But since it appears to contradict the view that marriage involves an exchange *between* groups and instead strengthens solidarity *within* a group, it seems to fall outside Lévi-Strauss's framework. Hence, I list it after elementary systems and before complex systems.

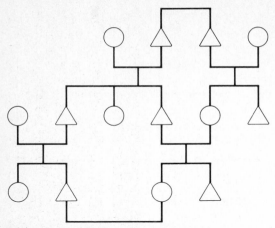

Figure 13.5   Patrilateral parallel-cousin marriage.

Complex Systems   Complex marriage systems are those with rules "not involving the positive determination of the type of preferred spouse" (Lévi-Strauss 1969:465). That is, complex systems, as noted above, simply state whom one should *not* marry (they do not provide formal rules about whom one should or must marry). Fox (1967:222–223) sums up as follows:

> In our own system, and in other systems which lack corporate kin-groups as the basic units of the society, then the prohibited relatives tend to be an ego-centered group of kin. These are either a motley collection such as our own, or a well-defined kindred . . . ; for example, all ego's kin up to second cousins or something such. As long as ego marries outside this category then there is no prescription applying to his marriage choice. The effect of this is, to put it graphically, to send people shooting off in all directions at once, and to link together many kindreds in a complex way. . . .
> . . . Many 'primitive' societies can be characterized in the same way, but because they are societies composed of corporate kinship groups—clans, lineages, phratries etc.—they work somewhat differently. Again, there are no positive rules and the simplest of them have only the rule of clan exogamy—thou shalt not marry members of thine own clan.

Marriage-Related Practices

It was stated earlier that in most instances it is more useful to consider marriage as a contract between groups than as a contract between individuals. The following are some commonly found customs associated with marriage that illustrate this point.

Marriage Payments   *Bridewealth or bride-price*   Bridewealth is a marriage payment made by the husband or, more often, the husband's group to the wife's group. No one is "buying" a wife. By the payment of goods, the husband or his group is securing in a socially recognized way his rights regarding his new wife and any children they may have. Bridewealth marks the transition of rights from one group to the other. It is a form of compensation paid by the husband's group to the wife's group for the loss of her labor, the loss of any children she might subsequently bear, etc. (Some anthropologists have focused on the fact that bridewealth establishes the husband's genetricial rights—i.e., the rights he has in the children borne by his wife—and have suggested that the payment is more aptly termed *child-wealth* or *progeny price*. They cite as evidence the fact that bridewealth is usually not found in matrilineal societies, since the husband's group does not secure rights over the woman's children. This ignores, however, the other rights, especially economic and sexual, that bridewealth establishes.)

Bridewealth, therefore, should not be thought of as one-sided, i.e., as only a payment made by the husband's group to the wife's group. It should be seen as an exchange, with valuables flowing both ways. It may be simply an exchange of rights for cows or camels (or whatever the bridewealth currency happens to be); but it may also involve the exchange of material goods in *both* directions, though in the latter case the goods that are given by the wife's group (say, for instance, a goat or a sheep) are usually of token value. (Viewed in this perspective, the American custom of exchanging rings during the wedding ceremony takes on a broader significance.)

Dowry A dowry is usually a payment of a different sort from bridewealth. Though some anthropologists (e.g., Taylor 1976:157) have equated dowry with property given to the husband's group by the wife's group, most anthropologists appear to consider dowry the woman's share of her inheritance from her natal group, a share she takes with her upon marriage. (This does not deny, of course, that the size of a woman's dowry may be significant in planning marital alliances.)

Bride service This is another custom by which the husband establishes the legitimacy of marital rights. It involves the groom's living with the bride's group for a specified period of time (which in some cases lasts until the birth of a child), working for the group, providing food, gifts, and so on.

Secondary Marriages *Levirate* In societies that practice the levirate, when a man dies, his kin group replaces him with another male as spouse for his widow. The levirate is often described as the practice whereby a deceased man's brother marries the widow (or, phrased in reference to the woman, the wife is expected to marry the brother of her deceased husband). But this is not necessarily quite accurate. Often she need not marry his brother (whether real or classificatory) but only some specified member of his kin group. Since the marriage contract involved the group, the group replaces the member who died.

Sororate In societies practicing the sororate, when a man's wife dies, her kin group replaces her with another woman from that group. Normally, the replacement need not be her sister.

Wife inheritance   This is something different from the sororate. In this case, when a man dies, his heir is expected to marry the widow. This is simply an "expression of a man's succession to the status and property rights" of the man he succeeds (Keesing and Keesing 1971:195).

In a matrilineal system, for example, a male ego does not inherit from his father (who is in a different kinship group from ego) but from his MB (who is a senior male in the same kinship group as ego). Along with property and rights, ego inherits obligations from his maternal uncle. One of these is to care for the deceased's wives. By marrying them, he acknowledges this obligation and honors the contract with the group or groups from which these women originally came.

FAMILY AND HOUSEHOLD

Family Groups

Ideally, the concepts "family" and "household" should be distinguished, with **household** referring to a domestic residential *group,* while **family,** minimally defined for cross-cultural applicability, refers to an intimate kinship unit (which may not constitute a distinct group) consisting of a mother and children. The father of the children (whether the genitor or the pater) need not be attached to this unit, though in most societies he is.

In reality, however, this distinction is difficult, if not impossible, to maintain. There is no known human society in which mother and child constitute a separate unit in themselves. The mother-child unit is always part of some larger *group* that contains adult members of both sexes, though the males may be brothers of the females and not their husbands.[6] Thus, anthropologists, after recognizing the conceptual distinction between *family* and *household* (by which they mean a residential group and "not necessarily the same dwelling, since a household may occupy several houses," Otterbein 1972:47), go on to discuss nuclear, extended, and joint *families* when they are usually talking about domestic *groups.*[7]

Therefore, in order to present an orderly account to the beginner in anthropology (who deserves such an account even if it does not accurately reflect the state of the field), I will refer to *family groups* and mean by this term households formed on the basis of kinship (whether affinal or consanguineal) that include the offspring of at least one of their adult members.

Types of Family Groups

We in Western society are accustomed to thinking of the basic family group as made up of a husband, a wife, and their children. In cross-cultural perspective, however, this arrangement is fairly rare. What is more common is a more complex elaboration of the mother-child unit. In this section, I will note the major variations in types of family organization, list the appropriate terms and definitions (even though all anthropologists do not agree on these), and provide a brief commentary.

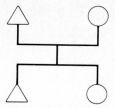

Figure 13.6   A nuclear family group.

Simple Family Groups   A *nuclear family group* is one composed of a man, a woman, and their children (Figure 13.6). It is most commonly found at the two ends of the evolutionary continuum—among hunter-gatherers and in industrial societies. Haviland (1975:177) comments on this:

> Certain parallels can be drawn between the contemporary nuclear family in industrial societies and families living on the bare edge of survival. In both cases, the family is an independent unit that must fend for itself; this creates a strong dependence of individual family members on one another. There is little help from outside in the event of emergencies or catastrophies. When their usefulness is at an end, the elderly are cared for only if it is feasible. In the event of death of the mother or father, life becomes precarious for the child. Yet this form of family is well adapted to a life that requires a high degree of mobility. For the Eskimo, this mobility permits the hunt for food; for Americans, it is probably the hunt for jobs and improved social status that requires a mobile form of family unit.

Keesing and Keesing (1971:199) suggest that the occurrence of nuclear family groups "can best be understood in terms of the *absence* of factors that produce more complex forms." Specifically, nuclear family groups occur where polygamy is absent (so that each person is limited to one spouse) and where unilineal descent as a basis for organizing groups is absent (so that the father and his children, for instance, are not members of one large-order kin group, while the mother is affiliated with another). In other words, in the absence of these factors, what emerges as the focal domestic unit is the nuclear family. Or, looked at from another angle and phrased positively, monogamous marriage, coupled with neolocal residence, results in nuclear family groups.

Complex or Compound Family Groups   Polygamous marriages or unilineal affiliation, or certain residence patterns in conjunction with either monogamous or polygamous marriage, produce more complex forms of family groups. There are several types (summarized in Table 13.1).

Family groups based on polygamous marriage   A *polygynous family group* is one which results when a man, his several wives, and his children by these wives live together (Figure 13.7*a*). Hence, a combination of polygy-

Table 13.1   Types of Family Groups as Results of Marriage and Residence Patterns

Type of marriage	+ Residence pattern	= Type of family group
Monogamy	Neolocal	Nuclear family group
Polygamy	Neolocal	Polygynous family group Polyandrous family group
Monogamy or polygamy	Coresident lineal relatives: Patrivirilocal Matrilocal Avunculocal Ambilocal	Extended family groups: Patrilocal extended family group Matrilocal extended family group Avunculocal extended family group Both patrilocal and matrilocal extended family groups
Monogamy or polygamy	Coresident collateral relatives	Joint family group
Monogamy or polygamy	Natolocal	Consanguine (uterine or matricentric) family group

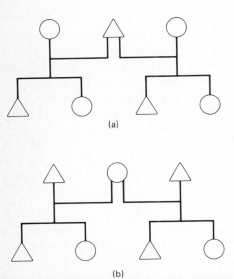

(a)

(b)

Figure 13.7   *Polygamous family groups: (a) polygynous; (b) polyandrous.*

A Toda polyandrous family group; southern India. *(Courtesy of the American Museum of Natural History.)*

ny and neolocal residence produces a polygynous family group. Since having several wives under the same roof can often lead to competition and jealousy, especially in regard to children, each wife with her own children may occupy a separate dwelling. These *matricentric households* are not independent. They are part of the larger residential unit and are only one element in the labor force this unit constitutes.

A **polyandrous family group** is produced when a woman, her several husbands, and her children all live together (Figure 13.7*b*). A combination of polyandry and neolocal residence results in a polyandrous family group. In this case, all the members may live under one roof, or the husbands may jointly occupy a separate "men's hut." The children, of course, reside with their mother.

Family groups based on common descent   Family groups based on common descent may utilize an intergenerational link, such as that between parent and child (*extended family*), or a sibling link (*joint family*).

An **extended family group** is one produced when two or more lineally related generations of persons with their spouses live together. There are three main types: patrilocal, matrilocal, and avunculocal.

A *patrilocal extended family group* results from a pattern of patrivirilocal residence and consists of a man, his son or sons, and the latter's wife or wives and children living together.[8] (See Figure 13.8*a*).

A *matrilocal extended family group* results from a pattern of matrilocal residence and consists of a woman, her daughter or daughters, and the latter's husband or husbands and children living together (Figure 13.8*b*).

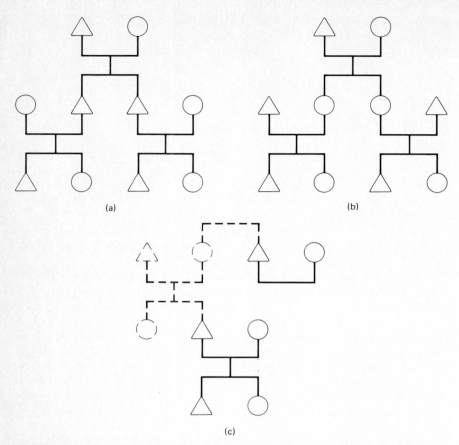

Figure 13.8 Extended family groups: *(a)* patrilocal; *(b)* matrilocal; *(c)* avunculocal (individuals indicated by solid lines are those constituting the group).

An *avunculocal extended family group* results from a pattern of avunculocal residence and consists of a man, his sister's son or sons, and the latter's wife or wives and children living together (Figure 13.8c).

A **joint family group** is one produced when two or more collaterally related persons with their spouses and children live together. The most common type is the *fraternal joint family group*. This consists of at least two brothers and their wives and children in coresidence (Figure 13.9).

It should be mentioned that joint and extended family groups, as well as those based on polygamous unions, are not mutually exclusive. A society might have a residential unit based on both common descent and plural marriage. The Herero are a case in point. They are polygynous (most men over forty have more than one wife). Each wife and her unmarried children occupy a separate hut (the husband has no hut of his own; he rotates

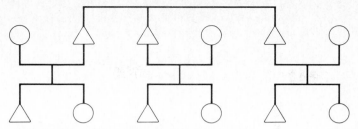

Figure 13.9 A fraternal joint family group.

among his wives' huts). The husband's married sons, with their wives and children, and his younger brothers, with their wives and children, also reside with him (though, of course, they occupy separate huts). All of these taken together, plus an occasional distant or poor relative, constitute a single residential unit called an *onganda* ("homestead") in the Herero language.

Complex family groups are characteristic of tribal societies. They provide an adequate labor force for cooperative economic activities such as clearing land, planting and tending crops, and herding domesticated animals; they are often the primary defensive groups; they provide for care of the aged and rearing of young; they are the basic focal units for ritual and other social activities. In short, they provide the primary social ambience within which people live and are the chief reference points for social identity.

FOOTNOTES

1 "Primary" is emphasized because of those societies, such as the Herero, who have, in addition to marriage, another kind of relationship between a man and a woman that allows the man to pay a fee to have the woman's children socially recognized as his legitimate offspring. He need not, however, marry the woman.

2 The phrase *at the same time* is added to exclude those societies in which serial monogamy occurs. *Serial monogamy* refers to the practice of taking several spouses in succession, though at any point in time a person only has one legal spouse. Serial monogamy appears to be characteristic, for example, of advanced industrial societies.

3 But E. Kathleen Gough (1959) claims that the situation among the Nayar, in which a woman goes through a marriage ceremony with a single male and thereafter is free to have sexual relations with any other male in his group, is a case of group marriage. Since all the other females in the woman's group are not legitimate sexual partners for all the men in the man's group, I am reluctant to call this group marriage.

The Marquesans, a Pacific society, were once thought to have group marriage. Among these people, both polyandry and polygyny are practiced. Hence, a woman may be married to two men at the same time that her husbands are each married to two women (Otterbein 1963). This falls short of the definition of group marriage, however, because each of the individuals involved has only one spouse in common with any of the others. All the women are not married to all the men.

4 Lévi-Strauss's prose is celebrated, at least among his English-speaking audience, for its incomprehensibility. Although a number of exegetical texts exist, I advise any student wishing an elementary grasp of the Lévi-Straussian approach to read Robin Fox's *Kinship and Marriage* (1967).

5 Anthropologists usually distinguish between prescriptive and preferential marriage. A *prescriptive* marriage system is one in which the rules state that an individual *must* marry into a designated category. In other words, marriage is prescribed. But a *preferential* system is one in which the rules specify into which category or categories an individual *should* marry, i.e., which is preferred.

6 A celebrated example is provided by the Nayars of India (Gough 1961). The primary residential and property-owning groups among the Nayar were segments of a matrilineage consisting of brothers and sisters, the sisters' children, and the sisters' daughters' children. The males who sired the children lived elsewhere, in their own uterine groups. (In other words, the Nayar practiced a pattern of natolocal residence.) Haviland (1975:176) calls this a "consanguine family."

7 This problem is mirrored in a staggering amount of terminological confusion. Indeed, it is rare to find two authors of introductory texts who agree in their definitions of terms. For example, for Keesing and Keesing (1971:201) *joint family* and *extended family* are synonymous terms. For other authors, the two terms are distinguishable, but which criteria are chosen to distinguish them vary. For some, *joint family* refers to collaterals (brothers) living together with their wives and children (Otterbein 1972:48); to others it is any kinspeople "living together in a single household, each with his or her own distinct spouse and offspring" (Hoebel 1972:434). To Pearson (1974:191), a joint family is an extended family living in a single house. To many writers *nuclear family* and *conjugal family* are synonymous. To Haviland (1975:176), a nuclear family is only one kind of conjugal family, and the latter is contrasted with *consanguine family*. To Pearson (1974:191) an extended family consists of a minimum of two generations, whereas most other authors hold that an extended family has a minimum of three generations. (See Glossary.)

8 Some authors choose to differentiate a subtype of extended family group called a *stem family*. This refers to a case in which only one married child, with his or her spouse or spouses, resides with the parent or parents.

Chapter 14

Religion

(Photograph by Ingrid Deich.)

THE PROBLEM OF DEFINITION

In discussing "religion," we are once more faced with the task of providing a definition that will help us to compare similar aspects of different societies, and at the same will be accurate enough in definition to fit any *particular* society. But, as with other human institutions, especially in nonliterate societies, religion is commingled with other spheres of behavior (such as economics, law, kinship, and politics). In addition, the task of differentiating "religion" from "religious-like" enterprises, such as magic, is a complicated one.

To what, then, shall we apply the term *religion?* A rapid perusal of about two dozen introductory texts and other literature in anthropology indicates that the typical, though not universally accepted, distinction used to designate an area of human conduct as religion is the belief in a supernatural or superhuman component of reality (what Goode 1964 calls "supernature") or, more specifically, a belief in supernatural or superhuman beings. Such a definition has a long history in anthropology and, in essence, is the same as that proposed by E. B. Tylor in his book *Primitive Culture* (1871), which is the first anthropological treatment of the subject. Tylor found what he called "animism" ("the general belief in spiritual beings") to be "practically sufficient" for a "definition of a minimum of religion." For James G. Frazer (1922:50), religion concerned the "propitiation or conciliation of powers superior to man." More recently, Spiro (1966:94) has identified a belief in "superhuman beings" as the "core variable which ought to be designated by any definition of religion."[1] Anthony Wallace (1966:5) says that religion is "a kind of human behavior . . . which can be classified as belief and ritual concerned with supernatural beings, powers, and forces." And, finally, James H. Leuba (quoted in Vetter 1958:157) observes: "It appeared to me that the only clear way of separating the religious from the rest of life was not by their end, but by the method or means they use to reach their end. That method is appeal to, and reliance upon, superhuman beings."

I will therefore follow precedent and use *religion* to refer to the way people deal with the supernatural (however the supernatural—i.e., something beyond the natural, material, visible world of human beings—may be identified within any culture).[2]

It must be pointed out, however, that because such a definition depends on identifying something as "supernatural," it is subject to a charge of ethnocentrism. That is, it is based on a cosmological orientation or world view that Westerners are generally comfortable with. We do not find it difficult to distinguish between the natural and the supernatural. But this can be very misleading, for many nonliterate peoples do not think this way. To them, the "natural" and "supernatural" realms are one interacting whole. In fact, for many peoples it would be "unnatural" (meaningless) to make such a distinction. Spirits, ghosts, deities, and intangible powers are a part of "normal" or ordinary everyday life. They are considered to be as real, as much a part of the real world, as anything else. Yet, if we as students of human beings are going to divide up human sociocultural systems conceptually for analytic purposes, I think we can usefully employ a reliance on the "supernatural" as the basis for segregating one aspect of human conduct, which we can call *religion,* so that we can examine it more closely. There is no real harm done as long as we always bear in mind that we are introducing a certain amount of distortion by separating one part from what is a highly interconnected system. Religion does not stand by itself, especially in primitive societies.

FUNCTIONS OF RELIGION

Keesing and Keesing (1971:302) correctly point out that "the religions of men vary enormously in the powers and agencies they posit in the universe and the ways men relate to them"; and they suggest that "it is perhaps futile to try to define 'religion' precisely or to seek a common denominator amidst this variability." They advocate, as others before them have done, that we ask "not what religions *are,* but what they *do* in human life."[3]

To summarize what religion does, Keesing and Keesing use a fourfold classification which I compress below into three categories: explanation, support, and psychological reinforcement.

Explanatory Functions

Through religion human beings seek to explain the inexplicable, such things as existence, sickness, death, and why objects fall down instead of up ("gravity," by the way, is not a solution for this last problem; it is simply another way of saying that objects fall down). In other words, religion addresses itself to answering the question, "Why?" Why did this happen at this time, in this place, to this person? Why not a day before or a day later? And why not to someone else?

Supportive Functions

Common beliefs and rituals contribute to the cohesion and solidarity of a society. Religion provides support and reinforcement for other institutions in a society and legitimates its values and goals (Keesing and Keesing label these the "validating functions" of religion). Religion provides consistence and coherence; it helps to draw things together—feelings, experience, perception—into a reasonably, though not perfectly, ordered whole. According to Keesing and Keesing (who refer to these as "integrative functions"), religion "weaves together many segments of the customs and beliefs of a people into an overall design. It establishes and validates basic premises about the world and man's place in it; and it relates the strivings and emotions of men to them" (p. 302).

Psychologically Reinforcing Functions

Because religion "provides an organized picture of the universe and establishes a more or less orderly relationship between man and his surroundings . . . [it] reduces fears and anxieties and gives man not only a greater feeling of security in the uncertain present, but as well hope of a tolerable future" (Beals and Hoijer 1965:597). Religion serves to alleviate fear, anxiety, uncertainty, and ignorance; it helps people to deal with luck, chance, sickness, death, spoiled crops, and unproductive hunts; it aids in combating the insecurity attendant upon pregnancy, birth, marriage, social success, and warfare.

BASIC TERMS

Before outlining variations in religious systems, I want to provide you with some terms that are part of the anthropologist's vocabulary when discussing religion. These are terms you will encounter when you read the professional literature on religion.

Personnel

A *shaman* (more popularly known as a "medicine man" or "witch doctor") is a part-time religious practitioner. That is, a shaman does not specialize in performing religious functions or perform these functions exclusively. Another characteristic sometimes used to identify a shaman is that he or she deals with the supernatural mainly as an individual and not as a spokesperson for, or representative of, the group.

A *priest* is a full-time religious practitioner, a specialist in performing religious functions. Priests, as opposed to shamans, are representatives of the group in ritual and deal with the supernatural on behalf of the group.

Acts

Ritual is sometimes used narrowly to refer to a single act of a religious performance. More broadly, the term may be used to refer to any prescribed, stylized, stereotyped way of performing some act, whether the act is religious or secular in nature.

Ceremony is used to denote a complex of rituals, "a number of interconnected and related rituals" (Beals and Hoijer 1965:594). In most of the literature, however, *ceremony* and *ritual* (and *rite* as well) are used interchangeably; the distinction is not rigidly adhered to.

Supernature

Deity or *god* refers to a supernatural being (1) that is named, (2) that has a separate identity all its own, (3) that receives offerings or prayers, (4) that is a source of power, and (5) that is always there to fulfill its functions for the society. (This definition is based on, and is only a slightly modified form of, that provided by Cohen 1971:177–178.)

A *high god* is "a supernatural being who created the universe and/or is

West African singer. *(Photograph by Ingrid Deich.)*

the ultimate governor of the universe. In some instances the high god may have created other supernatural beings who in turn produced the universe. Some high gods, after they created the universe, became inactive or no longer play an active part in the affairs of humans" (Otterbein 1972:96).

Ancestral spirits are the spirits of deceased ancestors. Where the belief in such supernatural beings is important in a society's religion, the ancestral spirits are considered to be interested and active participants in the affairs of the living.

Nonhuman spirits are supernatural beings that, though often possessing human characteristics, are not human in origin. Such spirits may be identi-fied with natural features of the physical environment—such as those beings that dwell in rocks, trees, or rivers—and may even reside in animals; or they may be unattached spirits that wander freely over the landscape. They may be benevolent and assist human beings in their activities, or they may be malevolent. If they are helpful to humans, they are actively sought out. A good example is the vision quest of the North American Plains Indians. A boy took his first significant step toward manhood by going alone into the wilderness and fasting for days until he had a vision in which a guardian spirit, often in the form of an animal, visited him, imparted a sacred song to him, and thereafter was his protector.

Animism is the belief in spiritual beings. These spirits may be what we would call the souls of people that continue after death, or they may be spirits that dwell in animals or places, or they may be free-wandering beings. *Animism* has sometimes been used in a more restricted sense to refer only to the practice of attributing a spiritual component to nonhuman phenomena (i.e., to other animals, plants, and inanimate objects). Following Tylor's original usage, I apply it to any belief in spiritual beings, including any and all of those defined above.

Animatism should not be confused with animism. Beals and Hoijer (1965:573) describe animatism as "the doctrine that certain objects or natural phenomena that we should consider inanimate are themselves capable of sentient action and movement. . . . The California Indian who believes that a tree may kill him if it so desires, by dropping one of its branches upon him, does not therefore venerate the tree nor believe that the tree contains a spirit to be worshiped. He merely avoids trees or exercises great care when passing under them." Other authors, following Marett's use of the term (1909, 1912), use *animatism* to refer to the concept of an impersonal supernatural power. I will therefore discuss this concept next.

An **impersonal supernatural power** (or **ISP**) is a supernatural power unconnected with any individual spirit. Although it is unseen, it is believed to be present everywhere, in both animate and inanimate objects and events. Like electricity, to which it is often compared, ISP is not the property of any one person or thing, but it can flow between objects. Beals and Hoijer (1965:569) say:

> One of the most interesting and widespread of religious phenomena is the belief in a generalized and impersonal force, influence, or power that exists invisibly throughout the universe, and that may be possessed, to a greater or lesser degree by gods, men, the forces of nature (such as the sun, moon, rain, or thunder), and natural objects such as pools, rivers, sticks, and stones. It should be emphasized that this force or power is wholly impersonal, that it is never embodied as such in a supreme god or deity. Gods may possess greater or lesser amounts of power, but they are never the embodiment of power.

An ISP is like some great reservoir of power in which people and things participate to a greater or lesser degree, a force that infuses people and things. It is not good or evil; it is amoral. It exists for no specific purpose; it simply is. (The ISP is a concept not dissimilar to the playwright and social critic George Bernard Shaw's "life force" or the philosopher Henri Bergson's *élan vital.*)

We often use *mana,* a Polynesian term, to refer to the concept of an ISP. (A fast canoe has mana. A successful man has mana. A good crop has mana.) The Algonkian Indians held a concept of ISP called *manitou* (which is often glossed as "great spirit" or "great power"). It is important to remember that an ISP is not worshiped or given offerings. It is similar to a principle or law of nature; it is *not* a supernatural being. It has no personal identity.

The ISP is a catchall concept; it can be used to explain anything remarkable, out of the ordinary, awe-inspiring, or thrilling. As such it is a wonderful explanatory device: it can account for everything.

Religion and Magic

Any introductory overview of the anthropology of religion must, because of past practice in the discipline, treat the subject of magic. Much verbiage has resulted from the effort to distinguish "magic" from "religion," though there are a significant number of investigators who claim that the distinction is spurious and of little use in understanding life-styles.[4] Goode (1964:50–54) has succinctly summarized both the observed similarities and the proposed distinctions between magic and religion.

Although there is good reason to discard the traditional separation of magic and religion in anthropology, an introduction such as this is not the appropriate place in which to do it. The two will be distinguished here.

The distinction I use is whether or not an appeal is made to a supernatural force or deity. This distinction is logically consistent with our definition of religion. Such a basis for distinguishing between magic and religion is far from novel. Burris (1931) used it in claiming that, in Vetter's words (1958:157), religion "invokes a god or personal agency of some sort" while magic does not. And for James Frazer, magic involves "no necessary idea of the supervention of a spiritual or personal agency," whereas religion concerns precisely such a notion (Bohannan 1963:318).

In other words, *magic* deals with the direct manipulation by human beings of cause and effect between what appear to the outside observer to be unrelated events (Keesing and Keesing 1971:305). Magic involves action that is based on the assumed ability of an individual or an object to produce desired effects in nature or in people. The effect is produced directly without the intervention of a third element (see Figure 14.1a). But in *religion* the assumption is that only the deity produces the desired effect; human beings cannot directly do so. An appeal is therefore made to the supernatural to bring about the end that is desired (see Figure 14.1b).[5]

In his monumental work *The Golden Bough*, Frazer divided what he called "sympathetic magic" into two major types in order to explain the rationale underlying beliefs in the effectiveness of magic.[6]

Imitative magic or **homeopathic magic** is the name given by Frazer to the belief that a desired effect can be produced simply by imitating it. This, he said, was based on the "law of similarity," which asserts that "like produces like, or . . . an effect resembles its cause" (p. 415). Sticking pins into a doll in order to kill or injure an enemy, "in the belief that just as the image suffers, so does the man, and that when it perishes he must die" (pp. 416–417), is an example of imitative magic.

Contagious magic refers to actions performed on an object in the belief that they will affect a person formerly in contact with that object. This belief is based on the "law of contagion": "things which have once been in

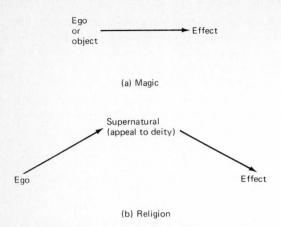

Figure 14.1   Distinction between magic and religion.

contact with each other continue to act on each other at a distance after the physical contact has been severed" (p. 415). "The most familiar example of Contagious Magic," Frazer says (p. 425), "is the magical sympathy which is supposed to exist between a man and any severed portion of his person, as his hair or nails; so that whoever gets possession of human hair or nails may work his will, at any distance, upon the person from whom they were cut."

Magic may be either benevolent or malevolent in intent. Beneficent magic is called *white magic;* a good example of white magic is curing in many nonliterate societies. Malevolent magic is called *black magic* or *sorcery,* and its aim is to bring harm or misfortune to its target. Black magic is usually distinguished from *witchcraft.* Both involve evildoing; but the magician usually acquires esoteric knowledge through some form of training, whereas witches are usually thought to have innate powers, a psychic gift by means of which they can produce effects with a minimum of, or no, paraphernalia. Witches are born, not made.

Lastly, there is a practice called *divination* which is common crossculturally. **Divination** refers to the practice of foretelling future events, obtaining information about past events, or penetrating the unknown through mystical means, such as "reading" tea leaves or palms, auguring, and interpreting the patterns made by sticks and stones that have been cast upon the ground. Sometimes divination involves the help of a supernatural being, and sometimes it does not. (If we want to adhere rigidly to our distinction between magic and religion, then, we have to say that divination can be "magical" in some cases and "religious" in others.)

APPROACHES TO RELIGION

If specific details are considered, many different approaches to the anthropological study of religion may be discerned. But, in general, these can all be subsumed under two headings: the social approach and the cultural approach (this division corresponds to the distinction made earlier between the "social realm" and the "cultural realm"). In the social approach, religion is seen as a reflection of, and support for, the social organization of the group under study (especially its economic and political aspects). In the cultural approach, religion is examined as a conceptual system apart from its social uses.

The Social Approach

It has long been recognized that the ways in which a people order their social relationships are reflected in their concept of the supernatural and in their religious beliefs. This correspondence has led many observers to conclude that religious beliefs provide a legitimating ideology which validates social organization and therefore helps to regulate social behavior.

One of the most influential modern exponents of this sort of theory of religion was Émile Durkheim. In his *Elementary Forms of the Religious Life* (1912, 1961), he suggested that in religion a society is actually setting up shrines to itself and is worshiping itself; in effect, society is the deity. People set up a symbol or totem which represents the group—their social identity—and the veneration of this totem is an acknowledgement of the authority of the group and the necessity for social unity. Through religion people recognize the legitimacy of the social and moral order and therefore help to maintain it.

In short, Durkheim (and Frazer before him) identified the religious realm with the social (primarily political) realm. Bohannan (1963:326) puts it succinctly when, in his discussion of Max Weber on religion, he says, "Indeed, if law or drama are life writ small for purposes of control or comprehension, then religion is life writ large for purposes of control and comprehension."

All approaches that focus on religion in its relation to the social order have as their basis some assumption similar to this. Specifically, they see religion in a double aspect:

Religion mirrors or parallels the social order; i.e., the form a religion takes in any society will be consistent with the social structure—the way people get food, organize labor, provide for decision making and the exercise of authority, and so on.

Religion serves to validate or reinforce this social order, to legitimate it as the proper way to live; and this helps to regulate social activities and contributes to the maintenance of social control.

If there is any validity to this approach, we ought to find some correlation between types of religion and types of societies. In what follows, I compare levels of sociocultural integration ("types of societies") with general characteristics of religion at these stages. And, indeed, there are certain correspondences. But let me offer an important qualification: the "fit" between evolutionary level and religion is not a neat one. Elements of the various religious forms identified below are found throughout the evolutionary scale. What follows, then, is an oversimplification; yet it does serve to introduce you to major variations of religious beliefs.

Band Societies   We previously characterized hunter-gatherers as having loosely structured, flexible groups, as being individualistic and egalitarian, and as having weak leadership of the first-among-equals sort lacking any real coercive authority. According to the social approach, religion should mirror and validate this social order. And in general we find that it does.

Polytheism   Hunter-gatherer religion is usually *polytheistic.* Polytheism is a religion in which many deities exist. In the polytheism of hunter-gatherers, each deity has authority in its own sphere and no deity is supreme. No deity can tell any of the others what to do. There may be a deity for rain, one for curing sickness, one for each species of hunted animal, and so on; but they are all separate and distinct. And the notion of a high god is normally absent. The world of the deities, therefore, reflects the world of human beings, where each person is basically his or her own authority and where there is no formal leadership.

In ritual, too, each person is his or her own religious functionary—i.e., each person maintains his or her own relationship to the supernatural.[7] There are no priests, although there are shamans among hunter-gatherers. There are few regular ceremonies of a group nature, and those that do occur are often spontaneous or concerned with immediate problems (such as the alleviation of a drought or the curing of a particularly threatening disease) or with life-cycle ceremonies. For the most part, however, people maintain their relationship to the deities on an individual and sporadic basis; that is, they perform a rite for a particular deity only when they come into contact with that deity by dealing with the sphere it controls—when hunting its animal, passing its tree, and so forth.

Tribal Societies   Tribal societies, in contrast to band societies, are made up of more tightly knit kin groups with a fair measure of stability (such as clans) and are characterized by leadership that varies from a weak, informal kind similar to that in band societies to stronger, better-defined forms such as chiefship. And religion, once again, mirrors this.

Ancestral veneration   *Ancestral veneration* (or ancestor worship) is the practice of maintaining a relationship with the spirits of deceased ancestors. It occurs most often in segmentary tribes which, you will recall from Chapter 11, have as their basic units (or primary segments) small, local communities. In ancestral veneration, each small group, such as a lineage, venerates its last deceased elder. Predeceased elders tend to lose their individual identities and join "the ancestors" as a body. The ancestors are considered to take a strong interest in the affairs of their living relatives and can influence these affairs for good or ill. In other words, they are considered to be active members of the society. It is not uncommon to find the notion of a distant, creator high god in conjunction with the practice of ancestral veneration. When the notion is present, the high god often has little to do with human beings and their social relations. These are the concern of the particular ancestor (or deity of the kin group; see below). It appears that the notion of a high god grows stronger the closer a society gets to centralized leadership.

Unitheism [8]   This type of religion is found in some tribal societies in which small kin groups, such as lineages, are incorporated into larger kin groups, such as clans, with the larger groups being the central corporate units in the society. In other words, the center of authority and social focus for cooperative labor activities has moved up in the organization of the tribe, and the religious organization changes to comply with this. In this form of religion, each of these larger kin groups maintains a relationship with only one deity (hence the term *unitheism*, meaning one deity per group).

Let us imagine a tribal society divided into four clans: eagle, bear, coyote, and buffalo. Members of the eagle clan recognize the existence of other gods but maintain an active relationship with only one, the god of the eagle clan. Members of the bear clan do not dispute the existence of this god, but they do not maintain a relationship with the eagle god. Instead, their religious activities are directed toward the god of the bear clan. Similarly for all the groups in the society: each has its own god, though the existence of other gods is accepted.

Thus unitheism is a form of polytheism in that *in* the society as a whole there are as many deities as there are constituent kin groups, but it differs from polytheism in that these many deities are not *for* the whole society; for each group does not worship *all* the deities but only the one associated with that group. Similarly, unitheism may be likened to monotheism in that there is just one deity per group, but it is unlike monotheism in that the society as a whole has not just one god but a number of gods.

Multitheism   There is another form of religion that should be mentioned here, but it has not, to my knowledge, been given a name. For expedience, therefore, I call it *multitheism*.[9] This refers to a particular orientation to the supernatural in which the existence of many gods is recognized but only one of them is worshiped by the society. In other words, the society is monotheistic, but its members conceive of the world as polytheistic. The ancient Hebrews exemplify this. The God of the Mountain was the only Hebrew god, but he was only one among many gods in the universe, gods that were worshiped by *other* societies.

State Societies   *Monotheism*   In those societies in which ᴀ state system has developed (and there is therefore a centralized political authority), this is mirrored in religion by *monotheism*, the belief in one deity. More precisely, we may say that in state societies there is a tendency toward monotheism. Since monotheism has obvious advantages for legitimating central authority, it is not surprising that states—and those societies developing toward statedom—favor a monotheistic religion. (The reader should bear in mind, however, the qualifications previously noted in Chapters 4, 6, and 8 concerning monotheism in state societies.)

A question arises at this point: How do we characterize socialist (specifically, communist) societies in terms of religion? Do we say that such societies are "atheistic," that they have entirely replaced religious ideology with a purely "materialistic" political ideology which serves the same validating and integrative functions that religion does in other societies? Can we say that communist societies are unique in that of all known human societies they alone are without "religion"? I don't know; but at least one anthropologist takes the view that these societies are *not* unique. Cohen says (1971:183):

> There are no known political systems without religious legitimation, whether we consider the political empire of the medieval Roman Catholic Church or the contemporary U.S.S.R. In the Soviet Union there is a state religious cult based on the veneration of Lenin; that the rulers of the Soviet Union have replaced Yahweh with Lenin's ghost in their national cult no more warrants a denial of its religious nature than would an assertion that the polytheistic Washo Indians . . . or the ancestor-venerating Tallensi . . . are without religion at all. The cult of Lenin has all the trappings of a national religion, the Soviets' claim to the contrary notwithstanding. There is a huge portrait of Lenin in the altar of the Leningrad Cathedral; Soviet citizens make pilgrimages to Lenin's tomb, a shrine abutting the seat of power in the Kremlin; his prophets periodically reinterpret his words: and the Soviet equation of the charge of anti-Leninism with an assault on the state's integrity differs not a whit from medieval religious inquisitions in Western Europe. These are essential ingredients of a religious cult. Most good Soviet citizens have a portrait of Lenin in their sitting rooms; I do not know if they keep one over their beds.

Melford Spiro (1966:88–89), however, looks at the question from another point of view: what does it matter if society X has "no religion"? He asks, "From what methodological principle does it follow that religion—or, for that matter, anything else—must be universal if it is to be studied comparatively?" He points out that the presence or absence of "religion" in any particular society is really dependent on how we define religion, and that "once we free the word 'religion' from all value judgements, there is reason neither for dismay nor for elation concerning the empirical distribution of religion attendant upon our definition." He suggests that finding "no religion" in one or several societies may have the positive effect of stimulating research.

Revitalization Movements   Many social movements to reinstate old social orders or to create new ones are often cast in a religious frame, further illustrating the linkage between social behavior and religious belief. These movements frequently result from contact with a technologically superior society, usually a colonial power, and arise as part of an attempt by the subordinate group to acquire the socioeconomic equity it feels it has been denied. These movements are called *revitalization* or *nativistic movements* because they attempt to resuscitate patterns of belief and behavior characteristic of a society or group before it came into contact with the dominant society and either changed voluntarily or was forced to alter its sociocultural system. The objective is to change and improve present living conditions by reviving the old ways, including the restoration of belief in traditional gods and the reinstitution of former rituals. Often the overcoming of present conditions and the onset of the new prosperity will be precipitated by the appearance of a forceful leader or messiah (hence, these movements are also known as *messianic* or *millenarian* movements).

The ethnographic literature is filled with cases of revitalization movements, but we need not look far for examples. Many American Indian groups, in recent years as well as in the past, have attempted to revitalize their old lifeways. Some have emphasized militaristic opposition to the dominant society, and others have advocated a quiet return to old beliefs and practices and faith in the gods to restore prosperity. The Black Muslim movement in the United States—a movement that looks to Africa (often an idealized Africa) for inspiration, a sense of unity, and identifying paraphernalia—is another example, one which indicates that nativistic movements are found not only in so-called primitive societies but also among subgroups in a larger society which feel themselves disadvantaged by the majority. The point is, however, that whatever particular cases may be chosen to exemplify revitalization movements, these movements have as their objective the improvement of down-to-earth material conditions but often use religious beliefs and references as a supporting or reinforcing ideology, as a vehicle for expressing their aims.

One type of social movement with pervasive religious overtones is known as the *cargo cult.* Cargo cults in their most spectacular form have been most frequently reported in Melanesia. These movements are usually characterized by the appearance of prophets who exhort the people to abandon their present European goods; break off their relationship with, and reliance on, colonialists; and return to the old beliefs. If they do so, the ancestors will return—often in steamships or airplanes—and bring prosperity with them in the form of abundant cargo of new European-type goods. Cargo cults, as Harris (1975a) notes, are a way of expressing a desire for improved material conditions when other avenues for securing improvement are closed off. (See Worsley 1959 and 1968 for descriptions of cargo cults.)

The Cultural Approach

A more recent approach views religion not only as a reflection of social reality but as a conceptual or ideational system deserving examination in and of itself apart from its social functions. Keesing and Keesing (1971:310) say, "Increasingly, we are perceiving that religions must be viewed as ideational systems, and their overall structure mapped. A focus on the parallels between religious and social has predisposed us to look at those segments of religious experience where the closest parallels occur, at the expense of the rest." They propose that "we look at religions as ideational systems with their own intricate structure of meaning, not [only] as reflections of something more tangible and real."

Claude Lévi-Strauss, the French anthropologist, is a major proponent of such a point of view. He argues that human beings use their creative, intellectual faculties to manipulate symbols in order to deal with the harsh realities of existence, to deal with contrasts such as that between life and death and that between body and soul. Thus Lévi-Strauss's argument is that religion, especially myth and ritual, has "a logic, structure, and richness we had not suspected" (Keesing and Keesing 1971:312) that is worth investigating for its own sake. There is structure in such cultural material that needs to be worked out and that is meaningful aside from social context because it tells us about the human mind and how it operates. Advocates of this position want to take apart belief systems to examine what the parts are and how they fit together into a logical system; and they want to uncover the assumptions or principles that underlie such systems. They hope that by taking apart cultural systems, such as religion, to see how they work, they will learn something about how the machine that built them—the human mind—works.

The cultural approach to religion is still so new, and its methodology so ill defined, that I cannot do more than present its tenets here. It is to be hoped that the advocates of this position will prove adequate to the tasks they have set themselves.

FOOTNOTES

1   Spiro's complete definition of religion is (1966:96) "an institution consisting of culturally patterned interaction with culturally postulated superhuman beings." He goes on to explain (p. 98) that "religion differs from other institutions in that its three component systems have reference to superhuman beings." According to Spiro, the three components of any institution are belief, action, and value systems (see footnote 4 in Chapter 3).

2   Edward Norbeck (1961:11) uses *supernatural* to refer to "all that is not natural, that which is regarded as extraordinary, not of the ordinary world, mysterious, and unexplained or unexplainable in ordinary terms."

3   Although sympathetic to the sentiment behind this suggestion, I am bothered by its dead-end implication. Spiro (1966:90) has observed that "unless he knows,

ostensively, what religion is, how can [an] anthropologist . . . know which, among a possible *n*, observations constitute observations of religious phenomena, rather than of some other phenomenal class, kinship, for example, or politics?"

4 Speaking of the energy and ink expended on distinguishing between "religion" and "magic," Vetter (1958:161–162, 168–169) says, "All this dichotomizing is nothing other than a more or less accurate pin-pointing of what the western, predominantly Christian-Jewish culture has rejected as not being properly or truly 'religious' out of the varied behaviors we find in other cultures that do not have an obviously instrumental or directly practical character. The evidence is unimpeachable that our separation of the magical from the religious is completely meaningless to the people of other cultures. Slight changes in attitudes or beliefs on the part of the practitioners of these magico-religious performances and we would change our classifications of them. These distinctions between magic and religion but mark the changes in our own culture that have been varying the techniques with which we meet particular problems. Whatever smacks a bit too strongly of methods or practices we no longer apply is now rejected and hence classified as 'magic.' . . .

    "Viewed objectively, there can be but one answer to this controversy over religion and magic: objectively there is no difference. As Goode put it, 'Magic and religion are not dichotomies, but represent a continuum, and are distinguished only ideal-typically.' In other words we, here in this culture, are making distinctions that certainly are not made elsewhere. And how does it happen that we are now making a distinction? Very simply: because the scientific method and habits of thought we have developed stand at sharp opposites to both magic and religion in the fundamental concepts of causality implied by both magic and religion, and where we *recognize* this incompatibility with science in any activities, we call them *magic;* where we as yet refuse to admit such incompatibility but insist that factors or forces are involved that do transcend our scientific framework we call it 'religion.'"

5 The phraseology I employ in distinguishing between magic and religion and the illustrative diagrams in Figure 14.1 are based on suggestions made by Yehudi A. Cohen (personal communication).

6 Page references in parentheses are to the excerpt from *The Golden Bough* entitled "Sympathetic Magic" in Lessa and Vogt (1972).

7 Of the Shoshonean Indians of the Great Basin, Steward says (1955:114): "The relationship between human beings and supernatural powers was conceived largely as a matter of individual concern. Every person hoped to acquire a supernatural power or guardian spirit. This power, manifest in the form of animals, plants, clouds, mountains, and other natural phenomena, came to him in dreams and gave him special abilities, such as gambling luck, hunting skill, endurance, and others of benefit to himself alone."

8 The term *unitheism* was coined by Yehudi A. Cohen and will be discussed by him in detail in a forthcoming publication. The term is used here with his permission. I am indebted to Professor Cohen for many suggestions which I have incorporated into this chapter; but he is, of course, in no way responsible for any shortcomings in my presentation.

9 The proliferation of descriptive terms and definitions has rightly been criticized

by many anthropologists. Bohannan (1963:328) says, "At best, all are *a priori* matrices in terms of which data can be viewed only with a greater or lesser discomfiture. At worst, they are totally effective blinders." Elsewhere (p. 326), he optimistically remarks, "We have finally emerged from terminological darkness to a situation in which the anthropological categories of primitive religion—animism, animatism, fetishism, totemism, and all the rest—can be cast aside. Anthropologists have at last discovered a means to translate the religious ideas of people without the curtain of *isms* that has so often hidden them in the past. That method is simple: first one must concentrate on the deed (ritual) in order to understand the explanation of the deed in terms given it by the practitioner (creed); one must set ritual and creed into their larger cultural context. Finally, one must compare rituals and creeds among societies—both in their substantive statements and in their symbolic reflections of the rest of culture."

Though I of course do not disagree with Bohannan, I think that the introduction of this little "ism" for expository purposes is excusable.

References

Adams, R. McC. 1966. *The Evolution of Urban Society: Early Mesopotamia and Prehispanic Mexico.* Chicago: Aldine.

Bacon, E. E. 1954. "Types of Pastoral Nomadism in Central and Southwest Asia," *Southwestern Journal of Anthropology,* **10**:44–68.

Balikci, A. 1970. *The Netsilik Eskimo.* Garden City, N.Y.: Natural History Press (Doubleday).

Barnouw, V. 1973. *Culture and Personality* (rev. ed.). Homewood, Ill.: Dorsey Press.

———. 1975. *An Introduction to Anthropology: Ethnology* (rev. ed.). Homewood, Ill.: Dorsey Press.

Barth, F. 1956. "Ecologic Relationships of Ethnic Groups in Swat, North Pakistan," *American Anthropologist,* **58**:1079–1089.

———. 1959–1960. "The Land Use Patterns of Migratory Tribes of South Persia," *Norsk Geografisk Tidsskrift,* **17**:2–11.

———. 1961. *Nomads of South Persia: The Basseri Tribe of the Khamseh Confederacy.* Boston: Little, Brown.

————. 1964. "Competition and Symbiosis in North East Baluchistan, *Folk*, **6**:15– 22.

Bates, D. G. 1971. "The Role of the State in Peasant-Nomad Mutualism," *Anthropological Quarterly*, **44**:109–131.

————. 1972. "Differential Access to Pasture in a Nomadic Society: The Yoruk of South-eastern Turkey," *Journal of Asian and African Studies*, **7**:48–59.

Beals, A. R. 1962. *Gopalpur: A South Indian Village*. New York: Holt, Rinehart and Winston.

————. 1974. *Village Life in South India: Cultural Design and Environmental Variation*. Chicago: Aldine.

Beals, R. L., and H. Hoijer. 1965. *An Introduction to Anthropology* (3d ed.). New York: Macmillan.

———— and ————. 1971. *An Introduction to Anthropology* (4th ed.) New York: Macmillan.

Beattie, J. 1964. *Other Cultures: Aims, Methods, and Achievements in Social Anthropology*. New York: Free Press.

Bee, R. L. 1974. *Patterns and Processes: An Introduction to Anthropological Strategies for Study of Sociocultural Change*. New York: Free Press.

Bennett, J. W. 1971. *Northern Plainsmen: Adaptive Strategy and Agrarian Life*. Chicago: Aldine.

Bernard, H. R. (ed.) 1975. *The Human Way: Readings in Anthropology*. New York: Macmillan.

Bicchieri, M. G. 1972. *Hunters and Gatherers Today*. New York: Holt, Rinehart and Winston.

Bock, P. K. 1969. *Modern Cultural Anthropology*. New York: Knopf.

Bohannan, P. 1963. *Social Anthropology*. New York: Holt, Rinehart and Winston.

————. 1964. *Africa and Africans*. Garden City, N.Y.: Natural History Press (Doubleday).

Browman, D. L. 1974. "Pastoral Nomadism in the Andes," *Current Anthropology*, **15**:188–196.

Brown J. K. 1963. "A Cross-Cultural Study of Female Initiation Rites," *American Anthropologist*, **65**:837–853.

Burris, E. 1931. *Taboo, Magic and Spirits*. New York: Macmillan.

Burton, R. V., and J. W. M. Whiting. 1961. "The Absent Father and Cross-Sex Identity," *Merrill-Palmer Quarterly of Behavior and Development*, **7**:85–95.

Carneiro, R. L. 1968. "The Transition from Hunting to Horticulture in the Amazon Basin," in *Proceedings of the Eighth International Congress of Anthropological and Ethnological Sciences*. (Reprinted in Cohen 1974:157–166.)

————. 1970. "A Theory of the Origin of the State," *Science*, **169**:733–738.

Chagnon, N. A. 1968. *Yanomamö: The Fierce People*. New York: Holt, Rinehart and Winston.

Chance, N. A. 1966. *The Eskimo of North Alaska*. New York: Holt, Rinehart and Winston.

Cohen, Y. A. 1964a. "The Establishment of Identity in a Social Nexus: The Special Case of Initiation Ceremonies and Their Relation to Value and Legal Systems," *American Anthropologist*, **66**:529–552.

————. 1964b. *The Transition from Childhood to Adolescence: Cross-Cultural Studies of Initiation Ceremonies, Legal Systems, and Incest Taboos*. Chicago: Aldine.

————. 1966. "On Alternative Views of the Individual in Culture-and-Personality Studies," *American Anthropologist* **68**:355–361.

————. (ed.) 1968. *Man in Adaptation: The Cultural Present* (1st ed.) Chicago: Aldine.

————. (ed.) 1971. *Man in Adaptation: The Institutional Framework.* Chicago: Aldine.

————. (ed.) 1974. *Man in Adaptation: The Cultural Present* (rev. ed.). Chicago: Aldine.

Cole, D. P. 1975. *Nomads of the Nomads: The Āl Murrah Bedouin of the Empty Quarter.* Chicago: Aldine.

Collins, J. J. 1975. *Anthropology: Culture, Society, and Evolution.* Englewood Cliffs, N.J.: Prentice-Hall.

Dalton, G. 1968 (orig. 1961). "Economic Theory and Primitive Society," in E. E. Le Clair and H. K. Schneider (eds.), *Economic Anthropology.* New York: Holt, Rinehart and Winston.

Damas, D. (ed.) 1969. *Band Societies.* Ottawa: National Museums of Canada, Bulletin No. 228.

Demos, J. 1970. *A Little Commonwealth: Family Life in Plymouth Colony.* New York: Oxford University Press.

Dentan, R. K. 1968. *The Semai: A Nonviolent People of Malaya.* New York: Holt, Rinehart and Winston.

Diaz, M. N. 1966. *Tonalá: Conservatism, Responsibility, and Authority in a Mexican Town.* Berkeley: University of California Press.

Downs, J. F. 1966. *The Two Worlds of the Washo: An Indian Tribe of California and Nevada.* New York: Holt, Rinehart and Winston.

Dozier, E. L. 1965. *Hano: A Tewa Indian Community in Arizona.* New York: Holt, Rinehart and Winston.

Drucker, P. 1955. *Indians of the Northwest Coast.* Garden City, N.Y.: Natural History Press.

Durkheim, E. 1961 (orig. 1912). *The Elementary Forms of the Religious Life.* New York: Collier.

Ekvall, R. B. 1968. *Fields on the Hoof: Nexus of Tibetan Nomadic Pastoralism.* New York: Holt, Rinehart and Winston.

Evans-Pritchard, E. E. 1951. *Kinship and Marriage among the Nuer.* Oxford: Clarendon Press.

Fortes, M. 1953. "The Structure of Unilineal Descent Groups," *American Anthropologist,* **55**:17–41.

Fox, R. 1967. *Kinship and Marriage: An Anthropological Perspective.* Baltimore; Penguin Books.

Frake, C. O. 1964. "A Structural Description of Subanum 'Religious Behavior,'" in W. H. Goodenough (ed.), *Explorations in Cultural Anthropology.* New York: McGraw-Hill.

Frazer, J. G. 1922. *The Golden Bough* (abridged). London: Macmillan.

Fried, M. H. 1967. *The Evolution of Political Society: An Essay in Political Anthropology.* New York: Random House.

————. 1968. "State: The Institution," *International Encyclopedia of the Social Sciences,* **15**:143–150.

Gade, D. W. 1969. "The Llama, Alpaca, and Vicuna: Fact vs. Fiction," *Journal of Geography,* **68**:339–343.

Gans, H. J. 1965 (orig. 1962). *The Urban Villagers: Group and Class in the Life of Italian-Americans.* New York: Free Press.

Garretson, L. R. 1976. *American Culture: An Anthropological Perspective.* Dubuque, Iowa: William C. Brown.

Geertz, C. 1971 (orig. 1963). *Agricultural Involution: The Processes of Ecological Change in Indonesia.* Berkeley: University of California Press.

Gibson, G. D. 1952. *The Social Organization of the Southwestern Bantu.* Doctoral thesis, University of Chicago.

Goode, W. J. 1964 (orig. 1951). *Religion among the Primitives.* New York: Free Press.

Goodenough, W. H. 1951. *Property, Kin, and Community on Truk.* Yale University Publications in Anthropology 46. (Reprinted by Archon Books, Hamden, Conn., 1966.)

———. 1961. "Comments on Cultural Evolution," *Daedalus,* **9**:521–528.

———. 1965. "Rethinking 'Status' and 'Role,'" in M. Banton (ed.), *The Relevance of Models for Social Anthropology.* London: Tavistock.

———. 1968. *Description and Comparison in Cultural Anthropology.* Chicago: Aldine.

———. 1969. "Frontiers of Cultural Anthropology," *Proceedings of the American Philosophical Society,* **113**:329–335.

———. 1971. "Culture, Language, and Society." Reading, Mass.: Addison-Wesley Modular Publications in Anthropology, No. 7.

Gordon, T. 1970. *P.E.T.: Parent Effectiveness Training.* New York: Wyden.

Gough, E. K. 1959. "The Nayars and the Definition of Marriage," *Journal of the Royal Anthropological Institute,* **89**:23–34.

———. 1961. "Nayar: Central Kerala" and "Nayar: North Kerala," in D. M. Schneider and E. K. Gough (eds.), *Matrilineal Kinship.* Berkeley: University of California Press.

Gould, R. A. (ed.) 1973. *Man's Many Ways: The Natural History Reader in Anthropology.* New York: Harper and Row.

Gulliver, P. H. 1953. "The Age-Set Organization of the Jie Tribe," *Journal of the Royal Anthropological Institute,* **84**:147–168.

———. 1958. "The Turkana Age Organization," *American Anthropologist,* **60**:900–922.

———. 1968. "Age Differentiation," *International Encyclopedia of the Social Sciences,* **1**:157–162.

Hammond, P. B. 1971. *An Introduction to Cultural and Social Anthropology.* New York: Macmillan.

———. 1975. *Cultural and Social Anthropology: Introductory Readings in Ethnology* (2d ed.). New York: Macmillan.

Harner, M. J. 1973 (orig. 1972). *The Jívaro: People of the Sacred Waterfall.* Garden City, N.Y.: Doubleday (Anchor).

Harris, M. 1968. *The Rise of Anthropological Theory.* New York: Thomas Y. Crowell.

———. 1975a. (orig. 1974). *Cows, Pigs, Wars and Witches: The Riddles of Culture.* New York: Vintage.

———. 1975b. *Culture, People, Nature: An Introduction to General Anthropology* (2d ed.). New York: Thomas Y. Crowell.

Hart, C. W. M., and A. R. Pilling. 1960. *The Tiwi of North Australia.* New York: Holt, Rinehart and Winston.

Harvey, E. B. 1975. *Industrial Society: Structures, Roles, Relations.* Homewood, Ill.: Dorsey Press.

Haviland, W. A. 1975. *Cultural Anthropology.* New York: Holt, Rinehart and Winston.

Heath, D. B. 1975. "Whatever Happened to 'Culture Change'?" *Reviews in Anthropology,* **2**:210–215.

Heider, K. G. 1970. *The Dugum Dani: A Papuan Culture in the Highlands of West New Guinea.* Viking Fund Publications in Anthropology, No. 49. Chicago: Aldine.

Hoebel, E. A. 1972. *Anthropology: The Study of Man.* New York: McGraw-Hill.

Holmberg, A. R. 1969 (orig. 1950). *Nomads of the Long Bow: The Siriono of Eastern Bolivia.* Garden City, N.Y.: Natural History Press.

Holmes, L. D. 1974. *Samoan Village.* New York: Holt, Rinehart and Winston.

Hostetler, J. A. 1968. *Amish Society.* Baltimore: John Hopkins.

Hostetler, J. A., and G. E. Huntington. 1967. *The Hutterites in North America.* New York: Holt, Rinehart and Winston.

———. 1971. *Children in Amish Society: Socialization and Community Education.* New York: Holt, Rinehart and Winston.

Hsu, C. 1965. *Ancient China in Transition: An Analysis of Social Mobility, 722–222 B.C.* Stanford: Stanford University Press.

Hughes, C. C. (ed.) 1976. *Custom-Made: Introductory Readings for Cultural Anthropology* (2d ed.). Chicago: Rand McNally.

Hunter, D. E., and P. Whitten (eds.). 1975. *Anthropology: Contemporary Perspectives.* Boston: Little, Brown.

Johnson, D. L. 1969. *The Nature of Nomadism.* Chicago: University of Chicago Press.

Keesing, R. M. 1967. "Statistical Models and Decision Models of Social Structure: A Kwaio Case," *Ethnology,* **6**:1–16.

———. 1973. "Toward a Model of Role Analysis," in R. Naroll and R. Cohen (eds.), *A Handbook of Method in Cultural Anthropology.* New York: Columbia University Press.

Keesing, R. M., and F. M. Keesing. 1971. *New Perspectives in Cultural Anthropology.* New York: Holt, Rinehart and Winston.

Keiser, R. L. 1969. *The Vice Lords: Warriors of the Streets.* New York: Holt, Rinehart and Winston.

Klima, G. J. 1970. *The Barabaig: East African Cattle-Herders.* New York: Holt, Rinehart and Winston.

Kottak, C. P. 1974. *Anthropology: The Exploration of Human Diversity.* New York: Random House.

Kroeber, A. L., and C. Kluckhohn. 1952. *Culture: A Critical Review of Concepts and Definitions.* Cambridge, Mass.: Harvard University Press. (Paperback edition published by Vintage, New York.)

Kroeber, A. L., et al. 1953. *Anthropology Today.* Chicago: University of Chicago Press.

Langdon, G. D. 1966. *Pilgrim Colony: A History of New Plymouth, 1620–1691.* New Haven: Yale University Press.

Lattimore, O. 1963. "Chingis Khan and the Mongol Conquests," *Scientific American,* **209**(2):54–68.

Lee, R. B. 1969. "!Kung Bushman Subsistence: An Input-Output Analysis," in D. Damas (ed.), *Ecological Essays.* Ottawa: National Museums of Canada, Bulletin No. 230.

Lee, R. B., and I. DeVore (eds.). 1968. *Man the Hunter.* Chicago: Aldine.

Leggesse, A. 1973. *Gada: Three Approaches to the Study of African Society.* New York: Free Press.

Lessa, W. A., and E. Z. Vogt (eds.). 1972. *Reader in Comparative Religion: An Anthropological Approach* (3d ed.). New York: Harper and Row.

Levine, N. D., et al. 1975. *Human Ecology.* North Scituate, Mass.: Duxbury Press.

LeVine, R. A. 1973. *Culture, Behavior, and Personality.* Chicago: Aldine. (British rights held by Hutchinson Publishing Group, London.)

Lévi-Strauss, C. 1969 (orig. 1949). *The Elementary Structures of Kinship* (J. H. Bell, J. R. von Sturmer, and R. Needham, trans.). Boston: Beacon Press.

Lewis, O. 1960. *Tepoztlan: Village in Mexico.* New York: Holt, Rinehart and Winston.

Lindesmith, A. R., A. L. Strauss, and N. K. Denzin. 1975. *Social Psychology* (4th ed.). Hinsdale, Ill.: Dryden Press.

Linton, R. 1937. "One Hundred Per Cent American," *The American Mercury,* **40**:427–449. (Reprinted in J. D. Jennings and E. A. Hoebel, eds., *Readings in Anthropology,* 2d ed. New York: McGraw-Hill, 1966.)

Little, K. 1957. "The Role of Voluntary Associations in West African Urbanization," *American Anthropologist,* **59**:579–594.

Löffler, R. 1971. "The Representative Mediator and the New Peasant," *American Anthropologist,* **73**:1077–1091.

Lynch, T. F. 1971. "Preceramic Transhumance in the Callejon de Huaylas, Peru," *American Antiquity,* **36**:139–148.

McGee, R. 1975. *Points of Departure: Basic Concepts in Sociology* (2d ed.). Hinsdale, Ill.: Dryden Press.

Mandelbaum, D. G., G. W. Lasker, and E. M. Albert (eds.). 1967. *The Teaching of Anthropology* (abridged ed.). Berkeley: University of California Press.

Manicas, P. T. 1974. *The Death of the State.* New York: Putnam.

Marett, R. R. 1909. *The Threshold of Religion.* London: Methuen.

———. 1912. *Anthropology.* New York: Henry Holt.

Mead, M. 1963. "Socialization and Enculturation," *Current Anthropology,* **4**:184–188.

———. 1966 (orig. 1963). "Anthropology and an Education for the Future," in J. D. Jennings and E. A. Hoebel (eds.), *Readings in Anthropology* (2d ed.). New York: McGraw-Hill.

Meggers, B. J. 1971. *Amazonia: Man and Culture in a Counterfeit Paradise.* Chicago: Aldine.

Middleton, J. 1965. *The Lugbara of Uganda.* New York: Holt, Rinehart and Winston.

Miner, H. 1956. "Body Ritual among the Nacirema," *American Anthropologist,* **58**:503–507.

Morgan, E. S. 1966. *The Puritan Family: Religious and Domestic Relations in Seventeenth-Century New England.* New York: Harper Torchbooks.

Murdock, G. P. 1947. "Bifurcate Merging, a Test of Five Theories, *American Anthropologist,* **49**:56–68.

———. 1949. *Social Structure.* New York: Free Press.

———. 1959. *Africa: Its People and Their Culture History,* New York: McGraw-Hill.

Nakane, C. 1970. *Japanese Society.* Berkeley: University of California Press.

Nance, J. 1975. *The Gentle Tasaday: A Stone Age People in the Philippine Rain Forest.* New York: Harcourt Brace Jovanovich.

Netting, R. McC.1971. "The Ecological Approach in Cultural Study." Reading, Mass.: Addison-Wesley Modular Publication 6.

Newman, P. L. 1965. *Knowing the Gururumba.* New York: Holt, Rinehart and Winston.

Norbeck, E. 1961. *Religion in Primitive Society.* New York: Harper and Row.

————. 1965. *Changing Japan.* New York: Holt, Rinehart and Winston.

————, D. E. Walker, and M. Cohen. 1962. "The Interpretation of Data: Puberty Rites," *American Anthropologist,* **64**:463–485.

Ohnuki-Tierney, E. 1974. *The Ainu of the Northwest Coast of Sakhalin.* New York: Holt, Rinehart and Winston.

Oswalt, W. H. 1972. *Other Peoples, Other Customs: World Ethnography and Its History.* New York: Holt, Rinehart and Winston.

Otterbein, K. F. 1963. "Marquesan Polyandry," *Marriage and Family Living,* **25**:155–159.

————. 1972. *Comparative Cultural Analysis.* New York: Holt, Rinehart and Winston.

Paige, K. E., and J. M. Paige. 1973. "The Politics of Birth Practices: A Strategic Analysis," *American Sociological Review,* **38**:663–677.

Pearson, R. 1974. *Introduction to Anthropology.* New York: Holt, Rinehart and Winston.

Pehrson, R. N. 1966. *The Social Organization of the Marri Baluch* (compiled by F. Barth). Viking Fund Publications in Anthropology, No. 43. Chicago: Aldine.

Poggie, J. J., G. H. Pelto, and P. J. Pelto (eds.). 1976. *The Evolution of Human Adaptations: Readings in Anthropology.* New York: Macmillan.

Polanyi, K. 1959. "Anthropology and Economic Theory," in M. Fried (ed.), *Readings in Anthropology* (vol. 2.). New York: Thomas Y. Crowell.

Powell, S. C. 1970 (orig. 1963). *Puritan Village: The Formation of a New England Town.* Middletown, Conn.: Wesleyan University Press.

R. A. I. (Royal Anthropological Institute of Great Britain and Ireland). 1956. *Notes and Queries on Anthropology* (6th edition). London: Routledge and Kegan Paul.

Richards, C. E. 1972. *Man in Perspective: An Introduction to Cultural Anthropology.* New York: Random House.

Rubel, P. G. 1969. "Herd Composition and Social Structure: On Building Models of Nomadic Pastoral Societies," *Man,* **4**:268–273.

Sahlins, M. D. 1960. "Evolution: Specific and General," in M. D. Sahlins and E. R. Service (eds.), *Evolution and Culture.* Ann Arbor: University of Michigan Press.

————. 1961. "The Segmentary Lineage: An Organization of Predatory Expansion," *American Anthropologist,* **63**:322–343.

————. 1965. "On the Sociology of Primitive Exchange," in M. Banton (ed.), *The Relevance of Models for Social Anthropology.* London: Tavistock.

————. 1968. *Tribesmen.* Englewood Cliffs, N.J.: Prentice-Hall.

Salzman, P. C. 1967. "Political Organization among Nomadic People," *Proceedings of the American Philosophical Society,* **111**:115–131.

————. 1971. "Movement and Resource Extraction among Pastoral Nomads: The Case of the Shah Nawaze Baluch," *Anthropological Quarterly,* **44**:185–197.

Sangree, W. H. 1965. "The Bantu Tiriki of Western Kenya," in J. A. Gibbs, Jr. (ed.), *Peoples of Africa.* New York: Holt, Rinehart and Winston. (Excerpted from W. H. Sangree. 1966. *Age, Prayer and Politics in Tiriki, Kenya.* London: Oxford University Press for the East African Institute of Social Research.)

Scheffler, H. W. 1966. "Ancestor Worship in Anthropology: or, Observations on Descent and Descent Groups," *Current Anthropology,* 7:541–551.

Schneider, E. V. 1969 (orig. 1957). *Industrial Society: The Social Relations and the Community* (2d ed.). New York: McGraw-Hill.

Schneider, H. K. 1957. "The Subsistence Role of Cattle among the Pakot and in East Africa." *American Anthropologist,* **59**:278–300.

Schusky, E. L. 1965. *Manual for Kinship Analysis.* New York: Holt, Rinehart and Winston.

———. 1975. *The Study of Cultural Anthropology.* New York: Holt, Rinehart and Winston.

Service, E. R. 1962. *Primitive Social Organization: An Evolutionary Perspective.* New York: Random House.

———. 1966. *The Hunters.* Englewood Cliffs, N.J.: Prentice-Hall.

———. 1971. *Profiles in Ethnology* (rev. ed.). New York: Harper and Row.

Shapiro, W. 1967. "Relational Affiliation in 'Unilineal' Descent Systems," *Man,* vol. 2.

Smith, T. C. 1959. *The Agrarian Origins of Modern Japan.* Stanford: Stanford University Press.

Spain, D. H. (ed.) 1975. *The Human Experience: Readings in Sociocultural Anthropology.* Homewood, Ill.: Dorsey Press.

Spencer, R. F. 1959. *The North Alaskan Eskimo: A Study in Ecology and Society.* Washington, D.C.: Bureau of American Ethnology, Bulletin No. 171.

Spencer, R. F., J. D. Jennings, et al. 1965. *The Native Americans.* New York: Harper and Row.

Spiro, M. E. 1966. "Religion: Problems of Definition and Explanation," in M. Banton (ed.), *Anthropological Approaches to the Study of Religion.* London: Tavistock.

Spooner, B. J. 1972. "The Status of Nomadism as a Cultural Phenomenon in the Middle East," *Journal of Asian and African Studies,* 7:122–131.

———. 1973. "The Cultural Ecology of Pastoral Nomads." Reading, Mass. Addison-Wesley Modular Publications in Anthropology, No. 45.

Spradley, J. P., and D. W. McCurdy. 1972. *The Cultural Experience: Ethnography in Complex Society.* Chicago: Science Research Associates.

——— and ———. 1974. *Conformity and Conflict: Readings in Cultural Anthropology* (2d ed.). Boston: Little, Brown.

——— and ———. 1975. *Anthropology: The Cultural Perspective.* New York: Wiley.

———, and B. J. Mann. 1975. *The Cocktail Waitress: Women's Work in a Man's World.* New York: Wiley.

———, and M. A. Rynkiewich (eds.). 1975. *The Nacirema: Readings on American Culture.* Boston: Little, Brown.

Stephens, W. N. 1961. "A Cross-Cultural Study of Menstrual Taboos," *Genetic Psychology Monographs,* **64**:385–416.

————. 1962. *The Oedipus Complex: Cross-Cultural Evidence.* Glencoe, Ill.: Free Press.

Steward, J. H. 1938. *Basin-Plateau Aboriginal Socio-Political Groups.* Washington, D.C.: Bureau of American Ethnology, Bulletin No. 120.

————. 1955. *Theory of Culture Change: The Methodology of Multilinear Evolution.* Urbana: University of Illinois Press.

Stewart, E. W. 1973. *Evolving Life Styles: An Introduction to Cultural Anthropology.* New York: McGraw-Hill.

Swartz, M. J., and D. K. Jordan. 1976. *Anthropology: Perspective on Humanity.* New York: Wiley.

Turnbull, C. M. 1961. *The Forest People: A Study of the Pygmies of the Congo.* New York: Simon and Schuster (Clarion).

Taylor, R. B. 1973. *Introduction to Cultural Anthropology.* Boston: Allyn and Bacon.

————. 1976. *Cultural Ways* (2d ed.). Boston: Allyn and Bacon.

Tylor, E. B. 1871. *Primitive Culture.* London: John Murray.

Van Gennep, A. 1960 (orig. 1908). *The Rites of Passage.* Chicago: University of Chicago Press.

Vanstone, J. W. 1974. *Athapascan Adaptations: Hunters and Fishermen of the Subarctic Forests.* Chicago: Aldine.

Verrill, A. H., and R. Verrill. 1967 (orig. 1953). *America's Ancient Civilizations.* New York: Capricorn Books.

Vetter, G. B. 1958. *Magic and Religion.* New York: Philosophical Library.

Vivelo, F. R. 1977. *The Herero of Western Botswana: Aspects of Change in a Group of Bantu-Speaking Cattle Herders.* American Ethnological Society, Monograph No. 61. St. Paul, Minn.: West.

Von Hagen, V. W. 1960. *World of the Maya.* New York: New American Library.

————. 1961a (orig. 1958). *The Aztec: Man and Tribe.* New York: New American Library.

————. 1961b (orig. 1957). *Realm of the Incas.* New York:New American Library.

Wallace, A. F. C. 1966. *Religion: An Anthropological View.* New York: Random House.

Watson, R. A., and P. J. Watson. 1969. *Man and Nature: An Anthropological Essay in Human Ecology.* New York: Harcourt Brace Jovanovich.

Webster, S. 1973. "Native Pastoralism in the South Andes," *Ethnology,* **12**:115–133.

Weiss, G. 1973. "A Scientific Concept of Culture," *American Anthropologist,* **75**:1376–1413.

White, L. A. 1962. *The Pueblo of Sia, New Mexico.* Washington, D.C.: Bureau of American Ethnology.

Whiting, J. W. M. 1961. "Socialization Process and Personality," in F. L. K. Hsu (ed.), *Psychological Anthropology.* Homewood, Ill.: Dorsey Press.

————. 1964. "Effects of Climate on Certain Cultural Practices," in W. H. Goodenough (ed.), *Explorations in Cultural Anthropology.* New York: McGraw-Hill.

————, R. Kluckhohn, and A. Anthony. 1958. "The Function of Male Initiation Ceremonies at Puberty," in E. E. Maccoby, T. M. Newcombe, and E. L. Hartley (eds.), *Readings in Social Psychology* (3d ed.). New York: Holt, Rinehart and Winston.

Williams, T. R. 1972. *Introduction to Socialization: Human Culture Transmitted.* St. Louis: C. V. Mosby.

Wolf, E. R. 1966. *Peasants.* Englewood Cliffs, N.J.: Prentice-Hall.

Worsley, P. M. 1959. "Cargo Cults," *Scientific American,* **200**:117–128.

———. 1968. *The Trumpet Shall Sound: A Study of "Cargo" Cults in Melanesia.* New York: Schocken.

Young, F. W. 1962. "The Function of Male Initiation Ceremonies: A Cross-Cultural Test of an Alternative Hypothesis," *American Journal of Sociology,* **67**:379–396.

———. 1965a. *Initiation Ceremonies: A Cross-Cultural Study of Status Dramatization.* Indianapolis: Bobbs-Merrill.

———. 1965b. "Menstrual Taboos and Social Rigidity," *Ethnology,* **4**:225–241.

Appendix 1

Summary Table

Summary Table

	?	5 million yrs. BP	9,000 to 11,000 yrs. BP	5,000 to 6,000 yrs. BP	200 yrs. BP
Adaptive strategy		Hunting-gathering	Horticulture Pastoral nomadism	Agriculture	Industrialism
			Increase in sophistication of technology; growing reliance on more powerful sources of energy; increase in complexity or organization of labor		
Political organization		Bands	Tribes	States (but often in conjunction with notable local autonomy)	States
			Increase in complexity of political institutions, in heterogeneity of population, in inequality, and in formal criteria for leadership		
Social control and resolution of conflicts		Based on interpersonal and small-group kin ties. Feuding.	Based on larger-order kin ties. Kin-phrased authority. Emergence of nonkin formal institutions (such as courts). Feuding and warfare.	Decreased reference to kin in favor of formal institutions. Warfare.	Formal, impersonal institutions. Warfare.
			Increased reliance on extrapersonal, formal mechanisms of control and increase of coercive authority		
Economic organization		Sexual division of labor. Reciprocity. Uniformity of consumption.	Sexual division of labor; some specialization. Reciprocity and redistribution (with peripheral markets). Mostly uniform consumption	Specialization of labor. Market exchange, redistribution, some reciprocity. Differential patterns of consumption.	Specialization of labor. Primarily market exchange; secondarily, redistribution. Conspicuous consumption.
			Increase in diversity of occupations, in amounts produced, distributed, and consumed, and in importance of trade based on a market principle		

Kinship and descent	Eskimo terminology. Cognatic descent. Large-scale kin groups generally absent.	Hawaiian, Iroquoian, Sudanese terminologies. Unilineal descent. Larger-order kin groups (such as lineages and clans).	Hawaiian, Iroquoian, Sudanese terminologies. Unilineal descent. Large-order kin groups present, but their influence decreasing.	Eskimo terminology. Cognatic descent. Large-scale kin groups absent.
	Kinship and descent are most important for ordering social relations in tribal societies, less important in bands, least important in states.			
Marriage	Mainly complex systems (Australian Aborigines a conspicuous exception). Both polygamy and monogamy, with latter predominant.	Mainly elementary systems. Polygamy usually preferred, though monogamous marriages occur frequently.	Elementary systems giving way to complex systems. Polygamy giving way to monogamy.	Complex systems. Monogamy only.
Family	Nuclear family groups are the rule; some complex.	Complex family groups.	Complex family groups.	Nuclear family groups.
Religion	Polytheism. Absence of a high god.	Polytheism, unitheism, multitheism, ancestral veneration. High god may be present but usually distant and unconcerned with mundane affairs.	Tendency toward monotheism, but still strong elements of polytheism, unitheism, ancestral veneration. High god usually present.	Monotheistic ideal.
	Increasing reliance on religious intermediaries or religious specialization; increase in complexity of religious ritual; growing bureaucratization of religious organization; more explicit theology			

Evaluating Incest Theories

"The tabu on the mating of brother and sister occurs everywhere, as does the tabu on mating between parent and child"—so state the authors of a recent introductory text in cultural anthropology (Hoebel and Frost 1976:172). *Because virtually every introductory text makes a similar assertion, because these texts devote a significant amount of space to "the incest taboo" and the influential role incest theory has played in anthropological thinking, and because the central importance of the subject rests on this assertion of universality, the following appendix is provided for the student. Among other things, it calls into serious question the claim that incest taboos are found everywhere.*

Since at least 1865 (with the publication of McLennan's *Primitive Marriage*) incest taboos have been a major focus of scholarly inquiry; and the study of incest taboos has had a general heuristic effect on theory within the social sciences, generating much debate about such overarching concerns as the emergence of culture and the origin of the human family, as well as problems of the origin, persistence, functions, and possible universality of the taboo itself. To put it mildly, interest in the topic of incest has always been lively.

It is my intention here to offer students a general framework for the discussion and evaluation of incest theories.[1] For far too long the literature on the subject has suffered from an overall lack of terminological as well as conceptual clarity: incest prohibitions have been confused with rules of exogamy, and marriage has been confused with mating. In short, the meaning of words and concepts used in the literature on incest has been poorly specified, and as a result there has been much confusion among investigators over just what it is they are talking about.[2] By focusing on such issues I hope not so much to clear up the problems definitively as to encourage new students to refine their predecessors' concepts about the study of these human sexual prohibitions.

TYPOLOGY OF ARGUMENTS

Before beginning, I first present a very brief review of the major types of arguments, each type followed by some examples of authors (whose works are listed in the accompanying bibliography) who I feel utilize to some degree that type of argument. (This typology owes much to the suggestions found in Aberle et al. 1963.) Not all theorists who employ a particular argument are listed, and any writer may use more than one type of argument in his or her interpretation. Consequently, some authors are listed more than once; others who might have been listed in various categories may only appear once. I am interested not in presenting a definitive classification but in providing some kind of general summary as a guide for anyone who wants to pursue the subject further.

Inbreeding

This argument asserts that close inbreeding is biologically deleterious: inbreeding would lead eventually to the extinction of its practitioners, while those who avoided inbreeding would survive to propagate themselves. After Westermarck, this idea seems to have died down for about thirty years until it was revived by Aberle et al. in 1963. It appears now to have been pretty well put to rest by Livingstone in 1969. The main reason for rejecting this argument is that inbreeding is not inherently deleterious. It merely brings out latent (recessive) traits in the breeding population, and these traits may be benficial or neutral as well as dangerous.

Proponents include: Aberle et al., Frazer, Morgan, Muller, and Westermarck.

Natural Aversion

This argument was first propounded by Westermarck. It holds that cosocialized, coresident children are naturally averse to sexual relations with one another in adulthood. The mechanism that causes or triggers this aversion is difficult to pin down.

Proponents include: Fox, Shepher, Talmon, Westermarck, Wolf, and Young.

Ecology; Demography

Next we have M. K. Slater's theory that intrafamilial mating, especially between parents and offspring, was unlikely because the life-span of "early man" was so short. By the time the offspring were old enough to mate with their parents, the latter probably would be dead. Mating with siblings would also have been unlikely, owing to spacing of births. But this reconstruction seems irrelevant. Even if "early man" was prevented from such mating, what was to prevent it when conditions changed? Wallis's hypothesis (suggested nine years before Slater's) argues from a similar demographic base and expands the argument to hold that the internal stability of the family is promoted by family exogamy.

Proponents include: M. K. Slater and Wallis.

Role Learning and Family Stability

Aberle et al. separate role learning and family stability into two types of theories, but here they are considered together. Interpretations based on these considerations are the ones that are most widely employed. The argument they offer is predicated in part on the nature of human beings, who require a long period of nurturance and learning before they are mature enough to function on their own. In general, and to simplify, we may represent proponents of such arguments as asserting something like the following: Socialization necessarily involves regulation of sexual activity to facilitate role learning; and if roles are confused by allowing unrestricted erotic relations within the family, parental authority will be undermined, the family will become disorganized, and so on. This argument is based on what may be an unwarranted assumption. A sexual relationship may not automatically involve a disruption of authority. Moreover, the argument says little about why brother-sister mating should be prohibited.

Proponents include: Aberle et al., Bagley, Coult, Count, Fox, Freud, Malinowski, Murdock, Parsons, Sahlins, Seligman, P. E. Slater, and Vetter.

Exchange for Alliance

Next we have all the arguments that have grown from Tylor's statement "marry out or be killed out." These theories assert that by marrying outside the natal or local group, human beings could better survive because friendly alliances would be created with other groups that might otherwise be enemies or because intergroup cooperation would be enhanced, etc. Confusion of "marrying out" with "mating out" is frequently evidenced in theories of this type. (See the discussion of terminology below.) An individual might be prohibited from marrying in the group but still be permitted to have sexual intercourse with its members. Besides, the argument operates on the assumption that groups involved in intermarriage are friendly—and this is not always so (for one example, see Meggitt 1964).

Proponents include: Freud, Fortune, Lévi-Strauss, Livingstone, Parsons, Sahlins, P. E. Slater, Tylor, White, and Young.

Ethology; Biobehavior

These theories are nearly as varied as the theorists who propose them; it is therefore difficult to generalize about them (some are dealt with later in this discussion). They share a broad characteristic, however: support for these theories is drawn from observations of the behavior of nonhuman primates and other animals and builds on the particular theorist's conception of the biological nature of human beings.

Proponents include: Count, Fox, Kortmulder, Shepher, and Wolf.

It should be apparent from this brief summary of existing theory on incest that we are dealing with a variety of phenomena that are often lumped together as "incest." Moreover, explanations for any one form of "incest" (see below) may be adequate within a given social setting but are not adequate outside that specific setting and should not be generalized to provide explanations for other forms of prohibitions.

In the next section, I describe some perspectives that I find useful in evaluating incest theories.

FRAME OF REFERENCE

Terminology

When I speak of *mating* I mean simply sexual intercourse, the act of copulation (*not* marriage). *Intrafamilial mating* is sexual intercourse within the nuclear family (excluding that between husband and wife)—i.e., mating between mother and son, father and daughter, or brother and sister. *Intrafamilial mating is not inherently incestuous. It must be so defined culturally.* Consequently, for conceptual as well as expository purposes, I use simply *mating* or *intrafamilial mating* when speaking generally or when rules against the mating are absent, and *incest* only when the mating is prohibited. (Thus, of course, incest is a nonexistent phenomenon among animals.) *Incest taboo* will be used here to refer to the rule of prohibition itself.[3]

Types of Intrafamilial Mating

Most theories on incest limit themselves to discussions of mating *within* the nuclear family—what was defined above as intrafamilial mating—or at least consider such mating as central, with other forms of prohibited mating seen as cross-culturally variable "extensions" of the intrafamilial taboo. If we assume that the mother's husband is also the actual genitor of her children (which I will do for the sake of simplicity of exposition), then we can isolate three possible intrafamilial mating dyads: mother-son (M-S), father-daughter (F-D), and brother-sister (B-Z).[4] It is important in any discussion of incest (i.e., *prohibited* intrafamilial mating) to recognize that these are three distinct relationships. Too frequently the distinctions have been overlooked, and all three have been discussed under a single label: "*the* incest taboo."

Origins, Persistence, Functions

The literature on "the incest taboo" has often proffered interpretations that confuse the origins, the persistence, and the functions of incest taboos. How and why the taboos arose, how and why they manage to continue to exist, and what the result of their persistent existence is (or what it is that they do) are separate problems and must be treated separately. Too often, however, social scientists have offered an explanation of origin as if it were an explanation of persistence or function; while others, concentrating on functions, have extrapolated backward to assume that function and origin are inseparable. It should be made clear that any argument which focuses on one of these does not necessarily elucidate any of the others. (Part of the problem stems from the English word *why,* which can mean both "how come?" and "what for?" Some other languages—German, for example—have different terms for these different meanings.)

Universality

Another issue that continually crops up in theoretical discussions of incest taboos is the matter of their universality. Is any form of incest taboo universal? The evidence is equivocal. For instance, in 1947 Slotkin presented evidence which, although not incontrovertible, indicates that mother-son, father-daughter, and brother-sister mating, as well as marriage, were widespread and legal among the ancient Persians. Middleton (1962) examined the legal documents of ancient Egypt and found that father-daughter and brother-sister marriages were *not* limited to the ruling family but were frequent, accepted forms of marriage among commoners as well. Bagley

(1969) mentions the Mormons in Utah before 1892, among whom marriage of men to daughters and sisters and of women to stepsons was extensively practiced with the consent of the Mormon community. Maisch (1972) reviews additional pertinent literature and reports on widespread, culturally permitted intrafamilial marriage (and hence, presumably, mating; though the converse—that mating entails marriage—obviously cannot be held) for pre- and post-Christian Egyptians (especially between, but apparently not limited to, brother and sister, p. 22), in ancient Peru (mother-son, father-daughter, and brother-sister, p. 22), among pre-Mosaic Hebrews (between agnatic siblings only, p. 23), and possibly in Athens before the time of Solon (brother-sister, p. 23). (Further examples are given by Maisch, p. 35).

These are only a few examples, but it is clear from them that it is quite possible that no form of the incest taboo is universal. Any theory must account—or at least allow—for this possibility. No theory can claim validity on the basis of the universality of the taboo when that very universality is in question.[5]

Guide for the Study of Incest

I should like now to delineate a framework I find useful as a general guide in examining the literature on the subject.

First, I insist on the value of conceptually separating the three types of intrafamilial mating. Taking the dyads one at a time, we can then evaluate any theory for its adequacy in explaining (1) the origins of the prohibition on mating between the two categories of persons, (2) the persistence of the prohibition, and (3) the functions or consequences of the prohibition. This is illustrated by Table Appendix 2.1.

If we keep such a table in mind, we are less likely to confuse, say, an explanation of the origins of one prohibition with an explanation of the functions of another—or even with an explanation of its own functions.

I suggest further[6] that each dyad be examined with regard to three possible regulatory mechanisms: *inhibition* (is there any evidence to indicate that the mating in question is somehow inhibited?); *prevention* (is the mating in question prevented by ecological conditions or by situations or indirectly related practices (cf. Merton's "latent function," 1941) in the society over which the individual has little or no control?); *prohibition* (is there a rule against the mating in question—is it in fact incest?).

Adding these considerations, our table can be expanded to look like Table Appendix 2.2.

Table Appendix 2.1

Type of Mating	Origins	Persistence	Functions
M-S			
B-Z			
F-D			

Table Appendix 2.2

Types of Dyads	Regulatory Mechanisms	Origins	Persistence	Functions
MS	Inhibition			
	Prevention			
	Prohibition			
B-Z	Inhibition			
	Prevention			
	Prohibition			
F-D	Inhibition			
	Prevention			
	Prohibition			

A very brief outline of the general applications of this suggested framework will serve to illustrate its intentions. (It should be stressed that none of the arguments mentioned below is accepted as valid. All are used simply as examples for expository purposes.)

USING THIS APPROACH: SOME EXAMPLES

The first problem with which we are confronted is that of origins. Bearing in mind that we are attempting to avoid wherever possible the teleological fallacy of equating function with origin, what do we look to for possible enlightenment? Besides the hominid fossil record (which has so far rewarded us with little substantial grounds for speculation), there are doubtless a number of fields of inquiry from which one might procure helpful data—e.g., small-group behavior and behavior in stress situations (Warren Shapiro, personal communication). But one particular source, primatology, has begun to yield some highly suggestive (though still inconclusive) data, at least for one of the mating dyads (M-S); and I shall begin my illustrations with such data.

M-S Mating

It may be, as Sade (1968) suggests, that there is in some nonhuman primates a mechanism of a sort to inhibit M-S mating. Sade's evidence from his observations of macaques on Cayo Santiago would certainly seem to support the proposition that something of this sort is present in his subjects. Whether, however, we may posit a similar inhibition for human beings—however rudimentary and however far back in our evolutionary past—is indeed an open matter. It is far from certain that we can accept the following suggestion of Sade (1968:37):

> We can speculate that a pre-existing condition became invested with symbolic content during hominization; the origin of at least the mother-son incest taboo may have been the elaboration of a phylogenetically older system which can still be observed operating at the monkey level or organization.

Indeed, neither is it certain that we can even accept the presence of some innate inhibitory mechanism in the monkeys themselves, for Sade's evidence suggests that the "inhibition" is operative only as long as the son remains subordinate to the mother. If their ranks are reversed and the son becomes dominant to the mother, M-S mating may occur. (It was in such instances of reversal of dominance that Sade observed M-S mating.)[7]

If subordinate males do not mate with any higher-ranking females, we need look no farther than the dominance structure for an explanation of the low frequency of mother-son mating. But this is not the case. Low-ranking males do mate with other higher-ranking females.

> It appears that a male is inhibited from mating with a higher ranking female only if she is his mother, since males will copulate with higher-ranking unrelated females. The inhibition is therefore specific to the parent-offspring relation. The role of infant reverberating in the relations of the adult male towards his mother is apparently incompatible with the role of mate. (Sade 1968:32)

Here, one might contend, is a more probable explanation of the near absence of M-S mating: reverberance of the infant role in the adult male. An adult male is unlikely to mate with his mother as long as he remains subordinate to her, since their role relationship is still one of mother-child. Apparently, as Sade suggests, the role of son is incompatible with that of mate. But when the dominance relationship is reversed, the male steps out of his subordinate role of son into one of dominant male to subordinate female. Reverberance of his infant role may then be less likely to occur to inhibit mating, since he no longer plays that role in other nonsexual (i.e., nonerotic) relations with his mother. Since, however, most males, regardless of what level they manage to attain in the overall dominance hierarchy, always remain subordinate to their own mothers (see, for example, Kawamura 1965), the reverberance of the infant role is probably sufficient to inhibit M-S mating.

Count, who sees human behavior as a product of "a symbolizing brain operating on a primate biogram" (1958:1073), had, a decade before Sade's article, suggested reverberance in humans as a factor inhibiting M-S mating:

> A mother-offspring mutualism that endures for over a decade of maturative learning in an animal with the endowment already noted [i.e., with a complex brain and high learning capacity] does not erase easily, even though other statuses meanwhile come into existence. . . . An earlier status may continue to influence personality as it tries to shape newer statuses; and we may term this continuance a "reverberance." (Count 1958:1075)

I interpret Count as asserting that the avoidance of M-S mating is probably originally an innate tendency which in human beings is reinforced, prolonged, and eventually replaced by learning. The long and thorough learning period in human beings, then, may help to explain why the observance of M-S incest taboos persists in human adults, although mother-son mating in nonhuman primates is no longer— or only incompletely—inhibited after a reversal in dominance. (But there is also some evidence—see Bagley 1969—that, given certain conditions, the assumption of a dominant role by an individual can lead to intrafamilial mating among humans that might otherwise be considered incestuous.)

Count, then, is presenting a biological interpretation that emphasizes the relation of human beings to other animals. His method is a cross-specific one. Human behavior is an elaboration of a biological substratum. (Such an interpretation, as Count himself recognizes, is more applicable to M-S behavior than the other two kinds of intrafamilial mating behavior discussed below.) Count's interpretation (whether correct or not) has the advantage of attempting to explain why avoidance of mating arises (it is in the primate biogram) and why it persists and becomes a taboo (it is reinforced through learning). His interpretation, if I understand it correctly, has the further important advantage of accounting for actual occurrence of M-S mating: if the innate tendency to avoid mating is not reinforced through proper socialization, then mating may occur.

Again, one might express doubt and not feel the necessity to posit any innate mechanism that initially inhibits M-S mating specifically. The concept of reverberance of the previous role (child) alone might be held sufficient to account for the inhibition—if there is one—of the later potential role (mate). The long learning period while the male is still in the subordinate role of child would probably be adequate of itself in most cases to inhibit his assuming an equal or dominant role as mate in relation to his mother.

It is *not* unlikely, however, that the young male's inchoate erotic desires are first directed toward the mother. (Little need be said on this point; the psychological literature on the subject is vast.) But the long socialization period has fixed the mother and son in a different, noncrotic role relationship. And, as Coult (1963:274) points out, "if an individual is to learn a new role in any situation, this is much more easily accomplished if the role is learned in relation to an individual who has not previously served as a stimulus that elicits another role."

The origin of the M-S inhibition, in this view, is adequately accounted for by the concept of role reverberance. Moreover, the inhibition is reinforced by the maintenance of the M-S role relationship during the long developmental and socialization period of the son. It thus tends to persist even after the son has reached manhood.

On the other hand, however, one may be more inclined toward Sade's and Count's concept of a biologically linked inhibition—as Shepher is (1971a, 1971b), but with an important modification emended. Shepher's opinion is that there is very probably a genetically programed predisposition for the human being to be "imprinted" against M-S mating. Thus, Shepher maintains that what is innate is not the inhibition itself but the tendency or predisposition toward such an inhibition. He holds this is true for the M-S dyad as well as for the B-Z dyad (which will be dealt with below).

So far I have discussed some likely reasons why there is probably a tendency for mother and son not to mate (what we may call the *M-S mating inhibition*). I have yet, however, to discuss in any detail the *taboo,* the *M-S mating prohibition.* I turn now to consider this problem.

Perhaps somewhere in the dim and distant long ago of our evolutionary past (and as research in various fields progresses, this proposition becomes less conditional and the past less dim and less distant), human social organization was not, as primatologists advise us, so different from that of nonhuman primates. The elemental social unit was probably mother and offspring (see, for example, Fox 1967a, 1967b). Adult males not the issue of the mother were not attached to this unit.

Certain pressures acted on this group. For one, I am accepting *for the purposes of demonstration* the idea of an innate predisposition toward an M-S mating inhibition. To this might also be added two probable *preventions:* the "demographic prevention" espoused by M. K. Slater (1959), that is, the idea that differences in age would have made M-S mating very unlikely, since by the time the son was old enough to mate, the mother was probably dead; and the "social prevention" effected through some expulsion or peripheralization of young adult males by the elder, more dominant males, thus limiting the younger males' sexual access to females. Both these preventions would support the inhibition by sexually separating the son and mother.

The argument might then run as follows: What is inhibited and prevented tends to be considered unnatural. Yet there is no guarantee that the "unnatural" behavior will not occur. Therefore, when the behavior does occur (or in anticipation of its occurrence), it is *prohibited:* it is reprehensible. The prohibition becomes incorporated into the content of socialization. It thus tends to persist. People get used to it. It becomes, generation after generation, a part of their individual psychology, as well as a part of the total normative structure of the society.

This, then, might account for the origins and persistence of the M-S incest taboo where it is present. What of those societies—if there are, or ever were, any— in which the taboo is absent, in which M-S mating is not prohibited? We might hypothesize that in such a society the tendency toward the M-S mating inhibition was for some reason never capitalized on and that tuition in this regard was not systematically incorporated into the socialization process.

There is here an analogy with imprinting in lower animals. The hypothesis outlined above suggests that there is a biological propensity to incorporate into the organism's behavioral structure a disinclination to M-S mating. If, however, the appropriate stimuli, either in the form of tuition or circumstance (what might be called *appropriate exposure* or *appropriate ambience*), are not present during the prepubertal "critical period" of maturation (Shepher 1971b, especially in regard to the B-Z dyad, suggests the age range from birth to six years), then the behavior will not become part of the organism's stock.

Therefore, the hypothesis is not invalidated if a society is found which allows M-S mating, as long as it can be shown also that the same society does not provide the appropriate exposure at the appropriate time (and these concepts will have to be more refined and operationally better defined as research in this area progresses).[8]

I have outlined a hypothesis concerning the origins and persistence of the M-S taboo, but this discussion has wider implications. Let us go on, then, to the second dyad, B-Z, which may be explained by a similar argument.

B-Z Mating

Some empirical data (e.g., Talmon 1964; Wolf 1966, 1968, 1970; Shepher 1971a, 1971b) suggest the presence of a tendency toward an inhibition against mating between individuals who have been cosocialized as children. Shepher's findings are particularly impressive. Children raised together in close contact during the "critical period," between birth and age six, tend of their own volition not to mate. We may therefore again resort to the obvious analogy of imprinting. (Shepher, however, maintains the phenomenon to be a case of *actual* imprinting. See Shepher 1971a and 1971b:225–246 for his argument and evidence.)

We may hypothesize that what I am labeling the B-Z mating inhibition probably arose and applied originally to uterine siblings alone since, as was asserted above, the primordial elemental social unit was very probably one of mother and offspring. The fact that the genitor of the children was probably unknown and that he probably sired children by various females would eliminate the possibility of a similar inhibition between agnatic siblings. The tendency toward inhibition, though originally one between uterine siblings, would operate among any group of cosocialized, coresident, freely interacting children.

Once we accept the neo-Westermarckian proposition that there is this tendency toward inhibition, the argument proceeds similarly to the one outlined above. Two preventions probably supported the tendency not to mate. First, there is Slater's "demographic prevention," mentioned above—the idea that owing to spacing of children, differences in age, and so on, uterine siblings would probably be prevented from mating. This hypothesis, however, applies with less force here because the age differences are not as great as that between mother and son. "Social prevention" (expulsion or peripheralization), though, seems equally applicable in this case.

The next step in this kind of argument proposes, once more, that what is inhibited is considered unnatural, and so is overtly prohibited. Socialization then establishes or ingrains the prohibition.

But what if no prohibition is imposed? What if socialization actually encourages erotic relationships? If one is inclined to place heavy emphasis on socialization and to deemphasize any kind of innate inhibitory tendency, one would expect mating to occur. If, on the other hand, one is persuaded that human beings are predisposed to incorporate this inhibition into their biopsychology, to become imprinted against the behavior (so long as the critical stimulus of free tactile interaction with peers is present from birth through age six), mating should not occur. Here the available evidence seems to support the latter view. Kibbutz children socialized together during the critical period of their first six years simply *do not mate* (Shepher 1971a, 1971b). Similar, though less dramatic, data have been reported by Wolf (1966, 1968, 1970).

But an additional complication presents itself in regard to the *prohibition*. Does the development of the taboo so closely parallel the M-S taboo, or does the prohibition arise from different circumstances? I allude to woman-exchange theories (those labeled *exchange for alliance* in the above typology). Do the dominant males impose the prohibition upon the younger males in order to have more females at their own sexual disposal or in order to have more young females to exchange with dominant males of another group? Here we confront the problem of confusing origins with functions. It was said above that a discussion of function does not necessarily tell us anything concerning origins. Neither, however, does a discussion of functions necessarily have nothing at all to tell us concerning origins. One view, which has grown increasingly popular, is that the prohibition was imposed by the dominant males in order to have females for exchange—that for cooperation, alliance, appeasement, the general generation of good will, or whatever, women were exchanged between groups. (There is no reason to recapitulate the argument; see the sources listed in the bibliography under the authors named above.)

But the grounds for this argument are questionable. The ethnographic evidence seems to indicate that such attempts at establishing political alliances through the exchange of women are a post-Neolithic development, whereas the literature on hunter-gatherers (our only living representatives comparable to human beings of the Paleolithic era) argues against the existence of exchange for alliance among early hominids (for the relevant literature on hunter-gatherers, see Lee and DeVore 1968 and references therein). The infrequency or total absence of intergroup warfare, the probable absence of territoriality, and the equally probable absence of control over productive property even argue against the need for such political alliances. (But one must bear in mind the nature of the fossil evidence. There seems to have been quite a lot of head crushing going on among our hominid ancestors. One might well imagine the need of one australopithecine or pithecanthropine male to appease another who is intent upon eating his brains by offering him an alternative prize.)

F-D Mating

We face the same problem when we consider the F-D dyad. Why a taboo on F-D mating? How did it arise? Before discussing the question of alliance here, let us once more set the hypothetical evolutionary scene.

The basic social unit must have changed somewhat. The process or event referred to as the "emergence of the human family" must have occurred: that is, there had to have been some kind of male-female pair-bonding for procreation. Whether it was temporary, permanent, polygynous, or monogamous is unimportant. What is of consequence is that the genitor was known—or at least a certain individual was identified as being responsible initially or subsequently as a "father" (pater). Otherwise we obviously cannot speak of an F-D dyad.

Further, we do not have grounds here for positing a tendency toward inhibition. Though no statistical cross-cultural comparative survey has been made of the occurrence of F-D mating, the generally held impression among investigators is that violation of the F-D incest taboo in most societies is considered the least reprehensible (with either M-S or B-Z mating, depending on the society, being considered the most horrifying). Moreover, the father stands in a dominant relationship to the daughter—as a male, as a socializer, and as a potential sexual partner.

Why, then, the F-D taboo? The alliance theory proposes that the fathers (dominant males) prohibited the sons (subordinate males) from mating with their sisters in order to have women for exchange purposes. To avoid the jealousy of their sons and possibly to have "unspoiled" women to exchange, they had likewise to deny themselves sexual rights over their daughters. Thus, the F-D taboo arose as a self-imposed prohibition, was incorporated into the socialization process, and persisted because of its practical utility (and afterwards because of the human predilection to retain old habits even beyond their utility, so long as they are not perceived as particularly detrimental).

But it is this very utility that is in question. It is doubtful that conditions in the Paleolithic era favored such exchange of women. And even if the conditions were present, are they valid grounds for an explanation of the origins of the taboo?

Wilson Wallis has made the following remarks (1950:278):

> It seems, then, more probable that marriage out led to perception of its advantages than that perception of its advantages led to this prevalent type of marriage.
>
> However that may be, do marriages commonly establish a closer relationship than hitherto existed between the intermarrying families? In our own culture they frequently do so. Are there many such instances in primitive groups? This matter, it appears, has been little investigated. One can recall many instances in which the intermarrying families seem to be, in consequence of the marriage, to some extent estranged from one another, at least to be put on the defensive and sometimes the offensive.
>
> It is my impression that frequently this is the case if bride purchase, or dowry, prevails. Here, to be sure, there are special considerations. How is it among the Eskimo, Bushmen, or Australians, among whom such property rights are absent or inconsequential? Does establishing these relations between families, with sequent obligations or rights, tend to ally them? And where, in such criss-crossing of families, are the lines of alliance drawn?

I am frankly at an impasse. Though aware of the teleological dangers of such an interpretation as exchange for alliance, and aware of the evidence that does not support this interpretation, I am nevertheless unable to offer a suitable alternative. I record the interpretation here by default, once again reminding the reader I do not advocate the content of the scheme, or the various hypotheses themselves, but rather the framework that helps us to analyze and evaluate the hypotheses. It was to illustrate this general frame of reference that Table Appendix 2.2 was provided. The table is blank, to emphasize that the framework rather than content is recommended.[9]

INCEST TABOOS AS STRUCTURAL CONSISTENCIES

Though it was not my intention in the previous sections to review and evaluate in detail the logical or empirical validity of any particular argument or class of arguments—for I was concerned only to describe a framework (which can then be used to facilitate such evaluations)—one cannot help being struck by the inadequacy of the abovementioned "explanations" of incest taboos. Perhaps this is because we have, so to speak, been barking up the wrong tree.

A more strictly structural approach to the study of intrafamilial mating and incest taboos (an approach that is inherently consonant with the possible nonuniversality of the taboos mentioned above) might run as follows.

No one type of sexual prohibition need be common to all societies. What is of apparent importance is that sexual activity *in general* be somehow regulated. In other words, human beings regulate their social activities; and human mating and mating patterns are social activities (though, of course, not only social activities). Therefore, human beings regulate their mating and mating patterns. Incest prohibitions, the argument might continue, are therefore best understood as an aspect of a society's set of regulatory prescriptions and proscriptions. They cannot be understood in isolation from the rest of a society's rules of behavior. They would, presumably, "make sense" when viewed as part of the entire set (cf. Cohen 1969). And, similarly, there would probably be no universal explanation for the varied prohibitions of erotic behavior that have been injudiciously lumped under the generic label of *incest taboos.*

In short, it might be contended that there is probably no universal incest taboo; that sexual prohibitions vary from society to society in accordance with the totality of regulations in any particular society; that to understand a society's incest taboos, one must analyze this totality and view the taboos in light of this totality; and that there is probably no valid cross-cultural generalization that can adequately explain "the incest taboo." [10]

This type of approach, however, has not been very much employed in the past (see Goody 1956), and most of the theoretical material on incest taboos has argued from completely different bases. [11]

FOOTNOTES FOR APPENDIX 2

1   I would be remiss if I did not mention that many of the remarks I make here are in part a product of my collaboration with Joseph Shepher on a related project, an unpublished anthology entitled *Incest Taboos: A Reader in Theory.* Indeed, I must acknowledge a great debt to Dr. Shepher for the numerous discussions we had regarding incest theory while we were compiling *Incest Taboos.* I probably could not have written this appendix without the benefit of his thought-provoking and incisive critiques. I must emphasize, however, that Dr. Shepher, though an important stimulus for me in producing this Appendix, is in no way responsible for whatever shortcomings it may have in its present form.

I acknowledge also the suggestions and criticisms of Yehudi A. Cohen, Robin Fox, Jane Lancaster, Gloria Levitas, Warren Shapiro, and Lionel Tiger—though I did not always heed their advice.

2   For one discussion of semantic and conceptual confusion on the subject—and the influence of this confusion on cross-cultural investigations—see Goody 1956. Schneider (1956:10–15) lucidly discusses some of these problems as well.

3   I of course do not mean to imply that *taboo* and *prohibition* are synonymous. It is recognized that the special characteristics of a taboo—such as that it is simultaneously attractive and repulsive and that it is surrounded by supernatural sanctions—are not qualities of all prohibitions.

4   Since in most societies vir, pater, and genitor are the same person, at this stage I do not distinguish between uterine and agnatic siblings; but I shall return later to this distinction.

5   I will return to the issue of universality at the end of this Appendix. Here I only want to suggest that at least some of the cases cited above seem to counter the repeated claim for the universality of incest taboos. Lévi-Strauss, for example, states (1969:9): "It is not so much, then, whether some groups allow marriages that others prohibit, but whether there are any groups in which no type of marriage whatever is prohibited. The answer must be completely in the negative, for two reasons: firstly, because marriage is never allowed between all near

relatives, but only between certain categories . . . ; secondly, because these consanguineous marriages are either temporary and ritualistic, or, when permanent and official, nevertheless remain the privilege of a very limited social category."

First of all, as already pointed out, marriage is not mating; and the issue is not whether or not all societies possess norms concerning whom one may or may not marry but whether there are societies in which intrafamilial mating of all types (i.e., mating between what I presume Lévi-Strauss to mean by "near relatives") is allowed. I do not claim that such cases have been conclusively established. I only wish to point out that enough data exist, if we are willing to look at them, to cause us to doubt universality and to stimulate empirical research into this question. We cannot simply ignore possible exceptions and *assume* universality for the sake of theoretical consistency.

6 These suggestions, of course, owe much to previous writers, especially to Robin Fox (1967a, 1967b, 1967c, 1968a, 1968b), to Joseph Shepher (1971b), and to David Schneider (1956:10–15).

7 According to Jane Lancaster (personal communication), recent observations of Japanese macaques have uncovered a much higher frequency of mother-son mating than Sade found and hence have led to conclusions contrary to Sade's. Since, however, these data are as yet unpublished and unavailable to me, I shall rely on Sade's material for my illustrations.

8 Thus the situation described by Wilson (1961) for one small Caribbean group might be dealt with as follows. Intrafamilial mating got its initial push when the smaller community was isolated from the larger community and deprived of a "normal" sexual outlet. (And such a situation has been shown by Bagley 1969 to be highly conducive to intrafamilial mating.) The generation growing up did so in an atmosphere of intrafamilial mating where socialization actually encouraged rather than discouraged such mating. Since there were no appropriate stimuli to elicit the genetic tendency not to mate within the family, intrafamilial mating continued. But it is significant that after the outside community resumed contact with the smaller community, the third generation began mating out. The outside community presumably provided the appropriate signals for the generation that was of the appropriate age. (The other reports that indicate the widespread practice of intrafamilial mating, such as Slotkin 1947 and Middleton 1962, do not supply information on socialization; consequently, their relevance here cannot be evaluated.)

9 It is not necessary to treat functions in themselves in any detail. They have been noteworthy in the literature primarily in connection with the origins of the taboo, and they have been mentioned in the above discussions in this respect.

10 Except in regard to functions (and, perhaps, in regard to persistence as well, since the two may in fact be closely related). For instance, consider the following. Incest prohibitions exist for the same functional reasons as prohibitions of masturbation—that is, to augment society's control over individuals (or that control exercised by those who speak in the name of the society). Intrafamilial mating (or even nonregulated mating) is more conducive to anarchy: a family that supplies its own sexual resources needs less from the rest of society than a family that must marry or mate out. And the less dependent individuals within a unit are upon exogenous sources for the satisfaction of their needs, the less

amenable they are to external controls. Marriageable and sexually accessible males and females are *resources* of a society and, like all important resources, they and their behavior are subject to regulations imposed by that society. Access to sexual or reproductive resources, like access to economic or productive resources, is a primary focus for social control in any group. (For a provocative essay, based on cross-cultural research, that argues for and illustrates the facilitating role sexual prohibitions play in social control, see Cohen 1969).

11   At the symposium on incest in Eastern Oceania at the Seventieth Annual Meetings of the American Anthropological Association in New York, a number of the participants made suggestions similar to those offered here and speculated that this approach—i.e., viewing incest prohibitions as part of a larger set of rules—will prove to be the only productive theoretical framework for the study of incest. Rodney Needham, as well, has argued similarly in a recent publication (1971).

REFERENCES FOR APPENDIX 2

Aberle, D. F., et al. 1963. 'The Incest Taboo and the Mating Patterns of Animals," *American Anthropologist,* **65**:253–265.

Bagley, C. 1969. "Incest Behavior and Incest Taboo," *Social Problems,* **16**:505–519.

Cohen, Y. A. 1969. "Ends and Means in Political Control: State Organizations and the Punishment of Adultery, Incest, and Violation of Celibacy," *American Anthropologist,* **71**:658–687.

Coult, A. D. 1963. "Causality and Cross-Sex Prohibitions," *American Anthropologist,* **65**:266–277.

Count, E. W. 1958. "The Biological Basis of Human Sociality," *American Anthropologist,* **60**:1049–1085.

Fortune, R. 1932. "Incest," *Encyclopedia of the Social Sciences,* **7**:620–622.

Fox, R. 1962. "Sibling Incest," *British Journal of Sociology,* **13**:128–150.

———. 1967a. "In the Beginning: Aspects of Hominid Behavioural Evolution," *Man,* **2**:415–433.

———. 1967b. *Kinship and Marriage: An Anthropological Perspective.* Baltimore: Penguin Books.

———. 1967c. *"Totem and Taboo* Reconsidered," in E. R. Leach (ed.), *The Structural Study of Totemism and Myth.* London: Tavistock.

———. 1968a. "The Evolution of Human Sexual Behavior," *The New York Times Magazine,* March 24.

———. 1968b. "Incest, Inhibition and Hominid Evolution." Paper presented at Wenner-Gren symposium in Burg Wartenstein.

Frazer, J. 1910. *Totemism and Exogamy* (4 vols.). London: Macmillan.

Freud, S. 1950. *Totem and Taboo.* London: Routledge and Kegan Paul.

Goody, J. 1956. "A Comparative Approach to Incest and Adultery," *British Journal of Sociology,* **7**:286–305.

Hoebel, E. A., and E. L. Frost. 1976. *Cultural and Social Anthropology.* New York: McGraw-Hill.

Kawamura, S. 1965. "Matriarchal Social Ranks in the Minoo-B Troop: A Study of Japanese Monkeys," in S. Altmann (ed.), *Japanese Monkeys: A Collection of Translations.* Atlanta, Ga.: Altmann.

Kortmulder, K. 1968. "An Ethological Theory of the Incest Taboo and Exogamy," *Current Anthropology,* **9**:437–450.

Lee, R. B., and I. DeVore (eds.). 1968. *Man the Hunter.* Chicago: Aldine.

Levi-Strauss, C. 1969. *The Elementary Structures of Kinship.* Boston: Beacon Press.

Livingstone, F. B. 1969. "Genetics, Ecology and the Origins of Incest and Exogamy," *Current Anthropology,* **10**:45–61.

McLennan, J. F. 1865. *Primitive Marriage: An Inquiry into the Origin of the Form of Capture in Marriage Ceremonies.* Edinburgh and London: Adam and Charles Black.

Maisch, H. 1972. *Incest.* New York: Stein and Day.

Malinowski, B. 1927. *Sex and Repression in Savage Society.* London: Routledge and Kegan Paul.

———. 1931. "Culture," *Encyclopedia of the Social Sciences,* **4**:621–646.

Meggitt, M. J. 1964. "Male-Female Relationships in the Highlands of Australian New Guinea," *American Anthropologist* **66** (no. 4, pt. 2):204–224.

Merton, R. K. 1941. "Intermarriage and Social Structure: Fact and Theory," *Psychiatry,* **4**:361–374.

Middleton, R. 1962. "Brother-Sister and Father-Daughter Marriage in Ancient Egypt," *American Sociological Review,* **27**:603–611.

Morgan, L. H. 1877. *Ancient Society.* New York: World.

Muller, H. F. 1931. "A Chronological Note on the Psysiological Explanation of the Prohibition of Incest," *Journal of Religious Psychology,* **6**:294–295.

Murdock, G. P. 1949. *Social Structure.* New York: Macmillan.

Needham, R. 1971. "Introduction," in R. Needham (ed.), *Rethinking Kinship and Marriage.* London: Tavistock.

Parsons, T. 1954. "The Incest Taboo in Relation to Social Structure and the Socialization of the Child," *British Journal of Sociology,* **5**:101–117.

Sade, D. S. 1968. "Inhibition of Son-Mother Mating among Free-Ranging Rhesus Monkeys," *Science and Psychoanalysis,* **12**:18–38.

Sahlins, M. D. 1959. "The Social Life of Monkeys, Apes, and Primitive Man," in J. N. Spuhler (ed.), *The Evolution of Man's Capacity for Culture.* Detroit: Wayne State University Press.

———. 1960. "The Origin of Society," *Scientific American,* **203**:76–89.

Schneider, D. M. 1956. "Attempts to Account for the Incest Taboo." Unpublished manuscript.

Seligman, B. Z. 1929. "Incest and Descent: Their Influence on Social Organization," *Journal of the Royal Anthropological Institute,* **59**:231–272.

———. 1932. "The Incest Barrier: Its Role in Social Organization," *British Journal of Psychology,* **22**:250–276.

———. 1935. "The Incest Taboo as a Social Regulation," *Sociological Review,* **27**:75–93.

Shepher, J. 1971a. "Mate Selection among Second Generation Kibbutz Adolescents and Adults: Incest Avoidance and Negative Imprinting," *Archives of Sexual Behavior,* **1**:293–307.

———. 1971b. *Self-Imposed Incest Avoidance and Exogamy in Second Generation Kibbutz Adults.* Doctoral thesis, Department of Anthropology, Rutgers University.

Slater, M. K. 1959. "Ecological Factors in the Origin of Incest," *American Anthropologist,* **61**:1042–1059.

Slater, P. E. 1963. "On Social Regression," *American Sociological Review,* **28**:339–364.

Slotkin, J. S. 1947. "On a Possible Lack of Incest Regulations in Old Iran," *American Anthropologist,* **49**:612–617.

Talmon, Y. 1964. "Mate Selection in Collective Settlements," *American Sociological Review,* **29**:491–508.

Tylor, E. B. 1888. "On a Method of Investigating the Development of Institutions; Applied to Laws of Marriage and Descent," *Journal of the Royal Anthropological Institute,* **18**:245–269.

Vetter, G. B. 1928. "The Incest Taboos," *Journal of Abnormal and Social Psychology,* **23**:232–240.

Wallis, W. 1950. "The Origin of Incest Rules," *American Anthropologist,* **52**:277–279.

Westermarck, E. 1922. *The History of Human Marriage* (3 vols.). London: Macmillan.

———. 1934a. "Recent Theories of Exogamy," *Sociological Review,* **26**:22–40.

———. 1934b. *Three Essays on Sex and Marriage.* London: Macmillan.

White, L. A. 1959. *The Evolution of Culture.* New York: McGraw-Hill.

Wilson, P. J. 1961. "Incest—A Case Study," *Social and Economic Studies,* **12**:200–209.

Wolf, A. P. 1966. "Childhood Association, Sexual Attraction, and Incest Taboo: A Chinese Case," *American Anthropologist,* **68**:883–893.

———. 1969. "Adopt a Daughter-in-Law, Marry a Sister: A Chinese Solution to the Problem of Incest Taboo," *American Anthropologist,* **70**:864–874.

———. 1970. "Childhood Association and Sexual Attraction: A Further Test of the Westermarck Hypothesis," *American Anthropologist,* **72**:503–515.

Young, F. W. 1967. "Incest Taboos and Social Solidarity," *American Journal of Sociology,* **72**:589–600.

Learning about Anthropology

An eight-step program with suggested readings, the purpose of which is to stimulate initial interest in the discipline of cultural anthropology and the phenomena with which it is concerned. The program is diagramed in Figure Appendix 3.1.

POPULAR ANTHROPOLOGY

1   Read, back to back, *The Gentle Tasaday* (Nance 1975) and *The Mountain People* (Turnbull 1972). Nance is a journalist. Although Turnbull is an anthropologist, his book is a journalistic and personal account of his fieldwork among the Ik in East Africa.

TECHNICAL INTRODUCTIONS

2   Read a thorough general introduction to the entire field of anthropology (physical, cultural, and archaeology). Several of those listed in Table I of the Preface to this handbook qualify.
3   Read and keep as a quick reference guide a short paperback introductory review of the field of cultural anthropology. (This handbook is designed as just such a guide. Referring to it for clarification during the course of your reading should minimize the chance of your being hindered by technical terminology and concepts.)

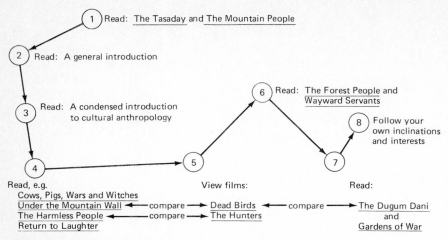

Figure Appendix 3.1   The eight-step program in outline.

POPULAR ANTHROPOLOGY

4   Read several additional anthropological books aimed at a general audience. Suggested: *Cows, Pigs, Wars and Witches* by Marvin Harris (1974), *Under the Mountain Wall* by Peter Matthiessen (1962), *Return to Laughter* by Eleanor Smith Bowen (1954), and *The Harmless People* by Elizabeth Marshall Thomas (1959). (The more enterprising neophyte may wish to subscribe to *Peoples of the Earth,* 1973, a twenty-volume work under the general editorship of Sir Edward Evans-Pritchard containing ethnographic sketches of peoples around the world accompanied by excellent color photographs.)

5   Try to see some ethnographic films such as *The Hunters* by John Marshall (compare this with the book *The Harmless People*) or *Dead Birds* by Robert Gardner (and compare this with the book *Under the Mountain Wall*). Most anthropologists welcome interested laymen; contact the anthropology department at your local college or university and ask if any films are scheduled to be shown and if you may attend the showings.

POPULAR VERSUS TECHNICAL ANTHROPOLOGY

6   Compare how a single anthropologist treats the same subject in a popular book and in a technical monograph. For example, compare Colin Turnbull's *Forest People* (1961) with his *Wayward Servants* (1965), both of which are accounts of the Mbuti Pygmies in Africa.

7   Compare how different authors handle the same subject in their books, both popular and technical. For example, you might compare Matthiessen's *Under the Mountain Wall* with *The Dugum Dani* by Karl G. Heider (1970) and with *Gardens of War: Life and Death in the New Guinea Stone Age* by Robert Gardner and Karl G. Heider (1969).

SINK OR SWIM

8   By this time you will have read enough anthropology to know whether you like
it or not. If you are intrigued, jump right in. Use the bibliographies in this
handbook and those in the publications mentioned above to select further readings on topics that interest you. Each piece you read will contain a bibliography
that will lead you to additional readings on the same topic or similar topics.
Eventually, you may even want to subscribe to a journal or two, such as the
American Anthropologist or *Current Anthropology.* Anthropology can be a fascinating hobby as well as a professional pursuit—in fact, anthropology originated
as a hobby.

REFERENCES FOR APPENDIX 3

Bowen, E. S. 1954. *Return to Laughter.* New York: Harper.

Evans-Pritchard, E. E. (ed.) 1973. *Peoples of the Earth.* Danbury, Conn.: Danbury
Press (Grolier Enterprises).

Gardner, R. 1963. *Dead Birds* (16 mm film). Cambridge: Film Study Center, Pea-
body Museum, Harvard University.

Gardner, R. and K. G. Heider. 1969. *Gardens of War: Life and Death in the New
Guinea Stone Age.* New York: Random House.

Harris, M. 1974. *Cows, Pigs, Wars and Witches: The Riddles of Culture.* New York:
Vintage.

Heider, K. G. 1970. *The Dugum Dani: A Papuan Culture in the Highlands of West
New Guinea.* Viking Fund Publications in Anthropology, No. 49. Chicago:
Aldine.

Marshall, J. 1956. *The Hunters* (16 mm film). Cambridge: Film Study Center, Pea-
body Museum, Harvard University.

Matthiessen, P. 1962. *Under the Mountain Wall: A Chronicle of Two Seasons in the
Stone Age.* New York: Viking.

Nance, J. 1975. *The Gentle Tasaday: A Stone Age People in the Philippine Rain
Forest.* New York: Harcourt Brace Jovanovich.

Turnbull, C. M. 1961. *The Forest People: A Study of the Pygmies of the Congo.* New
York: Simon and Schuster (Clarion).

———. 1965. *Wayward Servants: The Two Worlds of the African Pygmies.* Garden
City, N.Y.: Natural History Press (Doubleday).

———. 1972. *The Mountain People.* New York: Simon and Schuster. (Paperback
edition by Touchstone-Clarion.)

Thomas, E. M. 1959. *The Harmless People.* New York: Knopf. (Paperback edition
by Vintage.)

Glossary

Note: In this glossary, cross references are indicated by **boldface italic** type.

Acculturation   A term, applied to both individuals and whole societies, referring to changes in belief and behavior resulting from contact with one or more other societies. Often used more narrowly to refer to a contact situation in which one society is dominant, and the subordinate society or group adopts traits from the supraordinate one.

Acephalous   "Without a head"; refers to a type of *political organization* without a central authority or supraordinate administrative agency, such as exists in tribes (see *tribe*), which consist of a number of loosely connected, politically autonomous, local-level units.

Achieved status   A *status* in which membership is voluntary or attained through one's own efforts. (Cf. *ascribed status.*)

Action group or task group   A *group,* usually short-lived, formed for the purpose of accomplishing a specific objective. (See also *informal group.*)

Actual, or real, kinship A kinship relationship between persons who are able to demonstrate, usually to the satisfaction of an outside observer, an actual biological tie. (Cf. *fictive kinship* and *classificatory kinship.*)

Adaptation The process by means of which a population adjusts to the conditions of its *habitat* in order to maintain itself and contribute to its continued survival.

Adaptive strategy A particular complex of *technology* and *organization of labor* through which a society maintains itself in relation to its *habitat;* in other words, how the society "makes a living," its predominant strategy for survival—*hunting-gathering, horticulture, industrialism,* etc. Also called *ecological type.*

Adelphic polyandry See *fraternal polyandry.*

Adjacent generations Generations following immediately upon each other, i.e ., in consecutive order (parent-child). (Cf. *alternate generations.*)

Affinal kin Relatives through *marriage.* (Cf. *consanguineal kin.*)

Age grades Fixed categories (levels, stages) in which people are classified and through which they progress on the basis of culturally defined age ranges. For example, a society might distinguish "recent initiates," "young warriors," "senior warriors," and "elders." (See also *age sets, category.*)

Age sets Groups of persons (see *group*) who together occupy *age grades.* Each group has a separate name and identity and moves successively, as a unit, through the age-grade system of the society.

Aggregation or gathering Collectivities of persons who, by accident of circumstance, happen to be in the same place at the same time. In contrast to groups (see *group*), aggregations are without any internal *structure* or organization and consist of persons who are not interacting to achieve some common goal.

Agnatic descent See *patrilineal descent.*

Agnatic kin Persons (male or female) related through males; i.e., persons connected by at least one male *linking relative.* Agnatic relationships occur in all societies; such kin connections are not confined to societies with *patrilineal* (agnatic) *descent.* (Cf. *uterine kin.*)

Agriculture Most commonly, a form of plant cultivation employing the plow and draft animals. Sometimes cultivation, accompanied by terracing, crop rotation, fertilization, or irrigation. Occasionally, cultivation of grain, as opposed to root, crops. (Cf. *horticulture.*)

Alter In reckoning *kinship,* alter is the individual to whom the relationship is being traced. (Cf. *ego.*)

Alternate generations Every other generation (grandparent-grandchild). (Cf. *adjacent generations.*)

Ambilineage See *ramage.*

Ambilineal descent The term means "both-line descent" but refers to a form of *unilineal descent* in which a person may choose to trace descent *either* patrilineally or matrilineally (see *patrilineal descent, matrilineal descent*). More accurately, it is a form of *filiation* reckoned from either the father or the mother. Also called *optative descent.*

Ambilocal residence The term *ambilocal* means "both places" and refers to a form of residence in which the married couple as a unit resides with or near either the husband's parents or the wife's parents. Also called *bilocal.*

Ancestral veneration, or ancestor worship A form of polytheistic religion (see *polytheism*) in which people maintain an active relationship with the spirits of their deceased ancestors.

Animatism (1) The belief that inanimate objects are conscious beings and able to move under their own power. (2) More commonly, the belief in an *impersonal supernatural power* or force, such as *mana*. (Cf. *animism*.)

Animism The belief in any spiritual or supernatural beings. Sometimes used more narrowly to refer to the belief that nonhuman animals, plants, or inanimate objects possess spirits. (Cf. *animatism*.)

Anthropology The study of humanity, both biologically and culturally, including its origins, evolution, and present-day manifestations.

Apical ancestor The claimed ancestor of a *descent unit*; the progenitor who occupies the uppermost point (the apex) in a *kinship* diagram.

Archaeology A branch of *anthropology* dealing with the investigation and reconstruction of past human societies, mainly through excavation of physical remains.

Ascribed, or assigned, status A *status* in which membership is involuntary or assigned on the basis of attributes over which the person has no control, such as sex, age, ethnicity, etc. (Cf. *achieved status*.)

Associations Nonkin groups (see *group*) formed to pursue some continuing objective; e.g., a trading partnership, a *special-interest group, secret societies*. Membership in associations may be voluntary or involuntary.

Asymmetric marriage system See *generalized exchange.*

Authority In general, and regarding political institutions, the term refers to the legitimation of power, the recognized "right" to exercise control, to compel or prevent behavior. (Cf. *power*.)

Avoidance relationships Relationships governed by formal rules restricting interaction between designated categories of relatives or even imposing complete avoidance between them. (Cf. *joking relationships.)*

Avunculocal extended family group An *extended family group* based on *avunculocal residence;* i.e., minimally it consists of a man, his spouse or spouses, his sister's son or sons, and the latter's wife or wives and children all living together. (Cf. *matrilocal* and *patrilocal extended family group.)*

Avunculocal residence The term *avunculocal* means "mother's brother's place" and refers to a form of residence in which the married couple as a unit resides with or near the husband's mother's brother (thus, sometimes called *viriavunculocal* residence). Also refers to the practice, in some societies having *matrilineal descent* and *virilocal residence* for a married woman, whereby a woman's children at a certain age leave the natal household and residence with their mother to go to live with or near their mother's brother.

Balanced, or direct, reciprocity A form of economic exchange in which goods of commensurate value are exchanged within a specified period of time. (Cf. *generalized reciprocity.)*

Band A small, politically independent, coresident, eglitarian, face-to-face (i. e., primary) group of persons who are usually voluntarily associated on the bases of kinship and friendship. Bands normally consist of fewer than fifty persons organized without formally defined positions of leadership (see *primus inter pares*), characterized by economic self-sufficiency. Band organization is typical of hunter-gatherers.

Bifurcate collateral terminology A type of *kinship terminology,* also called Sudanese. See Chapter 12 of the text for major characteristics.

Bifurcate merging terminology A type of *kinship terminology,* also called Iroquois. See Chapter 12 of text for major characteristics.

Big man An unofficial leadership position (i.e., one not characterized by formal rules of occupancy or of succession) in tribal societies (see *tribe*). Achievement and retention of the position depend solely on personality and personal achievement.

Bilateral cross-cousin (MBD/FZD) marriage A form of *immediate direct exchange* in marriage. (See page 151 of the text for an explanation of abbreviations.)

Bilateral descent See *cognatic descent.*

Bilateral descent group See *cognatic descent group.*

Bilineal descent See *double descent.*

Bilocal residence See *ambilocal residence.*

Black magic A form of malevolent *magic,* the aim of which is to bring harm or misfortune to its target. Synonymous with *sorcery.* (Cf. *white magic.*)

Blood feud (1) Same as feud (see *feuding*). (2) Feuding that occurs specifically between kinship units (i.e., those that are organized on the basis of *kinship* or *descent*).

Bloodwealth Damages paid by one group as compensation for injuring or killing a member of another group.

Bond friendship A special relationship, established between social equals of the same sex and roughly the same age, involving mutual obligations and rights, such as hospitality, economic support, and gift giving. Also called *multipurpose association.*

Breeding population A group of people within an identifiable geographical locus who mate (breed; see *mating*) or marry more often among themselves than with persons from outside their group.

Bride price See *bridewealth.*

Bride service The practice whereby a man supplies a woman's group with his labor and perhaps gifts for a specified period of time in order to validate a *marriage.* Service may occur before marriage, after marriage, or both, and may or may not involve the husband's actually living with the wife's group.

Bridewealth Also called *bride price.* A marriage payment made by the groom or the groom's group to the bride's group. It serves to validate the marital union. (Sometimes confused with *childwealth* or progeny price.)

Cargo cult A type of *revitalization movement,* reported most often for Melanesia, characterized by the appearance of prophets who exhort the people to abandon their present European goods, break off their dependent relationship with colonialists, and return to the old beliefs. If the people do so, the ancestors are expected to return (often in ships or airplanes), bringing prosperity in the form of abundant cargo of new European-type goods.

Caste system A type of *social stratification,* according to which the society is divided into a hierarchically arranged number of fixed groups called *castes,* membership in which is ascribed by birth (i.e., membership is hereditary) and which thus afford little or no *social mobility.* Castes are usually endogamous (see *endogamy*) and associated with specified occupations. (Cf. *class system.*)

Category (social or cultural)   A classificatory unit, or collectivity of persons, membership in which is defined by some shared characteristic. As opposed to a *group,* the members of a category (i.e., persons who are classified together) do not interact with each other or do something together. (Cf. *group.*)

Ceremony   A series or complex of related rituals; *ritual* and *ceremony* are often used synonymously, however.

Chief   A type of leader in a tribal society (see *tribe*) organized on the basis of chiefdoms. It is an official position, a fixed office, governed by explicit rules of succession based on *descent.* A chief usually wields considerable *power.* (See *chiefdom.*)

Chiefdom   A form of tribal organization in which local communities are organized into larger territorial units, each headed by a leader known as a *chief.* In effect, the local communities are political subdivisions of the chiefdom; but each chiefdom is politically independent and separate from the other chiefdoms in the *tribe* (i.e., there is no supraordinate or central authority over the entire tribe).

Child lending   The practice of temporarily placing some of one's children in the homes of trusted friends and relatives to be cared for, while one reciprocates by caring for the children of others. The practice, however, is not confined to an exchange of children, for someone who is childless may be lent a child.

Childwealth   Payment establishing rights in children (see *right, genetricial rights*). May occur in conjunction with *marriage* or apart from a formal marital union. It involves payment of goods by a man or a man's group to a woman or a woman's group in order to legitimate the children as members of the man's *kin group.* Put another way, it filiates children to the man (see *filiation*). This is also known as *progeny price.* (Sometimes confused with *bridewealth* or bride price, probably because bridewealth usually entails childwealth—though the converse is not true.)

Circulating connubium   See *generalized exchange.*

City   A term having no precise definition. It refers to a high concentration of people in comparatively small land areas (some authors specify a density of 5,000 or more persons per square mile) living in communities in which houses are relatively permanent and substantial and are located close to one another along discernible streets.

Civilization   A term usually applied to a society manifesting several or all the following characteristics: (1) a particular kind of stratified political organization, usually a state system; (2) a particular kind of economic organization, usually one which incorporates occupational heterogeneity and in which markets and trade are important; (3) a particular kind of spatial organization and settlement pattern, usually one involving urbanization and monumental architecture; (4) a particular kind of religious organization, usually one with a monotheistic cast and a priestly bureaucracy; (5) writing.

Clan   A named *group* or *category* of persons of both sexes, membership in which is determined by *unilineal descent* or *filiation* to one parent, although the members cannot actually demonstrate their *descent* from the *apical ancestor* (cf. *lineage*). A clan is often composed of a number of related lineages. Formerly, *clan* was differentiated from *sib* on the basis of whether the members resided together (clan) or not (sib). Today *clan* and *sib* are often used synonymously.

Class system A type of *social stratification,* according to which the society is divided into a hierarchically arranged number of levels or strata called *classes,* in which membership, though initially determined by birth, may be changed through personal achievement (i.e., a class system is characterized, at least ideally, by *social mobility*). Classes are usually categories rather than groups. (Cf. *caste system.*)

Classificatory kinship A system of naming relatives in which persons are classified as *kin* although they are not biologically related; or a system in which several genealogical relatives are categorized together and referred to by the same kinship term. For example, in our own kinship system, we lump together father's sister, mother's sister, father's brother's wife, and mother's brother's wife under the single term *aunt.* Sometimes defined as a system in which terms for *lineal relatives* are "extended" to *collateral relatives.* (Cf. *descriptive kinship* and *actual kinship.*)

Cognatic descent A system of tracing *descent* through *all* progenitors, male and female, through both the mother *and* the father. Often referred to as *nonunilineal descent.* Also called *bilateral descent.* (Cf. *unilineal descent.*)

Cognatic descent group A group formed on the basis of *cognatic descent* or bilateral descent. Also called *bilateral* or *unrestricted* descent group.

Cognitive anthropology See *ethnoscience.*

Collateral relatives Literally, *collateral* means "side by side." It refers to *consanguineal kin* not in a direct line of *descent*; for example, cousins. That is, individuals who are related laterally (to the side) or "horizontally." (Cf. *lineal relatives.*)

Commingling of institutions A relatively high degree of overlap or integration, as opposed to segregation, in sociocultural systems. Various areas of belief and behavior tend to be interconnected and intermingled so that, for instance, religious activities, economic activities, and kinship activities are not readily distinguishable but are instead different aspects or functions of the same overall activity system. Accompanied by a *commingling of roles* for individuals. (Cf. *differentiation of institutions* and *differentiation of roles.*)

Commingling of roles A relatively high degree of overlap or integration, as opposed to segregation, in an individual's behavior. For instance, a person's activities tend to fulfill simultaneously religious, economic, and kinship functions. In other words, there tends to be a blending of the roles of worker, worshiper, parent, citizen, etc. A concomitant of the *commingling of institutions* in the society as a whole. (Cf. *differentiation of roles* and *differentiation of institutions.*)

Commonlocal residence A form of residence in which the married couple as a unit lives in a group in which both the husband's parents and the wife's parents also live.

Complex marriage systems Systems with negative rules prohibiting marriage between members of specified categories or groups of persons, but not specifying whom one should or must marry. (Cf. *elementary marriage system.*)

Componential analysis A technique of analysis that breaks down any domain of belief or behavior into its basic constituent elements, or components, in order to determine meaningful distinctions among the members of the domain, which are seen as different combinations (configurations or constellations) of these basic elements.

Confederacy A voluntary alliance of two or more politically autonomous tribes (see *tribe*).

Conjugal family group Most often, this term is used synonymously with *nuclear family group.* It is sometimes used to refer to any family group formed by *marriage,* as opposed to family groups based on ties of consanguinity among the members (see *consanguineal kin*).

Consanguineal kin Relatives by birth; those claiming *descent* from a common ancestor. (Cf. *affinal kin.*)

Consanguine family group A term used by some anthropologists to refer to a family unit formed on the basis of consanguinity (see *consanguineal kin*) as opposed to those formed by *marriage.* For example, a domestic group consisting of women, their offspring, and their brothers.

Consumption Patterns of behavior in a society pertaining to the use (as opposed to the *production* and *distribution*) of goods and services.

Conspicuous consumption Use or consumption of goods and services for public display rather than out of necesity; a way of demonstrating wealth and social standing.

Contagious magic Actions performed on an object in the belief that they will affect a person formerly in contact with that object. Based on Frazer's law of contagion: "Things which have once been in contact with each other continue to act on each other at a distance after the physical contact has been severed." (Cf. *imitative magic.*)

Corporate group In anthropology, a group whose defining characteristic is collective ownership or control of some valued commodity. Cross-culturally variable secondary characteristics include: (1) a group identity independent of the identities of its constituent members, (2) continued existence despite changes in personnel, and (3) face-to-face interaction among its members. A frequently mentioned tertiary characteristic is group *exogamy.*

Courts Assemblages of persons for the purpose of adjudicating disputes and dealing with transgressions of *law.*

Couvade A practice whereby a man retires to rest after his wife has given birth, as if he had just gone through the labor of childbirth (in some societies he may even simulate giving birth). The mother may also retire and recuperate, or she may resume her normal activities while her husband "recuperates."

Cross-cousins Persons who are children of opposite-sexed siblings; thus, the cross-cousins of *ego* are his or her FZC and MBC (see page 151 of the text for an explanation of abbreviations). (Cf. *parallel cousins.*)

Crow terminology A type of *kinship terminology,* usually found in conjunction with *matrilineal descent.* See Chapter 12 of the text for major characteristics.

Cultivation Raising crops for food; farming. (See *horticulture* and *agriculture.*)

Cultural anthropology (1) A major branch of *anthropology* dealing with the holistic and comparative study of *culture.* (2) A subdivision of anthropology synonymous with *ethnography* and *ethnology.* (3) A particular approach in anthropology concerned with the study of the human mind and how it works. As such, it is synonymous with cognitive anthropology *(ethnoscience)* and distinct from social anthropology, which is concerned more with *etic* interpretations of behavior than with the actors' conceptualizations or interpretations of their behavior.

Cultural ecology   (1) In *etic* terms, the study of *culture* as an adaptational device; i.e., the study of the interrelationships between sociocultural systems and their habitats (see *habitat*). (In this sense, often used synonymously with *human ecology.*) (2) In *emic* terms, the study of a people's cognitive orientation toward their habitat and their *adaptation* to it; i.e., how they view their relationship to the habitat. (Cf. *human ecology* and *social ecology.*)

Cultural relativism   A perspective on or approach to people's behavior and beliefs that attempts to evaluate these within the context of the sociocultural system in which they occur. It involves abstaining from judging a culture on the basis of criteria external to it, such as the standards of one's own culture. (Cf. *ethnocentrism.*)

Culture   (1) Shared patterns of learned belief and behavior constituting the total lifeway of a people; the totality of tools, acts, thoughts, and institutions of any given human population. (2) Some anthropologists choose to restrict this term only to an ideational or conceptual system; i.e., the shared system of ideas, knowledge, and beliefs by which people order their perceptions and experiences and make decisions, and in terms of which they act.

Culture area   A geographic region in which separate societies have similar cultures; i.e., an area in which a number of peoples share similar lifeways that, taken as a whole, contrast with lifeways in other areas. Culture areas are classificatory, not analytic, devices.

Cyclical age-set systems   Age-set systems in which the names used for *age sets* in the past may be used again for new age sets. (Cf. *progressive age-set systems.*)

Delayed direct exchange   A form of *restricted exchange* in marriage, in which the exchange of spouses does not occur simultaneously (in the same generation). In other words, men from group A marry women from group B in one generation; and then, in the next generation, men from group B marry women from group A. Also called *patrilateral cross-cousin (FZD) marriage* (see text, page 151, for an explanation of abbreviations).

Descent   A succession of genealogical links connecting a person with his or her ancestors. The way descent is reckoned or traced—i.e., which antecedents of a person are considered significant for social purposes—varies from society to society. (See *unilineal descent* and *cognatic descent.)*

Descent category   A classificatory unit including all those people who, by using the notions of *descent* prevalent in their culture, trace their relationship to a common ancestor. This term should not be confused with *descent group.*

Descent group   A group organized on the basis of the common ancestry of its members (i.e., their *descent* from a common ancestor) or consanguineal kinship. (See *consanguineal kin, kin group.*) In other words, people of common descent who use that descent as a basis of eligibility or recruitment for membership in a group form a descent group. This term should not be confused with *descent category.*

Descent unit, or descent-ordered unit   Any sociocultural unit—a *group* or *category*—formed or structured on the basis of the claimed common *descent* of its members. (See *descent category* and *descent group.*).

Descriptive kinship   A system of naming relatives in which each genealogical position has its own separate kinship term. Sometimes defined as a system in which terms for **lineal relatives** are distinct from those for **collateral relatives** and, as well, terms for **patrilateral** relatives are distinct from those for **matrilateral** relatives. (See **classificatory kinship.**)

Dibble   A pointed stick for digging.

Differentiation of institutions   A relatively high degree of discreteness or compartmentalization in sociocultural systems. Areas or sets of belief and behavior are associated with a particular **institution** and are kept separate from other institutions, i.e., there is little overlap among institutions, so that people tend to differentiate between religious activities and economic activities, economic activities and kinship activities, etc. Accompanied by a **differentiation of roles** for individuals. (Cf. **commingling of institutions** and **commingling of roles.**)

Differentiation of roles   A relatively high degree of discreteness or compartmentalization in individual behavior. An individual differentiates between, and attempts to keep separate, activities pertaining to economics and religion, politics and kinship, etc. A concomitant of the **differentiation of institutions** in the society as a whole. (Cf. **commingling of roles** and **commingling of institutions.**)

Direct exchange   See **restricted exchange.**

Distribution   The allocation of goods and services in a society (as opposed to their **production** and **consumption**).

Divination   The practice of foretelling future events, obtaining information about past events, or penetrating the unknown through mystical means, such as "reading" tea leaves or palms, auguring, and interpreting patterns made by sticks and stones or bones cast upon the ground. Sometimes divination involves the help of a supernatural being or force, and sometimes it does not.

Division of labor   How people are organized in a society for purposes of work; i.e., which individuals or groups perform which tasks. May be based simply on an ascribed characteristic (such as sex or age), or on acquired skills (as in the case of specialization), or on some combination of ascription and achievement. (See **specialization of labor.**)

Double descent   A form of **unilineal descent** combining principles of both **patrilineal** and **matrilineal descent.** In other words, a single **ego** traces descent through the father's line (i.e., the father is the **linking relative** between ego and ego's unilineal male forebears: F, FF, FFF, etc.) and at the same time traces descent through the mother's line (i.e., the mother is the linking relative between ego and ego's unilineal female forebears MM, MMM, etc.). (See text, page 151, for an explanation of abbreviations.) Also called **duolineal, bilineal,** and **double unilineal** descent. [Some anthropologists insist that groups (see **group**) based on both patrilineal and matrilineal descent must be present before a society can be said to have double descent. Other anthropologists consider the presence of descent categories (see **descent category**) based on both principles sufficient for identifying double descent.]

Double unilineal descent   See **double descent.**

Dowry   (1) A woman's share of inheritance (wealth, property) from her natal group, a share she takes with her upon marriage. (2) **Property** given by the bride's relatives to the groom or the groom's group upon marriage.

Dual descent   See **double descent.**

Dual organization   See *moiety.*

Dumb barter   A form of economic exchange in which a minimum of, or no, face-to-face contact occurs between the trading partners. Each party leaves and picks up trade goods at a designated area in the absence of the other party.

Duolineal descent   See *double descent.*

Duolocal residence   A type of residence in which the husband and wife, instead of living together, reside in separate groups.

Dyad   A two-person group; a pair.

Ecological niche   The particular complex of land and resources in a *habitat* exploited by a population and that population's manner of exploitation. Refers to a population's "place" in an *ecosystem.*

Ecological type   See *adaptive strategy.*

Ecology   The study of the relationship between an organism or a population of organisms and the environment. (See *cultural ecology, human ecology,* and *social ecology.*)

Economic organization   The allocation of resources, goods, and services among alternative ends: how potential *energy* in the *habitat* and in the human population is utilized for the *production, distribution,* and *consumption* of goods and services; the social relationships and behavior patterns these systems of activity entail; and related concepts such as *property,* ownership, and inheritance.

Ecosystem   The interconnected and interdependent whole formed by the multiplex relationships among populations of organisms, the land and resources they exploit, and their means of exploitation *(adaptation)* within a defined region *(habitat).* Probably best conceived of as a system of energy flow, in which *energy* is continually being tapped, converted, and utilized throughout a series of symbiotic links.

Egalitarian   Pertaining to groups in which there is roughly equal access to vital resources, goods, and services and there are no formal positions of coercive authority.

Ego   In reckoning *kinship,* ego is the individual from whom the relationship is being traced or who is tracing the relationship. Thus, in kinship diagrams or genealogical charts indicating a society's system of *kinship terminology, ego* refers to the individual from whose point of view we are labeling the diagram, the point of reference for tracing relationships. (Cf. *alter.*)

Egocentric unit   A unit *(group* or *category)* for which the defining focus is an individual, and in which membership is based on some relationship to that individual, such as is the case with a *kindred.* (Cf. *sociocentric units.*)

Elementary marriage systems   Systems with positive rules specifying marriage between members of designated categories or groups of persons; i.e., the rules specify whom one should or must marry. (Cf. *complex marriage systems.*)

Emic   Pertaining to the attempt to undersand patterns of belief and behavior from the native perspective, to interpret cultural data in a way that is meaningful to the members of the society being studied. Derived from the linguistics term *phonemics,* which refers to meaningful sounds in a language. (Cf. *etic;* see also *ethnoscience.*)

Empire   The type of political entity resulting from the conquest and incorporation by one *society* of other previously separate societies, so that groups that were formerly autonomous become dependent political subdivisions of the expanded **nation-state.**

Enculturation (1) In contradistinction to socialization, the transmission of a particular culture from one generation to another or from the initiated to the uninitiated. (2) Same as **socialization.** (3) Same as **internalization.**

Endogamy *Marriage* (not *mating*) within a defined social unit *(group* or *category).* Refers both to the rule requiring marriage within the unit and to the practice of such marriages. (Cf. *exogamy.*)

Energy (1) A moving, sustaining, or vital force. (2) The capacity for action or for doing work (i.e., the capacity to move a physical body). In humans, work is measured by the number of calories expended to perform some task.

Eskimo terminology A type of **kinship terminology,** also called *lineal,* often found in conjunction with **cognatic descent.** See Chapter 12 of the text for major characteristics.

Ethnocentrism The tendency to see one's own culture as central, as superior to other cultures, and as the measure or standard against which all other lifeways are evaluated. (Cf. *cultural relativism.*)

Ethnographic present The present tense used to describe societies as they were in the past, referring to such societies either (1) as they were observed when first encountered by Westerners or (2) as they were when the ethnographer writing the report conducted the fieldwork, when there is a notable time lapse between research and reporting.

Ethnography (1) Firsthand fieldwork conducted in a community, usually by means of **participant observation.** (2) The resultant description of a society or a culture. (Cf. *ethnology.*)

Ethnology The study of comparative ethnography; theorizing or generalizing about culture on the basis of data from a number of societies (in contradistinction to the primarily descriptive function of **ethnography**). To many British anthropologists, *ethnology* refers to the reconstruction of the history of a society or related societies in a given region.

Ethology The study of animal behavior. When the term is applied to humans, it usually refers to the study of nonverbal behavior.

Ethnoscience A theoretical and methodological approach to the study and interpretation of patterns of belief and behavior that utilizes an **emic** strategy; i.e., an attempt to understand foreign cultural systems from the insiders' perspective, with special focus on cognitive structures or systems of classification. Also referred to as *cognitive anthropology.*

Etic Pertaining to the attempt to understand patterns of belief and behavior in terms that are meaningful to the outside observer, to interpret cultural data according to some system of analysis that is independent of and external to the native system. Derived from the linguistics term *phonetics,* which refers to the recording of sounds used in language, regardless of whether the sounds are meaningful to the speakers of any particular language. (Cf. *emic.*)

Evolution, social evolution, cultural evolution Changes over long periods of time in the form of a species or class of things as seen in a series of successive representatives of that class. In regard to sociocultural systems, *evolution* refers to changes in forms of **adaptation.** (See **general evolution** and **specific evolution.**)

Evolutionary level or stage See **adaptive strategy.**

Exogamy *Marriage* (not *mating*) outside a defined social unit *(group* or *category).*

Refers both to the rule requiring marriage beyond the boundaries of the unit and to the practice of such marriage. (Cf. *endogamy*.)

Extended family group There is no consistent usage of this term in the anthropological literature, though the following definitions seem to be the most common. (1) A domestic group consisting of two or more coresident, lineally related family units; i.e., two or more generations of related persons and their spouses all living together (see *patrilocal, matrilocal,* and *avunculocal extended family groups;* cf. also *stem family*). (2) Any group including a *nuclear* or *polygamous family group* and at least one additional relative. (3) Any group of kin-connected families in close cooperation. (4) See *joint family group,* definition 1.

Extensive cultivation A form of cultivation (usually *shifting horticulture*) in which people move periodically from plot to plot, utilizing extensive areas of land for growing crops. That is, they do not remain in one area to work and rework the same land (see *intensive cultivation*).

Factory system An economic system in which production is broken down into stages and the product is broken down into component parts, and both stages and parts are standardized, so that the activities performed at one stage are distinct from those of other stages and the parts manufactured at each stage are interchangeable units that are eventually assembled into identical or similar end products. The emphasis is on mass production for mass distribution in anticipation of later mass consumption. (Several commentators have pointed out that the organization of social relations in general in industrial societies is based on a factory model.)

Family Usually, a domestic unit based on notions of kinship, either consanguineal or affinal (or both) (see *consanguineal kin, affinal kin*), real or classificatory (or both) (see *classificatory kinship, actual kinship*), consisting of adults and children. Types of family groups (see *nuclear, polygamous, extended,* and *joint family group*) may be interpreted as produced by a combination of marriage and residence patterns.

Family of orientation The *family* group into which one is born (natal family) or in which one is reared.

Family of procreation The *family* one establishes in *marriage.*

Feuding Small-scale armed combat, between factions within a community or between structurally equivalent communities, involving a limited number of participants and characterized by a continuing attack-retaliation relationship between the feuding groups.

Fictive or putative kinship (1) A claimed kinship relationship between persons unable to demonstrate any biological tie. In this sense, then, similar to *classificatory kinship.* (2) In contradistinction to both *actual kinship* and classificatory kinship, refers to treating an acknowledged nonkinsperson as kin (such as in godparenthood, blood brotherhood, etc.).

Filiation The social recognition of the relationship between a person and his or her parent. Often used by anthropologists in order to avoid confusion with *descent.* For example, in some societies group membership is not determined by descent from a distant ancestor but is governed by the rule that a child is a member of the same group of which his or her parent, mother or father, is a member.

Fission   The splitting or fragmenting of a group. Refers either to a large group splintering into several smaller, separate groups or to some members of a group leaving to join other groups. (Cf. *fusion.*)

Food collecting   Reliance on naturally occurring plants and undomesticated animals for food. (Cf. *food production,* and see *hunting-gathering.*)

Food production   The cultivation of plants *(horticulture, agriculture)* or the keeping of animals *(pastoralism)* for food. (Cf. *food collecting.*)

Formal group   A group in which the members share a common symbol or symbols representing the group and thus providing a sense of unity beyond the accomplishment of particular tasks. (Cf. *informal group.*)

Fraternal joint family group   A *joint family group* formed by the coresidence of at least two brothers, their wives, and their children.

Fraternal polyandry   A form of *polygamy* in which a woman is married to two or more brothers at the same time. (Cf. *sororal polygyny.*)

Fraternities (tribal)   Usually, involuntary associations based on sex; i.e., all adult males are required to become members. There are cases, however, of voluntary associations of males in tribal societies that anthropologists sometimes refer to as fraternities. (Cf. *sororities.*)

Fusion   The coming together of a number of small groups to form a larger group. (Cf. *fission.*)

General evolution   The overall changes in culture as a general phenomenon, or attribute of humans, as seen in successive forms culture has assumed in different places and at different times, indicating a developmental tendency toward larger and more complex systems of *adaptation.* (Cf. *specific evolution.*)

Generalized exchange   A *marriage* pattern in which men from group A marry women from group B, men from group B marry women from group C, and so on. Reversals in these established exchanges never occur; i.e., once A males marry B females, the relationship can never be reversed so that A females marry B males. Instead, B males marry C females. Also called *indirect exchange, asymmetric marriage system, circulating connubium,* and *matrilateral cross-cousin (MBD) marriage.* (See the text, page 151, for an explanation of abbreviations.)

Generalized, or delayed, reciprocity   A form of economic exchange in which goods or services are given by one party to another, with no expectation of an immediate or direct return of goods or services of equivalent value. (Cf. *balanced reciprocity.*)

Generational terminology   A type of *kinship terminology,* also called *Hawaiian.* See Chapter 12 of the text for major characteristics.

Genitricial rights   Rights a person or group holds in children. (See *right.*)

Genitor   The biological male parent. (Cf. *pater* and *vir.*)

God, or deity   A supernatural being that, usually, (1) is named, (2) has a separate identity all its own, (2) is a source of power, (3) receives offerings, prayers, or some such formal recognition of its power, and (4) is always there to fulfill its functions for the society.

Grammar   The set of rules that governs the arrangement of sounds to form intelligible statements (i.e., those that are meaningful to a native speaker of the language). (Cf. *speech.*)

Group (social)   A collectivity of persons who convene to do something together. A group, as opposed to a *category,* is a behavioral unit; i.e., the members interact.

Group marriage   Marriage of groups of men (two or more) to groups of women (two or more), such that all the men maintain relationships as husbands to all the women, and all the women maintain relationships as wives to all the men.

Guardian spirit   A supernatural being that serves as an individual's protector. (See *vision quest.*)

Habitat   Immediate surroundings, social and physical, in which a population lives; it is the external milieu to which the population adapts.

Hawaiian terminology   A type of *kinship terminology,* also called *generational.* See Chapter 12 of the text for major characteristics.

Headman   A type of typical community leader in tribal societies who exerts influence but little, if any, *power* or *authority.* In a *segmentary tribe* (a tribe organized into independent residential communities that are not incorporated into larger groupings such as chiefdoms), a headman typically has slight coercive ability. Instead, the headman derives executive functions from community consensus. In a more politically complex tribal society, such as a *chiefdom* (in which local residential communities are incorporated into a larger, usually stratified, pollitical entity), the headman's authority is normally greater but is derived from the headman's position as local representative of the *chief.* (The term *headman* is often used more generally to denote a local-level representative of some small community, regardless of the larger political system with which it is associated. Thus, anthropologists sometimes speak of a headman of a hunting-gathering band.)

High god   The supreme deity in a polytheistic religious system.

Holism   An attempt to study and understand any system as a whole—i.e., as composed of a number of interrelated, interactive, and interdependent parts.

Homeopathic magic   See *imitative magic.*

Hominids   Members of the family Hominidae, the taxonomic family in which human beings are classified.

Horizontal nomadism   A variant of *transhumance,* or seasonal movement among pastoralists (see *pastoralism*), in which herders and their animals move outward from a semipermanent or permanent cluster of dwellings (e.g., a village) to the surrounding open area, in search of pasturage and water, and eventually return to the original camp. (Cf. *vertical nomadism.*)

Horticulture   (Also known as *gardening.*) Usually, plant cultivation using hand tools, such as a hoe or digging stick; sometimes, cultivation of root, as opposed to grain, crops. (Cf. *agriculture.*)

Household   A domestic *group,* the members of which share a common area of residence (either a single dwelling or two or more dwellings situated closely together).

Human ecology   The study of the relationship between human populations and their habitats—how the physical environment influences the population's form of *adaptation* and its organization of social relations, and how the population's *adaptive strategy* affects the environment. (Cf. *cultural ecology.*)

Hunting-gathering   An *adaptive strategy* relying primarily on the collection of naturally occurring food sources, i.e., on gathering wild plants, hunting wild game, and fishing.

Hypergamy   Where *social stratification* exists, *hypergamy* refers to marriage between strata when the man is a member of the higher stratum. (Cf. *hypogamy.*)

Hypogamy Where *social stratification* exists, *hypogamy* refers to marriage between strata when the woman is a member of the higher stratum. (Cf. *hypergamy.*)

Imitative magic Magic based on the belief that a desired effect can be produced simply by imitating it, expressed by Frazer's law of similarity: "Like produces like, or . . . an effect resembles its cause." (Cf. *contagious magic.*)

Immediate direct exchange A form of *restricted exchange* in marriage where the exchange of spouses occurs simultaneously (or in the same generation). Also called *sister exchange* and *bilateral cross-cousin (MBD/FZD) marriage.* (See the text, page 151, for an explanation of abbreviations.)

Impersonal supernatural power A supernatural force or power that (1) has no consciousness or personality, for it is not a being or spirit; (2) is diffuse in nature and permeates both animate and inanimate, organic and inorganic, objects; (3) exists for no specific purpose; and (4) is neither good nor evil. Also referred to as *mana.* (See *animatism.*)

Incest Prohibited sexual intercourse *(mating)* between designated categories of *kin*—i.e., behavior prohibited by *incest taboos.*

Incest taboos Rules, usually believed to be reinforced by supernatural sanctions, prohibiting sexual intercourse *(mating)* between certain specified categories of relatives. (See also *incest.*)

Indirect exchange See *generalized exchange.*

Industrialism The use of inanimate energy sources (i.e., *energy* generated by means other than muscular action, whether animal or human) to operate machinery for the extraction and conversion of resources in a *factory system* of production. This form of adaptation first began on a large scale in Britain toward the end of the eighteenth century, although there is evidence of occasional or peripheral use of some industrial methods as early as 2,000 to 3,000 years ago (for instance, waterwheels in Greece about 2,300 years ago). The term *industrial revolution,* therefore, is reserved for the time, about 200 to 300 years ago, when reliance on industrialism first began to assume primary importance in *adaptation.*

Industrial revolution See *industrialism.*

Influence The capacity to sway decisions and modify others' behavior through example, argument, or counsel. (Cf. *power.*)

Informal group A group organized for a specific objective and having no sense of unity aside from that necessary to accomplish the objective. (Cf. *formal group.*)

Initiation ceremony A rite of passage marking the transition in status from nonmember to member in some identifiable social unit. The term is used most frequently in reference to the *rites of passage* from childhood to young adulthood (and hence is synonymous with *puberty rite*).

Institution An activity system or set of related and interdependent recurrent patterns of belief and behavior. An institution involves a functionally related constellation or configuration of behavioral, ideological, and cognitive subsystems concerning some sphere of activity that is analytically or empirically delimitable—e.g., economics (see *economic organization*), *religion, kinship.* (See also *commingling of institutions* and *differentiation of institutions.*)

Intensive cultivation A form of *cultivation* in which people continue to work and rework the same land. That is—by means of techniques such as crop rotation, land terracing, fertilization, or irrigation, with or without the use of the plow (see *horticulture* and *agriculture*)—they invest intensive effort growing in crops in a limited area, instead of moving from place to place to farm new areas (cf. *extensive cultivation*). Food production may be referred to as *labor-intensive cultivation,* that is, a form of cultivation requiring a high labor investment from humans and domesticated animals; or it may be called *capital-intensive cultivation,* a term which refers mainly to mechanized agriculture, where few people are needed to operate the machines that do most of the work.

Internalization   The process whereby a person makes his or her own the values, attitudes, goals, concepts, etc., that have been communicated as appropriate in the society; a form of psychological incorporation. Sometimes used synonymously with *enculturation* or *socialization.*

Iroquois terminology   A type of *kinship terminology,* also called *bifurcate merging.* See Chapter 12 of the text for major characteristics.

Joint family group   There is no consistent usage of this term in the anthropological literature, but the following definitions seem to be the most common: (1) A group of two or more collaterally related persons (such as siblings or cousins; see *collateral relatives*) with their spouses and children all living together. (2) Same as definition 1 under *extended family group.* (3) Same as definition 3 under *extended family group.*

Joking relationships   Those in which joking, teasing, intimate familiarity, and perhaps privileged access to personal belongings and sexual license or prerogatives are permitted between designated categories of relatives. (Cf. *avoidance relationships.*)

Jural   Pertaining to "legality," or formal public acceptability of behavior, and to rights (see *right*) and duties.

Juridical   Pertaining to *law* in general or its administration in particular.

Kin   Persons considered to be "relatives," i.e., connected by ties of *descent* or *marriage,* whether real or claimed.

Kindred   An egocentric category (as opposed to *group*; see *egocentric unit*) of kin, usually including both *matrilateral* and *patrilateral* relatives. That is, from each individual ego's point of view there is a circle of people he or she regards as *kin.*

Kin group   A group organized on the basis of consanguineal or affinal kinship (see *consanguineal kin, affinal kin*) or common *descent.* The term is often used interchangeably with *descent group.*

Kinship   The definition in any particular culture of "relatedness" among persons; i.e., relationships involving ties of *descent* and *marriage.*

Kinship, or relationship, terminology   A system for naming relatives; the set of terms of address or reference applied to *kin* in any society.

Law   In general, the mechanisms and procedures for dealing with transgressions of publicly recognized rules of behavior and for resolving disputes in a society. The term also refers to these rules or norms of behavior themselves. Some authors restrict the usage of *law* to those societies in which there exists a formally recognized political authority system, backed by the threat of force, with the capacity to impose institutionalized sanctions against violators of the legal code—thus implying, and sometimes stating, that where these conditions do not obtain, the society is considered to be without law. (This may be seen as a confusion between, on the one hand, law as any set of regular mechanisms for handling disputes and transgressions and, on the other hand, law as one particular set of such mechanisms and procedures having certain characteristics.)

Levirate A mechanism in some societies for the continuation of a *marriage* relationship between groups even after the death of the original husband. When a man dies, his *kin* group replaces him with another male as spouse for the widow. The new husband is often a brother (whether actual or classificatory; see *actual kinship, classificatory kinship*) but may, as well, be any male from the same kin group. (Cf. *sororate*.)

Life cycle The progression of the individual from birth through maturation and adulthood to death.

Lineage A descent-ordered unit (see *descent unit*), usually a *group,* generally having fewer members and of shallower genealogical depth than a clan. It is a group of persons of both sexes, in which membership is determined by *unilineal descent* and the members can trace their descent from the *apical ancestor* through a series of demonstrable genealogical links. A lineage is usually a localized (i.e., residential) group. (Cf. *clan.*)

Lineal relatives *Consanguineal kin* in a direct line of descent, such as grandparent, parent, child—i.e., individuals related "vertically." (Cf. *collateral relatives.*)

Lineal terminology A type of *kinship terminology,* also called *Eskimo,* often found in conjunction with *cognatic descent.* See Chapter 12 of the text for major characteristics.

Linguistics The study of language.

Linking relative Any individual through whom a kinship relationship is traced to another person, i.e., the relative connecting *ego* to *alter.*

Local, or residence, group A group of people who live together.

Magic The direct manipulation of cause and effect between phenomena whose connection is not demonstrable through independent means—i.e., between things or events that appear to an outside, scientifically inclined observer to be unrelated—such as affecting a person's well-being by pronouncing incantations over his or her image.

Mana The Malayo-Polynesian term for an *impersonal supernatural power.*

Manitou The Algonkin term for an *impersonal supernatural power.*

Market exchange A mode of economic exchange which involves the use of money (i.e., a recognized medium for exchange, one that is used to represent the value of a commodity); in which the relationship between buyers and sellers is based primarily on economics (rather than on kinship, friendship, etc.); and in which the price of goods and services varies with supply and demand (i.e., the amount of the commodity available for sale and how badly buyers want it) and, often, is regulated by some political authority.

Marketplace A place where people gather to conduct economic exchanges.

Marriage A socially recognized and normatively prescribed relationship between at least two persons (one culturally defined as male, the other as female) that defines and establishes economic, sexual, and other rights and duties each owes to the other or others and to other members of society and provides the *primary* or most usual mechanism in the society by which offspring are recognized as legitimate and accorded normal rights as members of their society.

Mating   Sexual intercourse. The term should not be confused with *marriage.*

Matriclan   A *clan* in which membership is determined by *matrilineal descent* or *filiation* to the mother.

Matrilateral   Pertaining to relatives on the "mother's side"; i.e., the mother is the *linking relative* between *ego* and collateral alters. (See *alter, collateral relatives;* cf. *patrilateral.*) The term is sometimes used when *matrilineal* is meant.

Matrilateral cross-cousin (MBD) marriage   See *generalized exchange.* (See the text, page 151, for an explanation of abbreviations.)

Matrilineage, or matrilineal lineage   A *lineage* formed on the basis of *matrilineal descent.* Also called *uterine lineage.*

Matrilineal descent   "Mother's-line descent"; a form of *unilineal descent* in which a person traces his or her descent through females only (M, MM, MMM, etc.; see the text, page 151, for an explanation of abbreviations); i.e., the mother is the *linking relative* between *ego* and ego's unilineal female forebears. Also called *uterine descent.*

Matrilocal extended family group   An *extended family group* based on *matrilocal residence;* minimally, it consists of a woman, with or without her spouse or spouses (depending on the particular anthropologist's definition), her daughters, and her daughters' husbands and children all living together. (Cf. *patrilocal* and *avunculocal extended family group.*)

Matrilocal residence   *Matrilocal* means "mother's place"; it refers to a form of residence in which the married couple as a unit resides with or near the wife's mother. Often confused with *uxorilocal residence.*

Matrisib   A *sib* in which membership is determined by *matrilineal descent* or *filiation* to the mother.

Medicine man   See *shaman.*

Messianic movement   A type of *revitalization movement* led by a charismatic savior or deliverer; or a movement prophesying the eventual appearance of such a leader, called a *messiah.*

Military society   A voluntary *association* of warriors.

Millenarian movement   A type of *revitalization movement* which asserts that the new order, once established, will last a thousand years. Belief in a messiah is also often associated with millenarism. (See *messianic movement.*)

Moiety   "Half." The term is used for those societies in which there is a division into two large social units (groups or categories). All persons in the society are at birth members of one or the other of these units. Membership may or may not be based on *descent* or *filiation.* A moiety is often, but not always, exogamous (see *exogamy*). (Also called *dual organization.*)

Monogamy   *Marriage* of one man to one woman.

Monotheism   A religious system in which there is a belief in only one *god.* (Cf. *polytheism, multitheism,* and *unitheism.*)

Multilineal descent   See *cognatic descent.*

Multipurpose association   See *bond friendship.*

Multitheism   A type of religion in which a society maintains a relationship with only one *god* (thus, the religion is similar to *monotheism*) but recognizes the existence of other gods for other societies (thus, a form of *polytheism*).

Nacirema *American* spelled backwards.

Natal family, or natal group See *family of orientation.*

Nativistic movement See *revitalization movement.*

Nation-state A society which has a centralized political system (the state) and is composed of a socially stratified, economically diversified. and otherwise heterogeneous population occupying a defined territory (the nation).

Natolocal residence *Natolocal* means "place of birth" and refers to a form of **duolocal residence** in which neither the husband nor the wife moves upon marriage but instead both continue to reside separately with their respective parents.

Negative reciprocity A form of economic exchange, dominated by the profit motive and the self-interest of each of the parties, in which each party attempts to get the better of the other.

Neolithic "New stone"; the term *Neolithic age* refers to (1) the use of polished stone tools, or (2) the domestication of plants and animals for food. The term *Neolithic revolution* refers to the time, from about 9,000 to 11,000 years ago, when humans in various areas of the world first began producing food. (Cf. *Paleolithic.*)

Neolocal residence *Neolocal* means "new place" and refers to a form of residence in which the married couple as a unit establishes a new household apart from the parents of either spouse.

Nomadism Movement in pursuit of resources, i.e., as a part of a group's *adaptive strategy.* Nomads, thus, have no permanent dwellings. (Cf. *sedentariness.*)

Nonunilineal descent See *cognatic descent.*

Norm, descriptive Statistical expression of actual behavior; i.e., the way people *normally* or usually behave in given situations, as opposed to ideas concerning the way they should or are generally expected to behave. (Cf. *norm, ideal.*)

Norm, ideal Ideas about, or a guide to, appropriate behavior. (Cf. *norm, descriptive.*)

Nuclear family group A domestic unit consisting of a man, a woman, and their children. Also called *elementary family* and *conjugal family.* (Cf. *extended, joint,* and *polygamous family group.*)

Omaha terminology A type of *kinship terminology,* usually found in conjunction with *patrilineal descent.* See Chapter 12 of the text for major characteristics.

Optative descent See *ambilineal descent.*

Optative descent group See *ramage.*

Organization of labor See *division of labor.*

Outcasts, or outcastes See *pariahs.*

Paleolithic "Old stone"; the term *Paleolithic age* refers to (1) the use of chipped, unpolished stone tools, or (2) the time, before 9,000 to 11,000 years ago, when humans everywhere relied solely on hunting and gathering for food. (Cf. *Neolithic.*)

Paleontology The study of fossils.

Parallel cousins Persons who are children of same-sexed siblings; thus the parallel cousins of *ego* are his or her FBC and MZC. (Cf. *cross-cousins;* and see the text, page 151, for an explanation of abbreviations.)

Parallel descent A form of *unilineal descent* in which females trace descent through females only, and males trace descent through males only. In other words, *in the same society*, females employ **matrilineal descent** and males employ **patrilineal descent.**

Pariahs   Persons excluded from the normal free range of social interaction with other members of society. They are considered unclean, polluted and polluting persons; and contact with them is considered defiling. (Also called *outcasts*, or *outcastes*, and *untouchables.*)

Participant observation   A technique in ethnographic fieldwork involving living among a group of people and participating in many of their activities, while observing and recording as much as possible of what occurs.

Pastoralism   An **adaptive strategy** dependent primarily on herds of large animals (sheep, goats, cattle, camels, reindeer, horses).

Pastoral nomadism   An **adaptive strategy** that combines **pastoralism** and **nomadism.** (Also called *nomadic pastoralism.*) Apparently not a self-sufficient strategy of adaptation but a regional specialization in areas where **cultivation** is also practiced, or a strategy employed by pastoralists who themselves engage in some additional form of making a living (cultivation, trade, wage labor, caravan transport).

Pater   A person socially defined as a "father"; often described as a "sociological father." The individual so identified, however, need not actually be of the male gender. (Cf. **genitor** and **vir.**)

Patriclan   A **clan** in which membership is determined by **patrilineal descent** or **filiation** to the father.

Patrilateral   Pertaining to relatives on the "father's side"; i.e., the father is the **linking relative** between **ego** and collateral alters. (See **alter, collateral relatives;** cf. **matrilateral.**) The term is sometimes used when **patrilineal** is meant.

Patrilateral cross-cousin (FZD) marriage   See **delayed direct exchange.** (See text, page 151, for an explanation of abbreviations.)

Patrilineage, or patrilineal lineage   A **lineage** formed on the basis of **patrilineal descent.** Also called *agnatic lineage.*

Patrilineal descent   "Father's-line descent"; a form of **unilineal descent** in which a person traces his or her descent through males only (F, FF, FFF, etc.; see the text, page 151, for an explanation of abbreviations). I.e., the father is the **linking relative** between **ego** and ego's unilineal male forebears. Also called *agnatic descent.*

Patrilocal extended family group   An **extended family group** based on **patrilocal residence;** minimally, it consists of a man, with or without his spouse or spouses (depending on the particular anthropologist's definition), his sons, and his sons' wives and children all living together. (Cf. **matrilocal** and **avunculocal extended family group.**)

Patrilocal residence   *Patrilocal* means "father's place" and refers to a form of residence in which the married couple as a unit resides with or near the husband's father (thus, also called *viripatrilocal* and *patrivirilocal residence*). The term is often confused with **virilocal** residence.

Patrisib   A **sib** in which membership is determined by **patrilineal descent** or **filiation** to the father.

Peasants   Usually, rural cultivators (see **cultivation**) in a nonindustrialized **nation-state** who farm primarily for their own subsistence but also participate in the society's market system.

Petty chieftain See *headman.*

Phratry A nonlocalized, named *descent unit, or descent-ordered unit* (usually a *category,* but may be a *group*) composed of two or more related clans or sibs (see *clan, sib.*) Phratries are often exogamous (see *exogamy*).

Physical anthropology A branch of *anthropology* dealing with humanity as a biological species—its physical evolution, its characteristics as a population of physical organisms, its physical variations.

Plural marriage See *polygamy.*

Political organization The way order and conformity are maintained in a society; i.e., those mechanisms most directly concerned with social control.

Polyandrous family group A *polygamous family group* formed by a woman, two or more husbands, and her children living together. (Cf. *polygynous family group.*)

Polyandry A form of *polygamy* in which one woman is married to two or more men at the same time. (Cf. *polygyny.*)

Polygamous family group A group formed by spouses in a polygamous union (see *polygamy*) and their children in coresidence. The group need not occupy only a single dwelling. See *polyandrous family group* and *polygynous family group.*

Polygamy The marriage of one person to two or more spouses at the same time. Subtypes are *polyandry* and *polygyny.* (Cf. *monogamy.*)

Polygynous family group A *polygamous family group* formed by a man, two or more wives, and his children living together. (Cf. *polyandrous family group.*)

Polygyny A form of *polygamy* in which one man is married to two or more women at the same time. (Cf. *polyandry.*)

Polytheism A religion in which there is the belief in more than one *god* or godlike supernatural being. (Cf. *monotheism.*)

Postpartum sex taboo The prohibition of sexual intercourse for one or both parents for a designated length of time after the birth of a child.

Potlatch A form of conspicuous consumption among Indians of the Northwest Coast of North America, in which *property* is given away or destroyed during feasts.

Power The ability to manipulate people, to compel or prevent behavior, with or without accompanying *authority.* As such, should be distinguished from *influence.*

Preferential marriage rules Rules, in *elementary marriage systems,* specifying whom (i.e., into which category or group) one *should* marry. In other words, rules designating preferred marriages. (Cf. *prescriptive marriage rules.*)

Prescriptive marriage rules Rules, in *elementary marriage systems,* specifying whom (i.e., into which category or group) one *must* marry. In other words, rules designating prescribed marriages. (Cf. *preferential marriage rules.*)

Priest A full-time religious practitioner; i.e., a specialist (see *specialists*). Secondary characteristics often used to identify a priest are (1) acting as a leader of group ritual, (2) being a spokesperson or representative of the group vis à vis the supernatural, (3) being a member of a formally structured, usually hierarchical, religious organization, and (4) deriving authority as a religious functionary from special training and under the auspices of the religious organization. (Cf. *shaman.*)

Primary group   A face-to-face group, i.e., one in which nearly all the members interact personally and directly. (Cf. *secondary group.*)

Primogeniture   Inheritance by the firstborn or oldest child. (Cf. *ultimogeniture.*)

Primus inter pares   "First among equals"; a type of informal leadership, typical of societies with *band* organization (mainly hunter-gatherers), in which the person accorded the title has no real *power* or *authority* but wields *influence* in the group because of his or her personality or achievements.

Production   Primarily, the way in which resources utilized by a society are converted into goods (for eventual *distribution* and *consumption*).

Progeny price   See *childwealth.*

Progressive age-set systems   Age-set systems in which the name for an age set (see *age sets*) is used only once; it may never be applied again to another group. (Cf. *cyclical age-set systems.*)

Property   Any object in which persons or groups hold rights (see *right*) of use or disposal.

Property rights   A proprietary relationship between a person or group and an object, in which the person or group claims the prerogative of use or disposal of the object.

Puberty rite   See *initiation ceremony.*

Raiding   A form of armed combat between small-scale territorial groups or residential communities, involving a relationship of attack and retaliation, which is often aimed at the acquisition of goods or resources (unlike *feuding,* which does not have primarily economic objectives).

Ramage   A *descent group* formed on the basis of *optative* or *ambilineal descent,* or *filiation* with one parent or the other. Also called *ambilineage* and *optative descent group.*

Reciprocal marriage system   See *retricted exchange.*

Reciprocity   Sometimes referred to as *gift giving.* Economic exchange between units (individuals or groups) of equivalent social standing in which goods and services of commensurate value are exchanged. (See *balanced reciprocity, generalized reciprocity,* and *negative reciprocity.*)

Redistribution   A mode of economic exchange or distribution in a society in which valued commodities are sent to an administrative center, from which they are then reallotted under the supervision of some authority. The term is sometimes used to refer to the movement of goods to any central locations (such as marketplaces), from which they then flow out to the general population.

Religion   Belief and behavior relating to the *supernatural.*

Residence rules   Regulations concerning where designated categories of persons are supposed to reside; in other words, norms regarding where people should live (in contradistinction to where they actually do live). Most often, anthropologists are interested in residence rules involving *marriage:* (1) rules concerning which partner moves upon marriage (see *virilocal, uxorilocal,* and *natolocal residence*); and (2) rules concerning where the newly married couple as a unit resides (see *patrilocal, matrilocal, avunculocal, ambilocal, neolocal,* and *commonlocal residence*).

Restricted exchange   A *marriage* pattern in which individual males and females from one group marry individual males and females from another group. In other words, the two groups exchange members as marriage partners. (Also known as *direct exchange, symmetric marriage system,* and *reciprocal marriage system.*) Major types of restricted exchange are ***immediate direct exchange*** and ***delayed direct exchange.***

Revitalization movement   An ideological and social movement aimed at reinstating a former social order or establishing a new one based on presumed ideals, or often an idealized view, of the past. Also called *nativistic movement.* (See also ***messianic movement, millenarian movement,*** and ***cargo cult.***)

Right   (1) A publicly recognized, granted privilege of either short-term or long-term duration. It is a social prerogative, existing because one social body confers it (either in response to demand or voluntarily) on another social body; or, viewed differently, it is the result of social convention or convenience, whereby at least two parties agree to accept certain behaviors as prerogatives of either or both of the contractors. In societies with institutionalized political structures (i.e., formal systems of power and authority), a right exists only through the grace of those who have the potential or actual power to abrogate it but, for one reason or another, choose not to do so. In this sense, rights are cross-culturally variable. (2) A prerogative believed to be innate, to inhere or reside intrinsically in an organism or population of organisms, without regard to sociocultural context (e.g., a prerogative believed to belong naturally to all people as members of the same species, or a prerogative considered to be attendant upon the condition of simply being alive). In this sense, rights are seen as absolutes.

Rites of desacralization   *Rites of passage* that must be undergone by a person who has somehow come into close contact with the ***supernatural.*** Since the supernatural, because of its intrinsic potency, is considered harmful to ordinary mortals, persons who have been touched by it must be "neutralized," both for their own sake and for the sake of any third party who later comes into contact with them. Until the rites of desacralization are performed, the contacted person is excluded from normal social intercourse. (Cf. *rites of purification.*)

Rites of intensification   Rites that function to intensify group ties or enhance group solidarity and cohesiveness. They are ceremonies that recur regularly and at designated times in a society, such as harvest rituals (hence, sometimes called *calendrical rites*), or those that are performed for a singular occasion or during a crisis, such as an epidemic. (Cf. *rites of passage.*)

Rites of passage   Ceremonies performed to mark the transition from one stage to another within the ***life cycle*** or to effect the passage of a person from a state of ritual abnormality to one of normality (as in ***rites of purification*** and ***rites of desacralization***). Hence, rites of passage (as opposed to ***rites of intensification***) are said to center on *individual* life crises.

Rites of purification   *Rites of passage* that must be undergone by a person who has somehow been ritually contaminated or defiled, in order for that person to become ritually pure once more. Until the rites are performed, the person remains ritually polluted and is excluded from normal social intercourse. (Cf. *rites of desacralization.*)

Ritual   (1) Broadly, any prescribed, stylized, stereotypical way of performing some act—e.g., saluting in a uniformed military organization. (The term is derived from Latin and means "by the numbers.") (2) Narrowly, a single act of a religious performance. (Cf. *ceremony,* with which *ritual* is often used interchangeably.)

Role (1) A particular set of expectations for appropriate behavior associated with a specific *status* or position in a social system. In this sense, then, similar to ideal norms (see *norm, ideal*) for the behavior of persons occupying a certain status. (2) The actual behavior of a person or persons in a specific status or position in a social system. Hence, the commonalities in behavior exhibited by persons occupying the same status constitute descriptive norms (see *norm, descriptive*). (3) Definitions 1 and 2 combined.

Secondary group A group in which not all members interact face to face; instead, the overall group is composed of a number of subgroups, with only some of their members in interaction with only some members of the other constituent subgroups. (Cf. *primary group.*)

Secret societies Nonkin *associations,* the members of which share some secret or esoteric knowledge which is denied to nonmembers and which is considered to give members special abilities or power. In some cases, membership itself is secret. (Some anthropologists define secret societies as voluntary associations, while others define them as involuntary.)

Sedentariness The characteristic of a group remaining settled in one place more or less permanently. (A neologism finding increasing favor among anthropologists as a synonym is *sedentism.*) The term *sedentary,* the adjectival form, is used also as a noun to denote a person who is sedentary. (Cf. *nomadism.*)

Segmentary lineage system A type of tribal organization based on *unilineal descent* in which social units are divided (or segmented) into successively smaller-scale units, down to local-level residential groups. Or, phrased differently, a type of organization in which social units combine into progressively larger, more inclusive units on a principle of unilineal descent (e.g., households into lineages, lineages into clans, clans into phratries; see *household, lineage, clan, phratry*), even back to a single ancestor or putative founder of the *tribe* who represents the society as a whole.

Segmentary tribe A tribal society (see *tribe*) in which the main constituent groups are local-level, relatively small communities (called *primary segments*) which, however, may form together for specific purposes (usually by means of a combination of *unilineal descent* and geographic proximity) into progressively larger, more inclusive kinship and territorial groups.

Senilicide The killing of old people.

Serial monogamy The practice of marrying several spouses in succession, but not simultaneously.

Shaman A part-time religious practitioner; i.e., a religious functionary who is not a specialist (see *specialists*). Other characteristics often used to identify shamans are (1) possessing special gifts, talents, or knowledge, such as the ability to converse with spirits, to cure the sick, or to work magic; (2) deriving abilities from personal contact with the *supernatural;* (3) acting more often as individuals than as spokespersons or representatives of the group when dealing with the supernatural; and (4) not being members of formal, bureaucratic religious organizations. (Cf. *priest.*)

Shifting horticulture A type of *cultivation* involving movement from plot to plot;

when soil in one area is exhausted, it is abandoned and people shift to another area to grow crops. The term is most commonly associated with *slash-and-burn horticulture.* (See also *extensive cultivation.*)

Sib   A *descent unit, or descent-ordered unit,* formerly differentiated from a clan; today the terms *clan* and *sib* are used synonymously. (See *clan* for basis of distinction.)

Silent trade   See *dumb barter.*

Sister exchange   See *immediate direct exchange.*

Slash-and-burn horticulture   A type of *cultivation* in which natural vegetation is cut and burned, with the ash left *in situ* to serve as fertilizer, to clear fields for gardening. (Also called *swidden cultivation.*) Each plot of land is used for a time and then allowed to lie fallow, while the people move to another area to repeat the process. (Hence, also called *shifting horticulture.*)

Slavery   Usually, a noncontractual relationship in which (1) there is a lack of reciprocal relations between slaves and masters, such that the bulk of the rights resides with one party (the master) and the duties with the other party (the slave); (2) the master exercises rights of proprietorship and disposition over the person of the slave; and (3) the relationship, with its attendant rights and duties, is supported by the society's political system and backed by threat of force.

Social ecology   The relationships among different groups of people within a defined area. (Cf. *cultural ecology* and *human ecology.*)

Socialization   (1) A generic term for the process of the transmission of culture (in contradistinction to the transmission of any particulare culture; cf. *enculturation*). (2) Same as enculturation. (3) Same as *internalization.*

Social mobility   The capacity, usually associated with class-stratified societies, of changing one's position in the social system; i.e., the ability to move up or down in the class structure (see *class system*) and the potential for acquiring or losing *status.*

Social stratification   The division of a society into a hierarchically arranged series of social strata or levels, which may be groups or categories (see *group, category*) the members of which have differential access to the resources, goods, and services, and any valued commodities available in the population as a whole. Stratification occurs in any sociocultural system in which the resources that the population relies on, or the techniques for extracting these resources and converting them into usable commodities, can be controlled by some members of the society. Thus, for example, all industrial societies are stratified. (See *caste system* and *class system.*)

Society   (1) Usually, an entity defined as some combination of the following: (a) a group or population of people, (b) who occupy a specified or distinct territory, (c) who share a similar language and set of customs, beliefs, institutions, and traditions, and (d) who have a strong sense of distinct group identity. (2) In this book (following Gerald Weiss), either a *breeding population* or a maximum political entity, whichever is larger in a particular instance.

Sociocentric units   The component parts of a social system when seen from an impersonal perspective—i.e., regardless of particular persons' affiliation to, or membership or participation in, these constituent elements. In other words, the divisions defined by the *structure* of a society. (Cf. *egocentric unit.*)

Song duel   A method for resolving conflict in some Eskimo societies. See Chapter 11 of the text for a description.

Sorcery   See *black magic.*

Sororal polygyny   A form of *polygamy* in which a man is married to two or more sisters at the same time. (Cf. *fraternal polyandry.*)

Sororate   A mechanism in some societies for the continuation of a *marriage* relationship between groups even after the death of the original wife. When a woman dies, her *kin group* replaces her with another female as spouse for the widower. The new wife is often a sister (whether actual or classificatory; see *actual kinship, classificatory kinship*) but may, as well, be any female from the same kin group. (Cf. *levirate.*)

Sororities (tribal)   Usually, involuntary *associations* based on sex; i.e., all adult females are required to become members. There are cases, however, of voluntary associations of females in tribal societies to which anthropologists sometimes refer as *sororities.* [Cf. *fraternities (tribal).*]

Special-interest group   A nonkin association (see *associations*) formed by persons who are in pursuit of the same goal or who share a particular interest, avocation, hobby, purpose, etc.

Specialists   Persons who perform one task or set of related tasks on a full-time basis and derive their livelihood from exchanging the products of their labor for other necessary services or goods produced by others.

Specialization of labor   An organization of labor in which individuals or groups are *specialists*—i.e., they engage in a single task or set of related tasks on a full-time basis—resulting in the production of a number of different goods and services. The society is thus divided into a number of specialized occupations, the practitioners of which exchange their particular goods or services (both economic and noneconomic) with each other.

Specific evolution   Sequences of change in form that have occurred in the cultures of specific human populations; or, phrased differently, changes in the *adaptive strategy* of a particular *society.* (Cf. *general evolution.*)

Speech   Series of meaningful sounds in a language; i.e., the actual sounds produced by a speaker when employing the grammatical rules as he or she knows them. (Cf. *grammar.*)

State society   A form of *political organization* in which for the entire society there is a single central political authority at the head of an administrative bureaucracy. (See *nation-state.*)

Status   (1) A recognized position in a society having a distinct *role* associated with it and carrying with it a certain amount of prestige relative to other such positions. A status is a slot in the *structure* of the society which is occupied by individuals. (2) More loosely, the rank or amount of prestige or esteem accorded to an individual by the members of society. (See *achieved status* and *ascribed status.*)

Status system   A hierarchical ordering, or arrangement, of statuses (see *status*) in a society.

Stem family group   Since some anthropologists restrict their meaning of *extended family group* to a domestic unit consisting of at least three generations of lineally related (see *lineal relatives*) married persons, the term *stem family* is used to refer either to (1) a group consisting of three lineally related generations, in which only the two adjacent generations each contain a married pair, or to (2) a group consisting of only one married child, with his or her spouse, residing with the parent or parents.

Structure   The arrangement of parts in a system; a blueprint of how any entity is constructed and the static, rather than dynamic, relations of its constituent elements or components.

Subsistence technology   Tools and techniques for gaining a livelihood, especially the manner of getting food. Similar to *adaptive strategy.*

Sudanese terminology   A type of *kinship terminology,* also called *bifurcate collateral.* See Chapter 12 of the text for major characteristics.

Supernatural, or supernature   A realm posited as existing beyond the material, visible, or objectively demonstrable world.

Swidden cultivation   See *slash-and-burn horticulture.*

Symmetric marriage system   See *restricted exchange.*

Taboo, or tabu   A Malayo-Polynesian term used by anthropologists to refer to a proscription (a rule of prohibition) usually supported by threat of supernatural retaliation in case of violation. Hence, not all prohibitions may be called taboos.

Technology   Tools and techniques for the extraction, conversion, and utilization of resources; i.e., the methods of extracting resources from the *habitat* and of producing and distributing goods and services. More broadly, and somewhat more abstractly, the variety of ways and means for harnessing *energy* and circulating it throughout a social system; in this sense, technology is inseparable from a society's *organization of labor.*

Territoriality   The assertion of rights of priority, proprietorship, and disposability over land and its resources, accompanied by willingness to defend this claim— by force, if necessary—against others viewed as intruders or usurpers.

Totemism   A special relationship that the members of a social unit (*group* or *category*) conceive to exist between their unit and some object in nature— usually a plant or animal, called the *totem*—that the unit is named after. Sometimes the object itself is treated as an ancestor or is considered to have been somehow closely associated with the human founder of the unit; and the members of the unit may be forbidden to kill or eat the object if it is an animal or plant.

Transhumance   This term has been used in a variety of ways. (1) The seasonal nomadic movement (see *nomadism*) of peoples practicing any of several adaptive strategies (see *adaptive strategy*). (2) Seasonal movement among peoples practicing *pastoralism,* as either a primary or a subsidiary component of their adaptive strategy. (3) Seasonal movement of pastoralists away from a permanent or semipermanent community, and their eventual return. (4) A seasonal shifting of pastoralists from low-altitude areas to high-altitude areas, with or without the existence of permanent or semipermanent communities in the lowlands. (See *horizontal nomadism* and *vertical nomadism.*)

Trial by ordeal   A method of ascertaining guilt or innocence or of testing a person's veracity by subjecting the person to some physically painful or dangerous ordeal.

Tribe   A loosely used term having no strict definition but most commonly applied to a type of *political organization* in which the society is composed of a number of geographically separated, politically (and often economically) independent communities or clusters of communities without any overarching central authority. Some measure of overall tribal identity is afforded by the similarities of language and custom that link the various segments into a loose whole and distinguish them as a cultural unit from other peoples with different languages and customs. The politically significant subdivisions of a tribe may be local-level residential communities (see **segmentary tribe**) or several communities in a defined territory each with a dominant political center (see **chiefdom**).

Ultimogeniture   Inheritance by the last-born or youngest child. (Cf. **primogeniture.**)

Unilateral kin   Either **matrilateral** or **patrilateral** relatives; i.e., collateral kin to whom relationship is traced through either the father or the mother as a **linking relative.** Unilateral ("one side") is used by some authors to mean unilineal ("one line"); for clarification compare **lineal relatives** with **collateral relatives,** and see also **unilineal descent.**

Unilineal descent   "One-line" descent; the tracing of descent through one parent and that parent's same-sexed progenitors, i.e., all males or all females. (But see **ambilineal descent.**) Varieties of unilineal descent include **patrilineal, matrilineal, double,** and **parallel descent.** (Cf. **cognatic,** or bilateral, **descent.**)

Unilineal descent group   A **descent group** based on some form of **unilineal descent.**

Unitheism   A form of polytheistic religion in tribal societies in which the society is divided into a number of relatively stable corporate groups, such as clans (see **corporate group, clan**), and each of these groups maintains a relationship with a single deity. Thus, for such a society, there are as many gods as there are kin groups. (Cf. **monotheism** and **multitheism.**)

Unrestricted descent group   See **cognatic descent group.**

Untouchables   See **pariahs.**

Uterine descent   See **matrilineal descent.**

Uterine kin   Persons (male or female) related through females; i.e., persons connected by one or more female linking relatives (see **linking relative**). Uterine relationships thus occur in all societies; such kin connections are not confined only to societies with **matrilineal** (uterine) **decent.** (Cf. **agnatic kin.**)

Uxorilocal residence   Uxorilocal means "wife's place" and refers to a form of residence in which the man moves upon marriage and takes up residence where his wife lives. Often confused with **matrilocal residence.**

Vertical nomadism   A variant of **transhumance,** or seasonal movement among pastoral nomads, in which herders and their animals move between low-altitude areas and high-altitude areas; for example, movement up a mountain slope in summer and down toward the valley in winter. (Cf. **horizontal nomadism.**)

Vir   Latin, "man." Often used by anthropologists to designate a woman's husband, regardless of whether he is the **genitor** or **pater** of her children.

Virilocal residence   Virilocal means "man's place" and refers to a form of residence in which the woman moves upon marriage and takes up residence where her husband lives. Often confused with **patrilocal residence.**

Vision quest   A phenomenon which was common among the North American Plains Indians. A young man would go alone into the wilderness and fast for days until he had a vision in which a **guardian spirit,** often in the form of an animal, visited him, imparted a sacred song to him, and thereafter served as his protector.

Warfare   Relatively long-term and large-scale armed combat between entire political communities (normally whole societies), in which large fighting forces are mobilized and in which fighting is an organized affair usually characterized by a formal hierarchy of leadership.

White magic   A form of benevolent *magic,* the aim of which is to effect some socially desirable, acceptable, or harmless result. For instance, white magic may be used in an effort to cure sickness. (Cf. *black magic.*)

Wife inheritance   A system by which the heir of a deceased man is obliged to marry the widow or widows.

Wife lending   The practice whereby men extend to each other rights of sexual access to their wives. A form of hospitality.

Witch   A person, male or female, with an inborn ability to cause harm or misfortune through magical—often purely psychic—means. (See *witchcraft.*)

Witchcraft   Most frequently, the exercise of the innate ability to produce harmful effects, either purposely or accidentally, through magical means. Thus, akin to sorcery (or *black magic*) but usually differentiated from it, since sorcerers undergo training to acquire their abilities, whereas witches are born with their abilities.

Work   See *energy,* definition 2.

Index